PUTTING RESEARCH TO WORK

In Your School

DAVID C. BERLINE
AND URSULA CASANOV.

PEARSON
SkyLight

Glenview, Illinois

Putting Research to Work in Your School

Published by SkyLight Professional Development
1900 E. Lake Ave., Glenview, IL 60025
Phone 800-348-4474, 847-657-7450
Fax 847-486-3183
info@skylightedu.com
http://www.skylightedu.com

LCCN 96-76991
ISBN 1-57517-064-7

1886
Item Number 1448

ZYXWVUTSRQPONMLKJI
06 05 04 03   15 14 13 12 11 10 9

About the Authors

David C. Berliner

David C. Berliner is Regents Professor of Education at Arizona State University. He has taught in Australia and Spain, as well as at numerous universities in the United States. David is a Fellow of the Center for Advanced Study in the Behavioral Sciences, and a past president of both the American Educational Research Association (AERA) and the Division of Educational Psychology of the American Psychological Association (APA). He is the recent recipient of awards for distinguished contributions from APA, AERA, and the National Education Association (NEA). He is coauthor of the bestseller *The Manufactured Crisis* and the text *Educational Psychology,* now in its fifth edition. David also coedited *The Handbook of Educational Psychology, Talks to Teachers,* and *Perspectives on Instructional Time.* In addition, he has authored more than one hundred published articles, technical reports, and book chapters.

Ursula Casanova

Ursula Casanova is Associate Professor in the Division of Educational Leadership and Policy Studies at Arizona State University. She was an elementary school teacher and principal in Rochester, New York, before being awarded a fellowship at the Institute for Educational Leadership in Washington, D.C., and then a position as Senior Research Associate at the National Institute of Education of the Department of Education. Ursula authored *Elementary School Secretaries: The Women in the Principal's Office* and coauthored *Schoolchildren at Risk; Bilingual Education: Politics, Practice and Research;* and—most recently—*Modern Fiction about Schoolteaching: An Anthology.* She also collaborated with her husband and colleague, David C. Berliner, in the development of the series *Readings in Educational Research,* which is intended to facilitate teachers' access to educational research.

■ Dedication

To those in our schools who strive to grow and develop against often insurmountable odds, and to all those who conduct research to help them.

■ Acknowledgments

This book was only possible because of the scholarship of many educational researchers. We thank them and hope we have been faithful to their intentions as we report their work. We also thank Leanna Landsmann who, as editor of *Instructor,* believed that educational research should be made available to teachers. The monthly columns we wrote for that magazine eventually grew into this book. We also owe a special debt of gratitude to Sheila Chávez who helped us with her well-honed research and organizational skills. Finally, we thank Robin Fogarty, vice president, and Julie Noblitt, managing/acquisitions editor, of IRI/Skylight Training and Publishing, Inc., for their interest and confidence in the value of this book for practitioners.

Contents

Section III: Learning

Section IV: Motivation

Preface

Approximately 100 years have passed since the first great American psychologist, William James, started giving his influential talks to teachers. In his weekly lectures he struggled to offer practicing teachers something of use from the psychology of that time. But James differentiated between psychology (a science) and teaching (an art). He believed that a science could not directly influence an art. Research emanating from psychology or any other social science, such as anthropology or sociology, he argued, could not directly inform a teacher about what to do— just as knowledge of the physics of light and the science of optometry could influence an artist only indirectly, not directly. According to James, the possessor of an *intermediate inventive mind* was needed to stand between science and art, or, as in our case, between research and practice. Such a person, whether in art or in teaching, could adapt, adopt, stretch, and tailor scientific research findings to the appropriate context, be it a canvas or particular classroom in school. This is what we have attempted in this book. Through our commentaries we have taken on the roles of "intermediate inventive minds" in order to bridge the distance between research and practice.

For several years we collected dozens of research findings from various scientific traditions, all relevant to teaching. In this book those studies are described, then followed by a discussion of how the findings might be applied in the classroom. All this is quite in keeping with James's edict—but it is not enough. Ultimately, practitioners need to apply their own inventive minds to the process of translation. Since each school (indeed each classroom) is unique, however, what is appropriate in each setting can best be determined only by those closest to it.

We believe that this book will be quite useful as a catalyst for discussions about professional concerns—a process found to be a powerful (and enjoyable) form of staff development. Such discussions can provide both instructional leaders and teachers at a school site with rare opportunities to evaluate their one-of-a-kind context, in order to determine the applicability and usefulness of this research. Our commentaries throughout are intended to help you in that process.

■ The Authors

Ursula Casanova has been a classroom teacher and school principal in urban settings. Currently she is Associate Professor of Educational Leadership and Policy Studies at Arizona State University. She provides herein the intermediate, inventive perspective that seeks to connect research findings to classroom practices. This book presents her interpretations and contextualizations of such findings, demonstrating the process you must follow if the research is to be useful in your own classroom. The research about which Professor Casanova comments is written in a forthright, non-technical style by David C. Berliner, Regents Professor of Education, at Arizona State University.

For six years we shared both our professional and personal lives, as coauthors of the column "Putting Research to Work," for *Instructor* magazine. That column, intended to help teachers to use research findings in order to inform their own practice, won an award from the American Educational Research Association. In this volume we have brought together a collection of those articles, newly edited and rewritten, as well as some new articles written expressly for this book. The book, originally published by Scholastic, has now found a new home at IRI/Skylight where we hope it will continue to be useful to practitioners.

■ The Articles

Each article in this book is an abridged and edited version of an original research study (original authors and sources are listed in the page-bottom references). Each was of necessity cut down dramatically in size and complexity, albeit without losing its important points. This potpourri of research articles and commentaries has been loosely organized into six categories. We present (1) eleven articles and commentaries about teaching, (2) eleven about instructional strategies, (3) nine about learning, and (4) eight about motivation. (Since the lines between teaching and instructional strategies are blurred, and both are concerned about student learning, and—further—motivation and learning are closely related topics, these four categories are, necessarily, loosely defined. The point is not whether the articles and commentaries fit neatly into these categories, but whether they are useful to you as a practicing classroom teacher.) In addition, we present (5) seven articles on school and society, and (6) five concerned with testing. Each of the six sections is preceded by a short introduction.

During the years spanned by the writing of the articles collected in this book, many thousands of research articles were published. The selection included here represents our choices from what we read of that vast array, and therefore our values. Our selection was not restricted to our national boundaries; you will find that our articles report about research from Finland, Israel, Japan, and various other countries. Their appropriateness suggests the commonality of experience that binds all educators. We also have made no attempt to select the "best" examples within any particular category. All the selections, however, can stand close scrutiny in regard to the rigor of their methods and the validity of their findings.

The articles you will find here were selected because they (1) dealt with issues that we believe to be relevant for teachers, (2) were of a style and range that could be easily synthesized within the space allotted, and (3) reflected our own philosophy of worthwhile educational practices. The third point is most important because it explains the lack of balance in the content. You will find, for example, that there are more articles related to culture in education, and to cooperative learning, than to other possible topics (such as direct instruction and assertive discipline). These choices represent our interest in these topics, and our belief that schools must be more than places where knowledge is transferred and stored. We believe, with John Dewey, that schools must also prepare children to be effective members of a democracy. Living with a heterogeneous society requires, we think, cultural flexibility and cooperation, both of which must be nurtured in our schools. The research articles we have chosen for this volume reflect these values.

■ The Readers

We are convinced that the readers of this book want to be knowledgeable professional educators. To be knowledgeable means staying up with what the research community has to offer. To be professional means having the courage to try new ideas and practices such as those presented here, and evaluating for yourself their usefulness. Not every research finding has relevance to your grade level or school, or for your kinds of students. But some findings may have such usefulness, and you are the only one who can identify them.

Because some findings require considerable teaching experience before they can be implemented, if you are just starting your career you may want to postpone trying some of the ideas you will read about in this book until you feel more secure in your professional role. Of course, some findings and practices can be implemented literally overnight, by any teacher working on his or her own—but others require such actions as teachers banding together as colleagues and changing existing school organization or school policy. Thus it might be especially helpful for some teachers to read and discuss these articles with one or more colleagues. (Getting into the habit of working together as professionals can also help break down the isolation that many teachers feel in their professional lives.)

Many of these articles and commentaries present ideas about such topics as culture and education, or involvement with parents. These cry out for immediate discussion, but *not* necessarily for immediate implementation. Similarly, some articles and commentaries may lead you to want to rethink, and even attempt to modify (for example), your school's grade-retention policy—but, again, you will need your colleagues to discuss with you how to do that.

Finally, learning with another person—or two, or several—usually is simply more fun than trying it alone. So we recommend the former, at least occasionally. As a matter of fact, learning with your colleagues may do more for your professional life than all the articles in this book.

■ Conclusion

We now invite you to join us as we examine and discuss research and its application. We urge you to be a critical reader of these articles: Neither the original researchers, nor ourselves as their synthesizers, has a monopoly on truth. *You* will need to be the one to decide what is right for you and your students. But we encourage you to bring an open mind to the process. Don't be too quick to judge what will work and what will not. At one time or another, all of us are misled by the looks of a foreign dish; it is only with open-minded testing that we learn to find it appetizing. And so it often is with new ideas. We may at first reject some that appear too different from what we are used to, but, if given a chance, they may turn out be quite compatible—and helpful.

It takes courage and self-confidence to try new things, whether food or ideas. However, as a teacher you probably have more than an ample supply of both characteristics.

SECTION 1

TEACHING

Introduction

For many years, teaching has been thought of as something you could discuss, like religion or philosophy, but not something you could study systematically, like biology or astronomy. In fact, at the turn of the twentieth century, when one of the first scientific studies of teaching in our country was presented (a study of the futility of most instruction in spelling), the audience is said to have booed the speaker! That audience was primarily made up of school administrators, most of whom believed that teaching was a *moral* endeavor, so that if you wanted to study it, you needed to use the methods of philosophy—logic, reason, and persuasion. You certainly never needed to go observe a classroom to determine what was good practice. It was a waste of time, they thought, to try to observe in classrooms, measure and quantify effects, control variables, and so forth. Moral endeavors were simply not studied that way.

There was also another popular belief, still with us today, that good teachers are born, not made—you either had it or you didn't! When this belief is held, teacher training is seen as a waste of time.

Both sets of beliefs have been shown to be nonsense: Teaching *can* be studied scientifically, like any other human endeavor; and, through education and training, dramatic changes in teachers' behavior *have* resulted. Teaching is still a moral calling, but that does not mean it cannot be studied. For the past twenty years, thousands of scientific studies of teaching and teachers have been completed, some of which have helped make struggling teachers competent, and competent teachers better at what they do.

Each idea or practice we briefly discuss here has a solid ground in one or more research studies. As knowledgeable professional educators, you need to be aware of these ideas and practices. But you will have to assess them and evaluate their utility in your own unique teaching environment. It is in that way, more than in any other, that scientific findings come to be applied to the art of teaching.

Only eleven out of a vast number of contemporary studies of teaching are presented in this section. Each of the articles selected provides direct benefits to teachers. We begin with two studies that remind us that some difficulties in teaching occur because of the vast individual differences that exist among the students in our classrooms. In our search to teach effectively in light of these incredible variations in learning

3

speed, motivation, background knowledge, home support, and so forth, *we* sometimes add to the problem. We may for instance treat all the children equally, denying their differences, or treat them so differently that we exaggerate their dissimilarities. In an era of cultural and linguistic diversity, and sharp difference between social classes, *all* the usual ways in which individuals differ seem to be magnified—and so this is an area of great concern to teachers. These two studies provide some nourishing food for thought.

Two additional studies are concerned with the teaching of learning strategies to students. Contemporary research has made an important finding—namely, that many students who do poorly in school have not been taught how to learn *in school.* They may function well in their parents' store, or competently care for their siblings, but fail many school tasks that require specific skills they have not needed to develop. Such students need to receive explicit instructions on *how* to learn in school. Schools are indeed unique learning environments, but not necessarily ones for which all children are adequately prepared.

Two studies are brief descriptions of easy-to-use teaching tips. One is about ways you can start classes more efficiently, allowing you to get more work done. The other describes ways you can improve your homework assignments, so that you get higher performance and more positive attitudes from students.

Another study in this section is about the teaching of science. In an era when teachers are under fire for not providing business with a scientifically literate work force, we must search for ways to do more and better instruction in science. This article provides clues about how to do that.

Four articles in this section deal with management issues. The teacher is, after all, a manager of learning environments. Good teaching cannot take place in poorly managed environments. The management of children, since they have been known to misbehave, is the focus of the first article. The second is on the management of time, a most precise instructional resource. The third concerns management of instruction in resource rooms, since problems of coordination need to be addressed so that children who need special teaching help will actually receive it. Fourth and finally, we present an article about organizational structure and teacher efficacy. There are some organizational structures that help teachers to avoid burnout and maintain enthusiasm. If you don't work in one of these you may need to band together with other teachers, to create such structures.

How Appropriate Are Most Teachers' Assignments?

■ Research

Adapted from Bennett, N., Desforges, C., Cockburn, A., & Wilkinson, B. (1984). *The quality of pupil learning experiences.* Hillsdale, N.J.: Lawrence Erlbaum Associates.

What kinds of tasks do highly regarded teachers assign to their primary students? Neville Bennett and his colleagues investigated that question in their intensive study of classroom life in grades 1–3 in British schools. Their data raise questions relevant to American schools as well.

To categorize the quality of work assigned, the researchers asked questions about each new task that students received in mathematics, reading, and language arts. They asked: Did the task present new material? Was either discovery or invention essential? Was the work intended for enrichment? Did the task require the student to revise completed work, or to practice a previously taught skill?

Overall, practice tasks predominated, as might be expected for youngsters beginning to learn language and mathematics skills. Noteworthy, however, was that only 7 percent of all new tasks were for enrichment. These researchers described enrichment tasks as those that require the transfer of a new skill to a new topic. (A typical enrichment activity might promote having a child who has just learned how to write a title for a class-written paragraph to write titles for a series of new paragraphs on different subjects.)

While these teachers asked their students to do relatively few transfer tasks, more startlingly, they assigned *hardly any* tasks (only .5 percent) requiring discovery or invention. These researchers described discovery tasks as those that, for example, promote having children who had been taught two-column subtraction to create the rule for three-column subtraction.

By interviewing teachers, the researchers discovered both which quality and what level of difficulty the teacher intended a task to have for students. After individually questioning and then testing children, they compared the teacher's intentions with the student's perception of a task's difficulty and purpose. What they found was most reassuring:

Teachers' and students' perceptions of purpose matched in 75 percent of cases!

It was when the researchers studied the other 25 percent of the tasks that they found something disquieting. First, from one-third to one-half of all tasks that teachers thought required new learning or transfer actually were practice tasks for the students. The mismatches showed a peculiar pattern. Teachers made fewest errors for the low-achieving students. The error rate doubled for students who were above average in achievement. The error rate tripled for high-achieving students! More than any others, the high achievers saw each of their tasks as having a purpose different from the one that their teacher intended.

Bennett's research team went on to study how teachers may over- or underestimate a student's ability to do certain tasks. Although, naturally, different teachers varied in their ability to accurately match a task with a student's achievement level, the teachers' overall accuracy was rather low. The cognitive requirements of the tasks meshed with students' ability levels in only 40 percent of the cases. About 30 percent of the tasks were too difficult for the student; about 25 percent were too easy. Thus, these data reveal how even well-regarded teachers have difficulty in choosing tasks that fit the ability levels of the students they teach. Furthermore, while these teachers were good at recognizing when they *over*estimated a student's ability, they seemed never to realize it when they *under*estimated it. Trained to watch for errors and misunderstandings, these teachers perceived no problems if children were working and not complaining!

Once again, the mismatches of difficulty with ability level were not random. Teachers *under*estimated the abilities of their *high*-achieving students on 41 percent of the tasks. They *over*estimated the abilities of their *low*-achieving students in 44 percent of the cases.

What this research indicates is that teachers have a tendency to homogenize their classes. They see their highest achievers as less able than they really are, and their lowest achievers as more able than they really are. Considering the size of the average class, this tendency is quite understandable. yet these misperceptions limit attainment for high achievers, and make school more difficult for low achievers.

Bennett and his colleagues concluded that even the well-regarded teachers in their study had too little insight into the levels and kinds of cognitive processing on and in which students engage. The researchers clearly recognized the complexity of teaching, and were very respectful of the teachers whom they studied. Their concern, however, was that the teachers could never hope to attain their goal of individualized instruction for children if they didn't become more adept at thinking about the cognitive demands of learning tasks in relation to the cognitive abilities of their students.

■ Practice

Each and every day, teachers are concerned with introducing new material, as well as giving students enough opportunities to discover, invent, transfer, and apply learning. Matching tasks with students is also something we think about every time we prepare a lesson plan. However, research tells us that although thinking about (and doing) these things is all to the good, we *still* have to consciously fight our tendency to homogenize a class. We have two good reasons to keep struggling against this "homogenization" inclination. First, students who are given inappropriate task are likely to behave badly, having become bored with the too-easy work, frustrated with the too-difficult. But even more importantly, mismatching tasks and students is patently counterproductive to learning.

How does a teacher go about improving his or her ability to select the right tasks for students? The first step is to carefully evaluate your students' competence. You can test ability with either commercial or teacher-made diagnostic tests. To reduce anxiety, though, you must let students know that the purpose of the test is to find out what they do *not* know, not to check their speed or to give a grade.

The next step is to distinguish between *careless* and *conceptual* errors. A repeated mistake is likely to reflect lack of understanding of the concept; an incidental error, carelessness. Students who find a task too easy might fail to give it their complete attention and make careless mistakes. To determine the student's instructional level, it's necessary to identify the specific concepts on which each student makes errors.

Matching a task to a student also requires that the task's level of difficulty be identified. You may find that the progression suggested by the textbook is not the most appropriate. That is, students might find some tasks found later in the textbook easier than those that are suggested to be done first. A couple of examples come to mind: A student whose home language is Spanish, a language closely related to Latin, will find Latin root words much easier to learn than the short Anglo-Saxon words typically introduced in early reading instruction. In another situation, urban students are likely to understand decimals before they comprehend fractions, primarily because they may have had responsibilities handling money. These and similar situations require that the teacher make the students consciously aware of the similarities between what they are familiar with and what they don't yet understand.

Teachers must also be alert to the possibility that a given task might involve more than one skill. A student may have the skills necessary to solve a math problem, but lack the reading skills necessary to understand it. And a recently arrived foreign-born child might not have the cultural references needed to understand a story.

In spite of your caution, you are still likely to misjudge some students. How will you know? Watch out for those who either complete their work in record time, or are still at it when everyone else has finished. Reevaluate those who refuse to complete their work—it may simply be too hard! Similarly, those who spend a lot of time fooling around may not be challenged enough. Finally, ask your students, individually and collectively, if they think a task is too easy or too hard.

Once you have identified the student's level of competence and the task's level of difficulty, you need to identify what the researchers call the quality of the task. Keep in mind that, according to this research, few of the tasks assigned by those "highly regarded" teachers required the application of previously learned skills. Even fewer encouraged discovery or invention. Take a critical look at the tasks you assign, and try to determine whether they are likely to accomplish what you intend. Are you limiting your students' progress with tasks that make them do the same thing over and over?

How can you help your students to transfer their skills from a known task to a new one? How can you help to use their curiosity and apply previously learned skills in discovering and inventing new solutions? The true measure of learning is the ability to apply what is learned. Generalization and transfer, not learning, is really our goal. To be able to do the same thing over and over only means that we can do that particular thing—a ditto page of sums, for example, or filling in the blanks in a work sheet. But the world outside school seldom requires *those* skills. What it does require is recognizing old problems in new forms, and thus dealing more readily with the unexpected. So that is what you need to emphasize in your teaching.

Ability Grouping: Does It Cause More Problems than It Solves?

■ Research

Adapted from Peterson, P. L., Wilkinson, L. C., & Hallinan, M. (Eds.), The social context of instruction; group organization and group processes. New York: Academic Press; and Rosenbaum, J. E. Social implications of educational grouping. In D. C. Berliner (Ed.), Review of Research in Education, Volume 9. Washington, D.C.: American Education Research Association.

Both tracking and grouping by ability are responses by schools and teachers to an inescapable fact of life: Students differ dramatically from one another. In some districts, tracking (ability-grouping by class) begins as early as the upper elementary grades. In many schools, children are grouped by ability within classes as early as first grade. In one famous (or infamous) study, a teacher grouped students on the eighth day of kindergarten, and the "low" group was still together in second grade.

But is homogeneous ability-grouping an effective response to student diversity? Contemporary researchers are now agreeing on this long-standing issue, and their research is showing that tracking and ability-grouping usually are quite detrimental to low-ability students.

In one study of tracking, low-track children were found to challenge their teachers, obstruct academic activity, and misuse educational resources more often than high-track children. When doing assigned, independent seatwork, low-track youngsters tended to discuss social, not academic, events. Meanwhile, in high-track classrooms, teachers and students were promulgating academic goals and standards.

One interpretation of these data is that low-track students cause schools and teachers to treat them in certain ways because of their behavior. Another interpretation is that a good deal of such student behavior is the result of school and teacher tracking practices.

In support of this second interpretation are many studies in which teachers were found to make fewer demands on low-track students, and to apply less exacting standards to themselves as teachers of low-track students. In one study, teachers complained more about the behavior of low-track students, but they did not discipline them as much as they disciplined high-track students. Another study found that teachers' evaluative comments to high-track students got lengthier, more elaborate, and more positive over the school year. During the same year, teachers progressively described low-track students in briefer and more pejorative terms.

In a number of studies the teachers simply appeared to be more serious about teaching their high-track students. While they would teach their low-track students basic skills with lots of drill, they offered their high-track students many concepts to learn, and a variety of ways to learn them. For example, in a unit on taxation, the high-track students learned how different taxation systems work, while low-track students learned to fill out forms! The work in the low track was easier, but also much more boring. And from a different set of studies about classroom management it was learned that a boring curriculum inevitably leads to management problems.

Complicating this research, however, is the finding that low-track students are also most likely to have been assigned the least-able teachers. The questions remain: Do low-ability students who are tracked cause teachers to treat them in ways that are not academically sound? Or does this behavior result from the educationally unsound behavior of teachers and schools? Most likely we are seeing *both* forces at work.

One place where homogeneous ability-tracking seems to be very beneficial, however, is in predominantly lower social-class schools. Here, tracking the high-ability students provides a context in which to promote the academic standards and norms of behavior they might not ordinarily encounter. In such schools, tracking results in higher rates of college attendance than when no tracking takes place.

Ability-grouping within a class presents problems similar to those of tracking. The low-ability group in a class usually accrues less time on learning tasks, and it experiences more behavioral interruptions. In one study of first-grade reading groups, the students predicted to have the most trouble learning to read were assigned to reading groups that contained the most immature, inattentive students. In these groups, teachers actually spent less time helping children read, and more time managing social and behavioral problems. Thus the social context of the group alone worked against the desired learning.

Studies also show that the pace of instruction is dramatically faster in high-ability groups, and that the difficulty of the tasks is greater, as well. Research has also revealed that in classroom discussions the low-ability students have fewer opportunities to respond, but are expected to answer more quickly when called on. Moreover, if low-ability students respond correctly, they are less likely to be praised. If they respond incorrectly, they are more likely to be criticized. Such is life when you wear the low ability label.

By the end of a year the small differences that are initially used to divide children into homogeneous high-, medium-, and low-ability groups often have become big ones. As currently used, ability groupings apparently increase diversity, rather than reduce it. The price paid by low-ability students needs to be carefully compared to the advantages that high-ability children might gain. This is particularly true since research usually shows no performance decrements for *high*-ability students in *hetero*geneous classes, but does show performance decrements for *low*-ability students in *homo*geneously grouped classes.

▬ Practice

The research cited above must be examined in the light of classroom realities. Every teacher faces diversity in the classroom. For some teachers, this diversity spans several grade levels; for others the span may be comparatively narrow. Where there is great diversity, some form of grouping seems unavoidable. Furthermore, in lower socioeconomic settings, where academic expectations may be generally low, tracking appears to be beneficial for at least the higher-ability students.

Given that tracking (again, class-by-class grouping) and ability-grouping within classes are so prevalent, it is perhaps most useful to devise ways to avoid the pitfalls uncovered by the research. One can begin by considering the reasons for forming different kinds of groups. While it might seem helpful to group children by ability in order to teach specific skills in math, we should remember that achievement in real life is not based solely on academic skills. This is sometimes forgotten in schools, where achievement in reading, for example, tends to become the sole criteria for judging competence. Groups ought to be organized in a variety of ways, academic ability being but one.

A group assigned to work on a science task may benefit from having at least some members who can read and write well, but might gain, too, from having rather more creative, physically dexterous, and socially astute students on the team as well. Similarly, a group organized for the purpose of writing a story would benefit from having students good at storytelling, as well as some skilled in writing—which is hardly the same trait.

Of course, it is not enough just to put groups together and give them a task. The teacher must first help students to recognize that *each of them* is necessary to the task's successful completion: Some students who lag academically need to be recognized for the skills they have that are not usually rewarded in the school setting. Children also need to learn how to work *together* in a cooperative group, the fact being that most of their school life is spent working competitively and individually. They need to learn how to listen to each other, how to be constructively critical when necessary, and how to join together and work cooperatively on some projects.

But what of those times when it is absolutely unavoidable to group by ability? Well, first make very sure that it is indeed *ability* that is being used as the criterion. I know of a situation wherein a young student was demoted to a lower reading group because he was not completing the assigned work and was often distracted during reading. This behavior was confused with a lack of ability to read the material. Putting him in a lower reading group in fact worsened the situation. He was then totally bored, and his achievement dropped. In addition, he began to dislike both school and reading. Fortunately, one teacher was alert to these changes and reassigned the child to a higher reading group. His behavior and his achievement then changed dramatically for the better.

There is a lesson here that is often forgotten—namely, that children are as likely to benefit from being accelerated as they are from reassignment to a lower achieving group. There is empirical evidence to support this counterintuitive claim, as well. For example, in one of the studies of grouping, the attention level of a child who was moved from a low to a high group was tracked throughout the course of the year. While in a low group with high levels of inattention, he was also inattentive at the same high levels. After moving to a high group where attention was higher, the boy's attention to academic tasks also increased. His individual patterns of attention and inattention eventually were similar to those of whichever group he was in. Students in low-ability and high-ability groups alike learn the norms of their respective groups.

Another thing to keep in mind is that groups do not have to be forever; they can arise out of the daily lesson. Children can change not only from one week to another, but from day to day. What one child now finds easy may be difficult for another—now. While such findings may be the basis for grouping today, it is hardly necessary (or wise) to stamp children with today's particular expectations for a long time. There is a danger that such expectations may be self-fulfilling.

Since research shows that assignment to groups may sometimes be detrimental to student achievement, teachers need to guard against negative effects of such. We must remember to treat children in the low-ability range with the same respect as those who achieve more easily. We need to recognize their particular skills, and consider their inadequacies as temporary hindrances that are likely to disappear with the help of interesting and challenging work. Our comments to *all* children ought to be both demanding of their best efforts, and encouraging.

Are There Any New Teaching Methods? Yes, and This One Produces Startling Results!

■ Research

Adapted from Palincsar, A. S., & Brown, A. L. (1984). Reciprocal teaching of comprehension-fostering and comprehension-monitoring activities. *Cognition and Instruction,* 1(2), 117–175.

Just when you think that every teaching method that is going to be invented already has been, along comes a new one. *This* one is called *reciprocal teaching.* Annemarie Palincsar and Ann Brown have demonstrated that remarkable student gains in comprehension can be achieved after relatively short periods of this type of instruction.

Cognitive scientists have noted that those who derive the most from reading instructional material have apparently developed their own personal comprehension strategies. These strategies inform them when they have wandered off, missed a point, are confused, cannot predict what is coming up, or are not following the gist of what is to be learned.

Palincsar and Brown thought that children who comprehend little of what they read might be missing both the comprehension-monitoring and comprehension-fostering strategies possessed by more efficient learners. To test their ideas they selected six seventh-grade children who could decode written words but were about two and one-half years behind their fellow students in terms of their standardized reading comprehension scores. The average IQ of these students was 83, varying from 67–99. Their grade equivalent achievement scores averaged 4.4.

These students were then taught four comprehension-fostering strategies: (1) summarize prose, ensuring a type of self-review; (2) ask main idea questions, and by answering these demonstrate comprehension; (3) clarify what was read, using their own words to restate and evaluate a passage; and (4) predict what would happen or be written next in the prose passage. All four comprehension-fostering activities emphasized bringing out the students' relevant background knowledge about the material to be learned.

Reciprocal teaching was the instructional method used, a method compatible with the developmental theories of the Russian scientist Lev Vygotsky. The development of a child's competence, said Vygotsky, depends on observations of, and coaching by, an expert. The expert, usually a parent or a teacher, provides the social support and the prompts necessary to bring a child to the most mature level that he or she is capable of reaching at that point in time. In effect, experts provide the scaffolding that the child needs in order to develop. Through modeling, verbal directions, and direct tutoring within a social context, the child learns to internalize the behavior to be learned, eventually resembling the mature learner. Reciprocal teaching relies on Vygotsky's theory, and provides a context for such interactions to occur within.

In this study a teacher and two children read instructional passages on such things as snakes, or camels, or the formation of the Hawaiian Islands. In the training sessions, students were asked to think of *questions* that a teacher might ask them, or that might appear on a test. They were also asked to *summarize* the main ideas. They learned to *predict* what was going to happen when, for example, a pit viper got close to a warm-blooded animal, or to *restate* why snakes have such flexibility in their bodies. On the first day of training the students gave very inadequate responses. For example, after reading about pit vipers, a child asked: "What is found in southeastern snakes; also the copperhead, rattlesnakes, vipers. They have—?" An ideal question would have been: "Why do they call some snakes pit vipers?" Another child summarized a paragraph on camels by saying: "What camels do." A better summary might have been: "It tells us about two kinds of camels—what they are like and where they live."

In the beginning the teacher would prompt the students, in an effort to get a response. The questions, summaries, paraphrases, and predictions elicited would be corrected. New and much better statements would be modeled. Students would practice giving the better responses. Verbal praise for matching the model was given. As the students got better at all four skills, the teacher would require each student to assume the role of leader of the training session. Teachers' and students' roles were then interchangeable—and thus the name "reciprocal teaching."

At the start of the study, on the daily classroom tests of comprehension of passages, the students' average score was 30 percent correct. At the end of instruction it was about 80 percent correct. On standardized test performance the students gained between 0-36 months. The average gain in comprehension was 15 months; the length of the training program was 15 days. *For 15 days' instruction an average of 15 months' growth was recorded!* Moreover, the students who received the reciprocal teaching experience showed gains in their social studies and science classes, dramatically changing their academic status in those subjects. Furthermore, the gains in comprehension were still evident eight weeks after training had ended.

These results are not from a single study. Similar effects occurred in a pilot study run before this one, and again in a study following the one just described. The evidence is persuasive: Most children with adequate decoding skills but low comprehension will profit from reciprocal teaching wherein comprehension-monitoring strategies are taught. You might want to add reciprocal teaching to your repertoire of methods.

▬ Practice

Are you the kind of teacher who is always seeking ways to improve your own teaching? If so, you probably are eager to try reciprocal teaching in your own classroom. It will encourage you even more to know that these researchers did not end their work by remaining in the laboratory. For their second study, Palincsar and Brown trained four teachers to use these instructional techniques in their classrooms, with their regular reading groups. After just three training sessions, the teachers began using these techniques with their students.

Although the teachers were at first very skeptical of their students' ability to participate in reciprocal teaching, their students did indeed achieve results similar to those reported above. Two of the teachers were regular classroom teachers, and two were resource-room teachers. At the end of the study, all four teachers were pleased with their students' ability to participate in this type of instruction, and with their progress—not only in reading comprehension, but in general "thinking" skills. All of the teachers said they would add these techniques to their instructional repertoire.

Three days of training cannot be adequately summarized in a short review. What follows is only a brief description of *some* of the techniques used in reciprocal teaching. You may want to try several of these ideas in your classroom, discuss them with your fellow teachers, and learn from your own experiences. The original article, and more recent references to reciprocal teaching, can also provide additional information.

What then were the components of reciprocal teaching? First, when introducing new material, the teacher would activate the students' prior knowledge with a brief discussion. Students' attention would be called to the title, on the basis of which they would be encouraged to make predictions. If the lesson was a continuation of an earlier one, they would be encouraged to discuss important points of the topic already covered. At this initial exercise, the adult teacher would appoint one student to lead a discussion of the first segment (usually a paragraph). The leader would read aloud while the group read silently.

After the reading, the student leader of the group would ask a question of the group—the type of question that might be asked by the teacher, or in a test. Next, the student leading the group would summarize the passage, and then offer a prediction (or ask for clarification, if necessary). The lesson would continue with different students taking the role of teacher.

The adult teacher's role throughout was to provide guidance to the student "teacher." The adult teacher might prompt the student: "What question do you think a teacher might ask?"; or the teacher might instruct the student: "Remember, a summary is a shortened version; it doesn't include detail"; or the teacher might modify the activity; "If you can't think of a question, maybe you can summarize first."

The adult teacher also provided praise and feedback specific to the student's participation: "Excellent prediction; let's see if you're right." Or, if the student did not quite have it yet, the teacher might say: "That was interesting information that I would call detail. Can you find the most important information?" After such feedback the adult teacher would model those activities that still needed improvement: "I would summarize by saying . . ." These sessions lasted approximately 30 minutes apiece during 20 days of lessons over four weeks.

As noted above, when the students began this type of instruction they had difficulty coming up with good questions, summarizing succinctly, and predicting well. However, as instruction progressed they improved very quickly, and their improvement was accompanied by the teacher's gradual withdrawal from the interaction. That is, with minimal coaching from the teacher, the students gradually took over the lesson. Interestingly, this transition happened much more quickly in heterogeneous groups than in others. When the reading groups included very capable readers who were also able to model these strategies, the less capable readers progressed much faster than those in homogeneous groups.

To summarize: Reciprocal teaching involves extensive modeling, by the teacher, of those comprehension-fostering and comprehension-monitoring activities used by expert readers. This method also forces students to respond even when they are not fully competent, thus allowing the teacher an opportunity to gauge their progress and provide feedback. In order to do this well, the teacher has to be sensitive to each student's needs at all stages of the process. Continuous diagnosis guides the teacher's own level of participation. Diagnosis in this sense involves not only initial estimates of a student's competence, but also continuous evaluation and revision that is responsive to his or her current level of participation. Palincsar and Brown call this "on-line diagnosis."

As a final note, it should be emphasized that when this method has been used, inadequate responses by students have not been considered as failures to perform a particular skill. Rather, they have been seen to be important sources of information that comprehension has not been proceeding as desired. Thus the teacher and the students clearly entered into an interaction in which they were mutually responsible for getting the task done. Responsibility for learning was shared, something that is rarely seen in the classrooms that we visit.

Are You Teaching Kids the Right Skills for Remembering?

■ Research

Adapted from Moely, B. E., Hart, S. S., Santulli, K., Leal, L., Johnson, T., Rao, N., & Burney, L. (1986). How do teachers teach memory skills? *Educational Psychologist,* 21 (1 & 2), 55–71.

Contemporary research informs us that most of us can learn to remember better. And, although developmental processes in memory capacity are clearly present in them, even relatively young children can be taught more sophisticated strategies by which to remember better. Because what most people have thought of as natural ability (e.g., some of us simply have good memories, and some do not) is, in fact, also a trainable skill.

Memory skills are needed for more than learning to name the capitals of the states. These skills are required for all kinds of cognitive activity, including the comprehension of analogies, the understanding of metaphors, and engaging in problem solving. Thus, it seemed eminently reasonable for Barbara Moely and her colleagues to study how elementary-school teachers teach skills that help students to learn and remember.

Sixty-nine teachers were studied as they carried out mathematics, reading, spelling, and language arts activities in classes ranging from kindergarten through sixth grade. Each teacher was observed for a total of five days, over several weeks. The instrument used to record classroom observations was designed to pick up a teacher's concern for three things. Did they (1) give suggestions about what kinds of cognitive processing students could use in a particular lesson; (2) provide a rationale for the use of a strategy; or (3) try to get students to verbalize their questions or problems about a learning task?

The findings are informative. Ten percent of the teachers studied never provided any sort of suggestion about strategies that students could use to learn and remember a task better. In fact, only about 2 percent of the classroom instructional activities were interpreted as examples of teachers giving students instruction in learning or memorizing strategies. This kind of verbal behavior, infrequent as it was, came more at the second and third grades than at other grades, and occurred more in mathematics than in the language-arts area.

The most frequent kind of strategy instruction was about using specific aids to solve specific problems (e.g., teaching children to use blocks or their fingers for counting when learning addition). Less often seen was instruction in general strategies applicable to a wide range of problems (e.g., teaching children how to use dictionaries and other reference works). A good many of the teachers' suggestions about strategies to use were designed to aid children in their role learning activities (e.g., children are told to repeat an exercise to learn it, or to write something ten times so they will not forget it). Teachers also taught about paying attention (e.g., "If you want to learn this, listen carefully!")

Less frequently mentioned by these teachers were strategies that children could use to learn how to check their own work for correctness, and strategies that could transform a "new" problem into a problem they clearly knew how to solve, and strategies that help students to monitor their own learning processes. These latter kinds of strategies for learning and remembering are probably among the most important cognitive skills we can learn—but they were rarely seen.

A more intensive study was made of the students of teachers in grades 1-3 who did or did not often suggest cognitive strategies. Low-, average-, and high-achieving students were administered an extensive set of memory tasks, some of which required that they be taught new cognitive strategies. The results of this part of the study were also quite interesting.

Students who came from classrooms where their teachers provided a good many suggestions about cognitive strategies to be used in learning and remembering were better able to verbalize about the nature of the training procedures, and performance in the task, than were the students from classes wherein teachers rarely suggested learning and memory strategies. It was as if the children of the teachers who provided more strategy instructions had learned how to do a bit of a task-analysis of the learning activities in which they were engaged. Furthermore, in several learning activities the average and low-achieving students whose teachers often made suggestions about cognitive processes and strategies showed longer maintenance of the new learning-memory strategies that they were taught. The average and low-achieving students from the classes in which teachers rarely discussed cognitive processes and strategies gave up their newly acquired strategies more easily. They reverted to their natural (often less adequate) ways of learning and remembering.

This study also informs us that cognitive strategies for learning and remembering are in fact taught by most (not all) teachers, but that even among those who provide such instruction it is an infrequent event. Moreover, when taught, these strategies are likely to be specific rather than general, and most often directed at issues of attention, practice, and repetition. Rarely were teachers seen to be exploring the cognitive strategies for learning and remembering that students used, yet it is precisely these strategies that we must better understand! It is unfortunately likely that many average and low-achieving students do not have the strategies that could best help them learn and remember their school work—strategies like those discussed in the development of reciprocal teaching (see pages 13–17).

This study also suggests that some changes in the typical behavior of teachers could produce some changes in students' behavior. We would hypothesize that were more instruction time spent focused on cognitive strategies for learning and memorizing, many more average and low-achieving students could be helped to learn and remember better.

■ Practice

The research reviewed above reminds us that there is more to teaching than content. It is so easy to forget that an important part of the teacher's work should be devoted to teaching the strategies that make learning possible. Since we *are* teachers, we probably have a history as successful learners. It is, therefore, easy to overlook the fact that our own learning success has depended on the use of strategies that have most often been unconscious. For example, I tend to remember telephone numbers with comparative ease, but I rarely think about just how I do this. If I observe myself (that is, if I use metamemory skills), I realize that I try to establish relationships between the numbers. If I have to remember two-nine-seven, I instantly think "$7 + 2 = 9$, but the 9 goes in the middle."

Of course, some of the relationships that I see would not be either readily apparent or useful to others, but only to me. The strategy in this particular case is the establishment of relationships. That strategy can be taught, but the way in which it is used will depend on the individual user. The point is that as successful learners we have developed strategies that we can teach our students if we try to make those strategies conscious. At the very least we help our students to see that personal strategies for remembering can be very useful, indeed.

Children also may unconsciously apply some strategies, though perhaps they apply them only to the things in which they are *really* interested. For example, they may be able to remember all the different models of cars, their specific characteristics, the years in which they were made, and many other details, that I for one find totally forgettable. They can also remember scores, and football lineups, and many other things, that clearly are not as important in the classroom as they are in their neighborhood. However, if they can remember all of that extracurricular detail, they certainly are using memory aids that can be useful in the classroom.

You can start by finding out how they remember, especially when they perform a feat such as recalling the entire last inning of the final game of any modern-day World Series. They will probably first tell you that they don't know how they remember—they just *do*. But if you pursue the question and prod them a bit, you may discover sophisticated strategies that they can learn to apply to classroom content, too. Sharing each and every student's own way of remembering could prove to be much more than an entertaining classroom activity.

However, there is more to learning than just memory. It is true that memory is an important component of learning, but there is a difference between "learning" and "remembering." We certainly want students to memorize facts (for example, multiplication facts). But mere memory is not our only goal. Students must also learn *how to use* facts—how to apply them to problems. In reading, we see that the skills used to remember knowledge are an inherent part of the still more complex skills called for in comprehension, inference, and drawing conclusions. The strategies we use in both memorizing and learning sometimes are similar, but at other times are different. And children need to learn about both.

To teach learning strategies, you might want to ask your students to predict what is going to happen next, or to establish relationships between what they are learning today and what they learned a week ago. For example: "Remember when we built that water pump? Remember how it works? Think back to what you know. Ask yourself whether there is anything about how the heart works that reminds you of that." Establishing linkages across subject matter and across topics makes remembering easier, but always be aware that children may not do this spontaneously. You need to model this kind of behavior, reward it when it is used, and build it into your instructional plans as often as possible.

Another useful learning and remembering strategy is visual cues. I will never forget the English teacher who had us open our composition books to the center and then write, in very large letters, "The second person singular always ends in 's.'" I don't think *any* of us ever forgot that.

Visual cues may be particularly important for children who have a stronger visual than aural memory. Much of what happens in the classroom depends on hearing accurately and on being able to learn from that. Teachers recognize this when they say "Are you listening?" But, for many children, listening may not be enough; they may need to see or to otherwise learn about strategies that can help them to visualize in their minds.

Are you one of those people who has trouble remembering directions to someone's house? You may need visual aids—a small map, for example. Alternatively, you can try to visualize the route in your head: "Get to the light, then turn right; go straight for two blocks, then turn left." I would never remember that unless I took the time to "see" it in my head. And, for at least some children, something like that may prove to be a very useful strategy.

It is important to remember that strategies for learning are no more a natural part of our thinking baggage than the dates of the Civil War. Some children grow up in homes where the Civil War is discussed so frequently that they never remember learning those dates. It is almost as though they always knew them. And so it is with learning strategies. Some children grow up in homes where they are taught many of these so early and so often that they appear to be a part of the kids' mental wherewithal. These children often do very well in school, and so we call them "intelligent," as though they had been born especially talented.

Some other children seem not to have the benefit of that early instruction. Their problems in school may appear to be due to some biological deficiency, when it is simply a deficiency in learning. We need to remind ourselves that knowing *how* to learn and memorize are extremely important skills, and that not all children come to school with them. In fact, sometimes students may even have such skills and not even know they do. We need to help these students to recognize that they *do* know how to memorize and learn in other contexts, help them to transfer those skills to school settings, and then go on to teach them pertinent strategies that will aid them in their efforts to better learn during all the rest of their school years, and beyond.

How to Make a Good Impression Every Day

■ Research

Adapted from Brooks, D. M., & Hawke, G. (1985). *Effective and in-effective session opening—teacher activity and task structures.* Paper presented at the American Educational Research Association meeting, Chicago, IL.

Douglas Brooks and Gay Hawke ran a study of an event common to everyday teaching. These researchers studied the ways in which some classroom teachers begin their lessons. What they found was a recogniz-able pattern for successfully opening a lesson that has implications for teachers at all grade levels.

On three occasions, three math teachers at the middle-school and junior-high levels were videotaped, and the openings of their lessons studied. Students' perceptions of their teachers were assessed, as were the students' achievement gains throughout the year. Two of the three teachers, a second-year teacher and a 32-year veteran, were experienc-ing management problems. The third teacher, with five years' experi-ence, had no history of difficulties.

When the videotapes were analyzed, it was found that the teacher with no management problems got the class started quickly, wasting no time from when the bell rang to roll-call. The teacher with 32 years of experience took twice as long to get the class started, and the second-year teacher took more than four times as long. Other researchers call this "transition time," and when it is too long, classes do not seem to function well.

Roll-call itself was done quickly and efficiently by the teacher with no management problems, but it took the second-year teacher about 2.5 times as long. The very experienced teacher took about five times as long to accomplish this task, despite the fact that she had probably performed this same task close to 30,000 times before (32 years x 5 classes a day x 180 days = 28,800). From the end of roll-call to the first substantive activity, the most effective organizer moved quickly once again, with both the second-year teacher and the veteran taking much longer to begin instruction (twice as long and nine times as long, respectively).

23

We can conclude from these data (and from other studies) that more and less successful classroom managers begin lessons and other kinds of instruction activities differently. First of all, the more successful lesson openings relied on routines, or scripts for behavior, that were virtually automatic. Automaticity of routines is very efficient. It is characteristic of experts in chess, ice skating, piano playing, and surgery. Once a well-practiced routine is running, it leaves a person's mind free to be concerned about more important things, which in the case of teachers are the instructional issues.

The effective lesson openings typically included a quick call to order in a businesslike tone of voice, fast-paced roll-taking, an opening remark that included behavioral and academic expectations for the students, an apparent anticipation of areas of confusion in the explanations given, and a call for questions. The more effective lesson openings were also characterized by more visual scanning to spot anything unusual before it became a management problem.

The least efficient lesson openings lacked effective day-to-day behavioral routines, and were characterized by slower calls to order in an unbusinesslike tone of voice. Visual scanning was often absent, roll-taking was time-consuming, and areas where explanations were going to be confusing were not anticipated.

When students in these three classes were asked questions about their teachers, it was apparent that they had been left with different first impressions. The teacher who started class faster was seen by her students as better prepared, as explaining material better, and as more organized and systematic in instruction. But something at least as important as efficiency and preparedness was also perceived. Students saw the more effective classroom manager not only as friendly, less punitive, more consistent and predictable, and more likely to admit mistakes, but also as someone who valued student feelings.

One hundred percent of her students rated this teacher as enjoying her job. Furthermore, when students were asked if they would like to have her for another course, 96 percent said yes. The percent of students of the *less* effective classroom managers who said they would want these teachers again was 57 and 32 respectively in the classes of the second-year and the experienced teacher. Finally, the students of the more effective manager had higher gains in achievement and in grade equivalencies.

The lesson is clear. Each and every day, businesslike lesson openings convey a seriousness of purpose and a respect for both learning and the learners. Such activities are not in the least incompatible with being an enthusiastic, friendly, caring, humane teacher.

Perhaps this analysis of how effective and ineffective classroom managers open their lessons will help you think about your own teaching. You may decide to practice some new lesson changes in order that the first impression your students receive, each and every day, is precisely the one you want to convey.

■ Practice

The study described above provides strong evidence that all-important first impressions are conveyed not only during the first days of the new school year, but also right down through the last ones.

Just as studies of effective schools have proved the importance of orderly, efficient environments wherein teachers communicate high expectations and a sense of purpose, this study finds the same characteristics at work at the classroom level. The happiest finding is the preference that students demonstrated for such an environment. They voiced this appreciation, and their achievement gains showed it, too.

Those of us who have continuing problems during opening exercises may well be aware of deficiencies—but, if so, how to improve? Here again this study can be helpful: The following subtasks appeared to make a difference.

Routinization. If a task is accomplished daily in a similar manner, matter-of-factly and swiftly, students will know exactly what to expect and how to respond. Thus you will avoid unnecessary interruptions and confusion. Just as brushing our teeth, getting dressed, and preparing breakfast in a routinized fashion allows us to plan our day, we can also free our minds by routinizing daily school tasks. Our discussions and our responses to student needs ought to be characterized by spontaneity, creativity, and improvisation. But our housekeeping tasks need not be done that way.

Visual scanning. The effortlessness of routines can allow time for visual scanning, a way to gauge the collective attitudes of the group: Is everyone high in expectation of a long weekend? Is the group reacting to a national tragedy? Teachers can also gauge individual attitudes: Is Lisa uncharacteristically quiet? Does Tommy appear restless? These observations can help you to target instruction and responses throughout the day.

Businesslike tone of voice. No whining, no harshness—just use a direct, matter-of-fact style.

Behavioral and academic expectations. State daily reminders of behavior expectations, as well as expectations for the day's tasks.

Anticipation of confusion. By reviewing homework you can often guess what's going to cause confusion. If many students make similar mistakes, you can address the source of error and avoid later interruptions. Sometimes, of course, problems may be caused by sudden logistical alterations (like changes in the usual schedule). Keep in mind that calling for questions before initiating the day's instruction gives students the opportunity to clarify issues you haven't anticipated to be problematical.

Are you doing these things? If so, how well? You can probably answer the first question and begin to assess your own opening exercises. To answer the second, you may want to discuss the idea with a fellow teacher, or plan to visit each other's classrooms during opening exercises. You may start by deciding whether you do the five subtasks, or you may choose to have your colleague describe for you how you accomplished just one. Keep in mind that the time period we are discussing is only a few minutes, but apparently a *very important* few minutes. Also remember that the purpose of the observations is to describe and learn, not to rank or evaluate each other.

Another way in which you can gain from your colleagues is by observing an excellent teacher (or such teachers). In this way, the collective experience of teaching can be passed on to incoming professionals— something we need to do more often. (Think, for example, of medical residencies and law clerkships.)

Opening exercises can become great opportunities. This research makes clear that the rewards for improving this unavoidable daily task appear to warrant our best efforts.

Why What You Write on Homework Papers Counts

▪ Research

Adapted from Elawar, M., & Corno, L. (1985). A factorial experiment in teachers' written feedback on student homework. *Journal of Educational Psychology, 77*(2), 162–173.

The title of this article could have been "Little Things Mean a Lot!" In this case the little thing was a little feedback by teachers to students. The research conducted by Maria Elawar and Lynn Corno in 18 sixth-grade classes in Venezuela demonstrated what happened to children's math achievement when individualized feedback on homework was given. It was an ambitious project, for each teacher had from 34–45 children per class.

One group of teachers simply corrected and scored their students' homework. The others were trained to give a different kind of feedback. They asked themselves four questions when they reviewed their students' homework assignments: (1) What is the key error? (2) What is the probable reason for the error? (3) How can I guide the student to avoid the error in the future? (4) What did the student do well that could be noted? These are good questions for teachers to learn to ask as they review their students' homework.

The feedback was quite specific. For instance, on an assignment in which children were asked to draw pictures of their work, teachers might write such comments as "You know how to solve the problem—the formula is correct—but you have not demonstrated that you understand how one fraction multiplied by another can give you an answer that is smaller than either of the numbers multiplied ($1/2$ x $1/2$ = $1/4$). I'm pleased that you know the formula so well!"

Homework was assigned three times a week for ten weeks, and three mathematics achievement tests were given during the course of the study. The researchers measured the students' mathematics achievement, enjoyment of mathematics, anxiety about math, self-concept, and attitude toward school. They also measured the teachers' attitudes toward the teaching of mathematics. What the researchers wanted to know was: Did this kind of feedback make a difference?

What they found was that *on every one* of the achievement tests, the students who had gotten personal and pertinent feedback about their homework errors outperformed the students who received only their scores as feedback on their homework. In addition, the students who were getting the personal and targeted comments rated their enjoyment of mathematics, and the value of mathematics to the world, much higher than they did before they started getting this kind of feedback. But the findings did not stop there. These students showed a reduced anxiety about mathematics, and an improvement in both their self-concept and their attitude toward school. And the teachers expressed more positive attitudes toward teaching mathematics!

The effect of the feedback was positive for children at all levels of ability. Moreover, there was some evidence that the feedback reduced the slight gap in achievement and attitude that had previously separated sixth-grade boys and girls. In short, the study was a resounding success.

This study was not Elawar and Corno's first: It replicated an earlier one (done in the United States) in which they found that the same kind of feedback improved the second-language learning of college students. Both of their studies, and dozens more done by others, remind us that pertinent individual feedback, aimed at correcting errors made during learning, positively affects the learners' performance and attitude alike. Even though we know this, however, we have evidence that in some classrooms very little such feedback is given. We realize it takes a lot of effort to provide this kind of feedback, but it's worth it. Little things like that really do mean a lot.

▬ Practice

Providing the specific feedback that was so effective in the Venezuelan study is within the reach of any interested teacher. While it is easier and faster to do quick corrections that only indicate right and wrong answers, specific written feedback helps students to focus on their weaknesses, and correct these through their own efforts. Thus the time spent in giving feedback should eventually result in savings in classroom instructional time. It is also likely that improvements in student attitude will have a positive impact on classroom climate.

If the reality of time constraints looms large for you, but you'd still like to try what appears to be very useful practice, you might want to target your efforts toward those students who are having the most difficulty.

That is, you could continue to assign, correct, and return homework to all students, but begin to write specific comments to those you feel will benefit from that practice the most—and watch the rewarding results.

Another possibility is to give specific feedback each time to a different small group of students chosen at random. Not every last one would get comments each time, but at least everyone will have felt your personal attention no later than each fourth or fifth time he or she has submitted work.

The four feedback questions used by these researchers provide a convenient guide for teachers to learn ways to comment on student work. Apropos of the first question, it is particularly important to identify the key error made by the student. Because the student will need to know exactly what to concentrate on, your comments must be specific, too. It is not enough, for example, to indicate where students should have written a complete sentence. You must indicate what they must add to *make* the fragment a complete sentence. Likewise, "You have problems with subtraction" is not specific enough, but "You have problems borrowing" makes the error clear to the student. (If a student has made *more* than one error, you may need to resist the inclination to point them all out. It is discouraging to get back a paper whereon nothing seems to be right.) Help the students to understand that your comments will be focused on one mistake, even though there well may be others.

The second feedback question requires the identification of the pattern that leads to errors. When does the student make these errors? For example, you may notice that the student consistently makes mistakes in borrowing from zero. The reason might be that he or she does not understand the procedure.

A brief comment regarding such a procedure may respond to the third feedback question used in the training: How can I guide the student to avoid the error in the future? Your comment might be: "Remember that when you borrow to make the zero become ten, you are taking away units from the next column." This kind of specific feedback gives the student a tool to use when performing this operation in the next assignment. It will also focus attention on those problems the student finds particularly troublesome.

Finally, (in line with the fourth feedback question), do not forget to add a positive comment about the student's work. And make sure that such remarks are academic in nature. "Neat work!" does not qualify as a useful, positive statement, but "Good work: You remembered to apply the rules for borrowing!" does.

The research discussed here is similar to other research on classroom feedback. That research also emphasizes the need for feedback to be directed to the student's work, stated in specific terms but balanced with positive comments. Students are quite willing to accept corrections as long as these are specific to their work rather than general remarks that contribute to feelings of incompetence. Apparently the guidance that students in the Venezuelan study received from their teachers made them feel competent to correct their own errors and, therefore, able both to learn and to *enjoy learning* the subject matter.

Students, as all the rest of us, tend to like those activities in which they succeed. As a matter of fact, the teachers in this study, though working harder, felt rather better about teaching mathematics. This was probably because they felt more successful, too. The personalized comments seem to be such a little thing, but they also seem to do a lot for both students and their teachers.

How to Increase Scientific Literacy: Teach It!

■ Research

Adapted from Mitman, A. L., Mergendollar, J. R., Marchman, V. A., & Packer, M. J. (1987). Instruction addressing the components of scientific literacy and its relation to student outcomes. *American Educational Research Journal, 24,* 611–633.

When educators talk about scientific literacy they frequently stress, in the same breath, the future employability of today's young students, and the economic survival of the nation. With so much apparently riding on the shoulders of our youth, one research team questioned whether teaching for scientific literacy actually occurs to any meaningful degree in public schools. This team defined scientific literacy as scientific content plus four different contexts for understanding and valuing that content: (1) impact on society, (2) knowledge about the reasoning processes used by scientists, (3) knowledge about the historical development of science, and (4) development of positive attitudes toward science.

The team examined the science lessons of 11 seventh-grade teachers with between 1 and 24 years experience who taught in predominantly middle-class schools in Utah and California. Each teacher taught a year-long course in life science. Their textbooks differed, and all brought in a variety of supplementary materials to help them in teaching scientific topics. Each teacher was observed while teaching two different topics. (For example, one teacher was observed while she taught cell structure and function for ten days, and then was observed again when she taught the human circulatory system over a six-day period.)

The dramatic results of the observations were extremely consistent—regardless of teacher or topic. These science teachers *almost always* taught only content. During the first observations, 96.8 percent of the presentation time covered content; during the second, 98.1 percent.

Despite the rhetoric and pressure to develop scientific literacy among their students, these teachers were overwhelmingly concerned with communicating scientific facts and figures, concepts and principles. In the very few instances when the teachers contextualized science instruction, observers described the sessions as very low in quality.

Worksheet and examination items yielded bleak evidence. Of 1,898 worksheet items or test questions used to teach the two topics, only 96 (5.1 percent) put course material in context. Moreover, teachers primarily used recitation and seatwork to teach. Demonstrations took up only about 1.5 percent of the presentation time; laboratory experiences an average of only 10 percent.

When they learned the purpose of the study during the debriefing period, these well-trained science teachers cited fact- and vocabulary-oriented textbooks, lack of time to develop the other components (which they did not appear to value as highly as content), and inadequacy of training as reasons for not teaching all the components of scientific literacy.

These may be reasonable explanations, but they cannot be allowed to direct our teaching. To increase the level of scientific literacy in the country, we must overcome such limitations. Scientific literacy, not just scientific "facts," must be taught directly.

▬ Practice

Many students don't see the relationship between what they learn in school, and their own lives. In science instruction this is particularly dangerous because many social issues require scientific knowledge. To prepare them for the future, we must find ways to help students bridge the gap between the science classroom and real world. How can we do this? Let's look at some examples that were identified by these researchers.

Perhaps the most important concepts for children to understand about the *societal impact of science* is that scientific inventions have social consequences. Pesticides, for example, should not be thought of only as chemical compounds, but as chemical compounds whose misuse can have a serious impact on our daily lives—an undesirable result the thought of which often forces us to balance productivity against health concerns.

To demonstrate this concern to young children, you might spray colored water on a pile of sand. They will see that, though the sand may look prettier, the water that flows out from it hasn't been cleared by the sand's filtering action. Explain that the water may also be less healthy, or at least less palatable, than before. Let older children debate similar scientific issues with social implications at a higher level.

The reasoning processes of science are basic to general logical reasoning as well. By observing, recording, analyzing, making inferences, hypothesizing, and experimenting, our students learn that these are not arbitrary processes, but ones that can be useful throughout their lives.

Older children can relate the process of scientific reasoning to—for example—their interest in cars. An unexpected noise must be listened to carefully (in lieu of observation or diagnostic testing). The mechanic determines when the aberration occurs: During acceleration? At certain speeds? While idling? By analyzing the data the mechanic infers the cause of the problem (hypotheses), and then attempts a solution, repeating this process if necessary until an effective solution is (hopefully) found.

Younger children can understand the scientific process when you begin an investigation with questions like these: Why does a mixture of flour and water sometimes turn into bread, and other times into paste? How can we find out what makes the difference?

Help students to see the *social historical development of science* as an evolving process, not merely as a chronology of facts. In discussing the scientific developments of aircraft, for example, you can relate how concepts of flight drawn by da Vinci during the Renaissance remained mere curiosities until the development of the gasoline engine. Only then could scientists combine engineering design with a propellant system to make flight possible.

Continuing the discussion of science in its social context, you can explain the rapid development of these flying machines as well. Although the first successful flight occurred as a private venture in the United

States, the Germans saw the military potential of the airplane—mainly as an instrument of war. And, because of World War I, they outdistanced other countries in its early development.

Finally, help students to develop a *positive attitude toward science* by showing them how science can satisfy their curiosity about themselves, and indeed the world in which they live, too.

In summary: Besides the content of science, you need to teach (1) the societal impact of science, (2) the reasoning processes used by scientists, (3) the developmental history of science, and (4) positive attitudes toward science as a means of understanding natural, biological, and social phenomena that affect us all. You will need to stress that science is challenging and exciting, but tell your students it's more like a detective story than a miracle. Let them know that such mysteries usually yield to accepted techniques that *anyone* can learn. Your students will then be able to be full participants in a society wherein science is a daily concern. And perhaps, as they are encouraged to grow in their scientific knowledge, they will realize that many mysteries remain to be solved, and they might be the ones to solve them.

What Do We Know About Well-Managed Classrooms?

■ Research

Adapted from Kounin, J. (1970). *Discipline and group management in classrooms.* NY: Holt, Rinehart & Winston; and Evertson, C. M., Emmer, E. T., Clements, B. S., Sanford, J. P., & Worsham, M. E. (1984). *Classroom management for elementary teachers.* Englewood Cliffs, NJ: Prentice-Hall.

In the early 1960s Jacob Kounin completed his basic research on how teachers keep order and maintain attention. His findings were extended by other researchers in the early 1970s, turned into teacher-training materials in the late 1970s, and successfully field-tested by Carolyn Evertson and her colleagues in the early 1980s.

The upshot of the research was that good classroom managers actually prevented most management problems from occurring by keeping events from escalating out of control. They prevented problems, first of all, by sensible room arrangement. High traffic areas were free of congestion and widely separated. Good classroom managers also made sure they had clear sight of all student work areas at all times. They organized their classrooms to have easy access to frequently used teaching materials and student supplies. Finally, they ensured that all students could easily see and hear instructional demonstrations and displays. These teachers simply did not let the physical arrangement of their classrooms take shape by happenstance or tradition.

Every social group needs shared rules and procedures in order to function well. Classrooms are not exceptions. More proficient classroom managers did a better job of clearly communicating to their students the rules about gum-chewing, going to the bathroom, or changing classrooms. They actually modeled the procedures for getting out of one's seat, getting attention when having a problem, and using the library. The most serious of school rules (say, rules about running in the hallways) were written out, as were the penalties for violations of those rules. Research has confirmed that students take more responsibility for their own behavior when the need for rules and procedures is made clear to them—and when their teachers make sure the rules are really sensible before they discuss them.

The everyday tasks of instruction were carried out differently by the better managers. That is, they told students such things as the dates when things were due, the level of neatness required, what they should do when absent, and how much work was expected for particular assignments. The better managers also monitored student progress on instructional tasks more closely. To accomplish this, they maintained accurate record-keeping systems. And when assignments were completed, they gave prompt feedback about the acceptability of the work. However, these teachers did not accept work that did not meet their standards.

The more effective managers had a variety of rewards available, and used them frequently to designate *real* accomplishment. They also knew what sort of penalties to use for different situations, since even the best managers sometimes had to invoke penalties. For violations of certain rules and procedures they were ready to reduce grades or scores, invoke a loss of privileges, provide detention, give demerits, or confiscate materials.

Not only was a system for rewards and penalties well thought out, but it was consistently in use. Frequent use of penalties by a teacher was an indicator of management problems. When inappropriate behavior occurred in class, the better managers always handled the problem promptly, often simply by standing next to a student to closely monitor him or her, or by signaling a student nonverbally. They also seemed to have learned that it was better to simply ignore inappropriate student behavior if it was likely to be of short duration, was not likely to spread around the class, was a minor deviation, or would interrupt other valued activities if reacted to.

Researchers have found that good managers can be spotted on the first day of school. The key signs are that they teach rules and procedures; they are in the room (and often at the door) when children come in, rather than entering later when noise levels are higher; they sometimes have name tags ready; they have procedures to catch up new children assigned to the class during the first few weeks; to reduce anxiety among their students during the first few days of school they plan success-filled whole-group activities; and they never leave their class alone during the first week of school.

In short, from the opening bell to the end of the day, the better classroom managers are thinking ahead. While maintaining a pleasant classroom atmosphere, these teachers keep planning how to organize, manage, and control activities in order to facilitate instruction. They also insure that the instructional program is interesting and that the goals of the program are achievable by most students. Management is much easier when the curriculum is interesting and success in it is possible. So the best managers of classrooms also were excellent in designing instruction.

■ Practice

A well-managed classroom is always a pleasure to visit and, like a well-crafted object, appears seamless. The research described above does much to explain where the seams are and where and how you can improve your classroom management.

You do not have to wait until next fall to take a close look at your classroom, but before you decide to change your arrangement, rules, and expectations, you will want to examine whether the instructional program in use is appropriate to your students. You need to remember that *no* amount of management skill can make up for poor instruction.

Your rules have to mesh with your goals for your students and with your own personal style. A teacher who usually prefers working with small groups while other students work independently will require a different room arrangement from one who usually prefers whole-group instruction. The room arrangement must be appropriate for your purposes. If you want students to work independently, you want to set up areas where this can be accomplished with minimal distraction. If you want to do whole-class instruction, a U-shape arrangement is much more likely to encourage total class involvement than are the traditional rows.

Once you have decided on an arrangement, try to determine whether your plan allows each of your students to see and hear when you are speaking to the class. You may want to sit in different seats in your room, trying to experience that space from your students' point of view.

Another important preventive measure is to clearly establish the rules and procedures of your classroom. Do not be concerned if your colleagues do not support the same rules. Children are flexible and able to understand differences in expectations. It is your own consistency that is important, so you need to make your own rules explicit. Again, those rules need to be guided by your instructional goals. Some teachers encourage a higher degree of independence; others prefer to maintain tighter control over their students' behavior. You make the decision first, and then plan accordingly.

It is not enough to have standards if they are not made explicit through instruction, repeated often, and prominently displayed. Students whose native language is not English, or who come from homes where expectations are widely different from school expectations, may require additional explanations. Newcomers to the classroom also deserve special consideration. In contemporary society every classroom has a good deal of turnover every year. So newcomers are frequent—especially in the schools that serve the poorest students. Therefore, assigning a buddy is a good way to facilitate a new student's appearance, as well as to ensure the passing-on of the rules.

What you expect in behavior should be related to what you expect in academic output. In a mastery learning program, for example, a student has a flexible amount of time to complete the work, but *must* achieve mastery. Other instructional programs limit the time available for learning, but accept a wide range of achievement levels which are translated into grades. If you know what your goals are, what you consider important, and how you will evaluate accomplishment, you will be able to share your values with your students, and to use your procedures consistently.

A clear set of expectations **needs** to be accompanied by an equally clear set of rewards and penalties. These should also be compatible with the instructional goals. Rewards that excuse students from school work are counterproductive. To free children from a reading assignment because they read an extra book the last time suggests that reading is unpleasant. Additional library time or a new book would be more appropriate. Rewards are especially important for those students who are at the low end of the achievement curve. Top achievers usually are amply rewarded. Low achievers need to be recognized for their efforts, also.

Unfortunately, even the best teacher/managers must sometimes resort to penalties, the range of which carefully escalates from a private interaction between student and teacher to an increasing public censure involving as a last resort the principal and parents. For minor problems, they have a repertory of remedies—like standing close to a distracted child, ignoring minor infractions that are not likely to spread, and using signals such as lowering the voice or giving a particular look.

Successful managers, as the research indicates, avoid problems from Day One. They are ready and waiting for their students. Some of them use checklists to ensure that they are taking care of all contingencies, that they are not forgetting to mention some important classroom routine. It is, of course, best to start out the year in this way, but don't worry if you haven't done that. If you need to make changes, tomorrow can be the beginning of your new system of management, provided that you make the changes clear to your students—perhaps even enlist their help. Students who participate in establishing rules find them fairer, and obey them more often.

You will learn what students consider fair if you involve them in helping to set up rules that you *all* live with. We caution against one thing: Rules can be coercive; they can teach obedience and stifle creativity. We have seen some very well-managed and very dull classrooms. The trick is to have an efficient management system *and* a lively, creative classroom. These are not incompatible goals.

Managing Instructional Time

■ Research

Adapted from Berliner, D. C. (1979). Tempus educare. In P. L. Peterson & H. J. Walberg (Eds.), *Research on teaching*. Berkeley, CA: McCutchan; and Fisher, C. W. and Berliner, D. C. (Eds.) (1985), *Perspectives on instructional time*. White Plains, NY: Longman.

Educational researchers think of time in classrooms in the same way that an accountant thinks of expenses in a business. Keeping track of where a business person's money goes, or where a teacher's time goes, is a good way to find out what that person thinks are necessary expenditures. Saving money or time is important because both are scarce and finite resources. Frivolous expenditures of either bring in the auditors or the parents.

For decades there has been a national concern about time management. That concern has surfaced again as a result of some research in which time expenditures in classrooms were recorded. The researchers found enormous variability in the ways time was used by different teachers, even when the teachers were in the same schools working with the same types of children. Described here are five time-based variables that researchers have related to student achievement.

Allocation of time to subject matter. In secondary schools, the number and length of periods allocated to different subject-matter areas usually are set by the districts. Elementary- and some middle-school teachers, however, personally decide how much time will actually be spent on (for example) reading, science, and physical education. Researchers found that one elementary-school teacher regularly spent 45 minutes per day in reading and language arts, while another in the same district regularly spent 137 minutes per day. Other descriptive data showed that one teacher regularly allocated 16 minutes per day to mathematics, while another teacher was able to regularly find 71 minutes each day to allocate to mathematics. The conclusion of a number of researchers was that the opportunity to learn language arts or mathematics was vastly different in different classrooms. Generally, students who are allocated more time—who have greater opportunity to learn—achieve more. This is probably why many countries perform better than does the United States in international comparisons of mathematics and science achievement.

Allocation of time within subject matter area. Every teacher, primary- or secondary-school, decides how much time to spend on the content areas *within* a subject-matter area. Researchers found that one teacher of reading and language arts spent 50 hours over the school year teaching comprehension skills, while another teacher spent only five hours in such activities. One teacher provided 30 hours of writing instruction, while another teacher of similar studies provided only about seven hours during the entire school year. In mathematics, one teacher was found to spend seven hours teaching fractions, while another spent *no time at all* teaching fractions to her students. The conclusion here is that the emphasis given to a specific content area often increases or limits a particular student's opportunity to master that content. Researchers are generally in agreement that opportunity to learn some particular content area is one of the most powerful determiners of achievement that is under the control of teachers and schools.

Time-on-task. After looking at how much time is allocated to different subjects and on content areas within a subject, we must check also on how much children are paying attention to the tasks at hand. Research tells us that, in the typical class, students will attend to what they are supposed to about 70 percent of the time. The attending behavior of students is very different, however, in different classes. The range is from 35–90 percent. This means that if a school subject is allocated 50 minutes, in a class where students attend 90 percent of the time, 45 minutes of instruction will actually be "delivered" to the students. In a class where students attend only 40 percent of the time, only 20 minutes of instruction will actually be "delivered."

Thus the differences in the amount of instruction that students actually receive may be 25 minutes a day, or two hours a week, or 80 hours per school year! When classrooms show big differences in time-on-task, they will also show big differences in student achievement.

Transition time. This is the time it takes students to begin a new period or a new subject, and it also is the time lost when students are putting their things away or getting ready to leave. Time-on-task during transitions is almost zero. No learning is expected, so transition time should be kept low. Researchers have shown, however, that students in one self-contained classroom spent as much as 75 minutes a day on transitions alone. And it is not usual to find a secondary-school period of 50 minutes reduced by 20 minutes for transitions into and out of the subject. Since these kinds of transitions lower time-on-task, they lower achievement, too. It is quite possible, however, to make transitions more quickly without turning schools into factories.

Successful time. Many researchers are convinced that for the early elementary grades, say grades 1–5, a very high percent practice time should be time during which children are successful. The time spent on workbooks, reading circles, recitations, and homework should result in correct responses from students. Research has determined that the percent of time that young children spend in high-success activities is positively related to achievement. For teachers of the early grades this means ensuring that a great deal of time is allocated to "easy" work—work that provides high percentages of successful time. The evidence is not as clear-cut in grades 6–12. Perhaps these older students, with more ego-strength, require less success. But young students need lots of success experiences, and students at any age are not likely to profit from time spent in experiences that lead to failure.

These five variables should start you thinking about how student achievement might improve through better time management.

■ Practice

It's not surprising that research indicates that students achieve better in areas where they have spent the most time. What *is* surprising is what the enormous variability in time use suggests: that decisions about the use of time in the classroom are not consciously directed toward the instructional goals of the schools!

But before we apply any of the time-management findings, we should note that simply adding school hours or days is not an appropriate interpretation of this research. The issues are *efficiency* and *achievement of goals within the time available.* Our efforts should be directed at making better use of the time that we *already* have.

Schoolwide decisions about the use of time must come first. What are the most pressing needs of the school population? Should there be grade-level differences in time allocation? How can we deal with fast and slow students? Responses to these three questions help in setting guidelines for the allocation of time to subject areas, to special classes, and to schoolwide activities alike.

Decisions about the amount of time to be spent on specific content areas should also be made by a school faculty. It is particularly important to decide the sequence to be followed in instruction. At which grade level will fractions be introduced? What must be covered before then? What ought to follow? Are there some skills that tend to be neglected—writing, perhaps memorization—that we want to emphasize across the grades? Remember "coverage" and "emphasis" and "neglect" are words we use to describe time allocations.

Classroom decisions about time allocations must be made on the basis of the characteristics of the particular group of students in each room. These are the decisions over which individual teachers have the most control. Even if our school offers no clear guidelines, we still need to think about what we do with our time, what our students' needs are, and what they will be expected to master.

Our first task is to find out how we are using time now, by monitoring classroom activities for a few days and by asking ourselves these questions: How closely do I stay to my schedule? Am I giving enough attention to those areas that students must master by the end of the year? How much time is used for transitions? Careful records of how we use time can provide a baseline from which teachers can begin to make changes. Audio- and videotape recordings can help answer questions about how time is allocated, and whether or not transitions are smooth.

A more difficult task is to monitor the attending rate of students. The monitoring of students' time-on-task should be done by colleagues who can visit each other's classes for perhaps 30 minutes at a time, four or five different times. The colleague should focus on six to eight students and check whether or not they are paying attention to a task at a given moment. The decisions should be made quickly, using common sense notions about what constitutes attending behavior. It will take under two minutes to check all eight students; then the cycle should be repeated throughout the 30 minutes. Let's say fourteen cycles occurred and a student was judged on-task ten times. The attending rate of each student is the number of checks divided by the total number possible: $10/14 = 73$ percent. Averaging the percentages over the six or eight students studied will give a group rate. Records of four or five such sessions, preferably at different times of day, will give a rough idea of the percent of time when students are attending. If it is not as high as is desirable, teachers can then begin to think of ways to increase their students' time-on-task.

Finally, we need to look at the success rate of students by examining their written work, workbooks, and tests. Are our young students consistently getting less than 75 percent correct? Do we find ourselves needing to reteach very often? Do our students complain that "It's too

41

hard"? Remember that a high level of success (80 percent or above) tends to be associated with higher achievement, especially at the elementary level. It is probably also important to provide for high levels of success for the less academically successful of *any* age.

Time-on-task does not mean that school should become a dreary chore for teachers and students, any more than keeping a budget should result in a joyless lifestyle. It does mean giving conscious attention to the use of the limited time available. Since opportunity to learn is one of the best predictors of achievement, teachers must ensure that, by managing time sensibly, their students have the opportunities to acquire the knowledge and skills that we ask them to learn.

What Kind of Resource Is Your Resource Room?

■ Research

Adapted from Haynes, M. C., & Jenkins, J. (1986). Reading instruction in special education resource rooms. *American Educational Research Journal, 23,* 161–191.

The number of children thought to need remedial help of one sort or another has grown enormously. For example, the number of students identified as learning-disabled has grown from 120,000 to nearly two million in about 20 years. With the increase in identification of special populations has come an increase in special kinds of remediation. Effectiveness of remedial programs, however, has *not* been easy to document. To help understand what goes on in some remedial programs, Mariana Haynes and Joseph Jenkins looked at reading instruction in 28 resource rooms designed to serve fourth through sixth-grade mildly handicapped students. Twenty-three of these resource-room programs were located in an urban district; the remaining five were in a suburban district. All of the mildly handicapped students in these schools who received reading instruction in a resource room were included in the sample. Classroom observations were made in the resource rooms only during reading instruction.

Descriptive data revealed that the minutes per day of actual reading instruction in a resource room varied a great deal for students, ranging from 11 to 180 minutes. Variation of time spent in reading instruction in the resource room should be due to need—but the correlation between a measure of reading achievement and hours of instruction was very low. This suggested that ". . . scheduling practices may be determined more by teacher and school context factors, than by child characteristics. If this interpretation is correct, then resource services may not . . . function in the way they are ordinarily described (i.e., services based on student need)."

Observation also revealed that 56 percent of the time spent within the reading resource room was *not* spent reading at all, but on other things, including management, waiting, being out of the room, other academic work, etc. Fifty-two percent of the time the students were in resource rooms, they were doing seatwork. They received one-to-one instruction only 16 percent of the time, despite the fact that teacher-student ratios were about 6:1. From the observations it appeared that students received direct reading instruction (i.e., demonstration or feedback) 5 percent of the time, and were directly monitored by the teacher (listened to or questioned) 17 percent of the time. "The picture of reading instruction that emerges from these resource rooms is of students working independently; receiving little feedback, few explanations or demonstrations from their teacher; and actually reading letters, words, or text only 25 percent of the time."

Differences in instruction were evident when the urban and suburban districts were compared. The major difference between the programs in these districts was that a direct instruction curriculum was extensively used in the suburban districts. For each hour spent in the resource room an urban student could expect 14.4 minutes of direct reading, while the average suburban child received 38.7 minutes. Apparently, agreement on a single philosophy and instructional approach had a large effect on instructional practices.

Although many of the regular and special education teachers who shared the same students believed that reading instruction primarily occurred in the resource program, this was not the case. Students appeared to read as much in regular classrooms as they did in resource rooms, and they actually received more reading instruction in their regular classroom. Related research, cited by Haynes and Jenkins, suggests that remedial and regular class reading instruction is not usually aligned. For example, one study showed that only 50 percent of remedial and regular class teachers knew what reading series the other used, and only 27 percent knew the book their students used in the other setting, despite their shared responsibility for the students' reading instruction. Furthermore, in that study, the instruction goals of the regular classroom teacher and the remedial teacher were found *not* to be congruent for 60 percent of the students. Haynes and Jenkins, in their study, also noted coordination problems. Only 15 percent of the handicapped students had the same curriculum in both the regular classroom and in the resource room. Resource room teachers believed that one-third of their students had no reading instruction in the regular classroom, but that simply was not true.

It is sensible to assume that handicapped students require more and different kinds of reading instruction than their nonhandicapped peers. There is no evidence from this study that such was the case. The resource rooms managed to give the handicapped students enough extra reading time to provide them about the same amount of time as their nonhandicapped peers. If they needed more time in order to reduce the differential between them and their nonhandicapped peers, they were not getting that. Furthermore, the kind of instruction in the resource rooms does not seem very "special" when compared to regular classroom instruction.

This study suggests that we must question whether the resources provided in some resource rooms are appropriate for the problems that exist. The data from this study, however, also inform us that the variability across resource rooms makes any categorical statement about them impossible. School administrators, regular classroom teachers, and resource-room teachers need an articulated curriculum, a cohesive philosophy for the two classrooms, and regular meetings on what is best for the handicapped child. A lack of coordination not only seems to produce no effects, but also probably increases the complexity of the environment for the handicapped child. And the last thing a handicapped child needs is more complexity!

■ Practice

Classroom teachers assume that the small class size and homogeneous grouping of resource rooms allows their students to get more, and more individualized, instruction than they can provide in the regular classroom. Haynes and Jenkins, however, point out three problems that interfere with the achievement of these goals: (1) the lack of relationship between student need and the time that students spend in some resource rooms, (2) the lack of relationship between student need and instructional methods in some resource rooms, and (3) the lack of coordination between resource-room teachers and classroom teachers. Let us discuss each of these issues.

How do we decide how much time a student should spend in a resource room? It appears that this decision is often made on the basis of a predetermined schedule. Children from Teacher X's class are to come in between 10:00 and 11:00 A.M., for example. But what of the students' needs? If all the students in Teacher X's class need the same amount of instruction, then it is appropriate that they all come for the same amount of time. If, as is more likely, the children vary in their need for additional help, then forcing them all into a preset schedule will facilitate only program administration, not student learning.

Let us remember that the purpose of resource rooms is to provide intensive instruction that supplements the regular classroom program. The amount and type of instruction should be closely related to the amount and type of need exhibited by the child. Providing for those needs calls for creative solutions on the part of the administrators and teachers. It means that you begin planning by examining *student needs,* and let the *schedule* follow. Or it may mean having *no* set schedule. Instead, the resource teacher could post a weekly "menu" of offerings tailored to the needs of the total group of students with whom he or she works. Each teacher could then send students to the resource room during the time when the featured instruction matches their diagnosed needs. There are many ways to accomplish the task. What is necessary is a clear acceptance of the importance of adjusting the school program to the students, rather than the other way around.

Similarly, and also beginning with student needs, it is to be expected that students who need resource-room services have not responded well to the instruction received in the classroom. We assume that they have special needs that are not served well in large classroom groups. Class size in resource rooms is kept small so that teachers can provide individual attention to their special students. Unfortunately, it appears that many teachers are assigned to resource rooms without *any* previous training in methods appropriate for small-group instruction! Thus, they often continue to use methods and materials appropriate to groups of 30 or so students. Small groups should make possible direct teacher involvement with *all* students during instruction.

Discussion groups and cooperative learning activities also become much more manageable in resource-room settings. Those are the types of activities that regular classroom teachers often replace with seatwork in their efforts to manage a large group of students. The work of the resource room teacher is not easy, but he or she does have the advantage of reduced numbers and more specific instructional tasks. One would expect that, as a result, effective resource-room instruction would be noticeably different from regular classroom instruction. If it is not, then it is probably not responsive to the special needs of students.

If resources are to provide a supplement to classroom instruction, then there must be close coordination between classroom and resource teachers. We often think of resource rooms as places for remediation; it may be more useful to think of them as places for re-mediation—that is, as places where new and different ways can be tried to mediate the instructional task, rather than just repeating unsuccessful approaches. If a student has problems in the classroom with, say, isolating sounds in reading, the resource teacher may want to try a different approach (for example, a whole-language approach to reading).

Too often, remediation translates as repetition, and students who have failed in the classroom just continue to fail again. An alternative approach is to use the resource-room time for preteaching. The classroom teacher can share instructional plans with the resource teacher, who can then introduce the concept to the student *before* it is presented in the regular classroom. When the new material is presented in the classroom, the student who has been exposed to the material beforehand can participate more fully in the classroom activities. In the process, students can gain both in confidence and in status among their peers.

But implementing novel approaches in the resource room requires close coordination between teachers. Resource-room teachers need to know what has worked and what has not worked in the classroom. They also need to learn from the classroom teachers—who will usually know them best—about their students' likes and dislikes. Likewise, the classroom teacher needs to be informed about instruction taking place in the resource room. The resource teacher may discover, for example, that Tom enjoys the rhythm of rhyming words, and that therefore poetry can help to lead him to reading. The classroom teacher can then apply that knowledge to Tom's classroom activities. Through joint planning, teachers can ensure effective instruction for *all* the students they share.

Resource rooms can provide valuable support for both students and their regular classroom teachers. But this can only happen if resource teachers take full advantage of their setting and provide, in a join effort with the classroom teachers, alternative instruction that is truly responsive to students' special needs.

Teacher Efficacy: How Can Teachers Make a Difference?

■ Research

Adapted from Ashton, P., & Webb, R. B. (1986). *Making a difference: Teachers' sense of efficacy and student achievement.* White Plains, NY: Longman.

"Most of a student's motivation and performance depends on his or her home environment. When it comes right down to it, a teacher can't do much."

What is your response to that statement? Read it again. Do you: (a) strongly agree, (b) agree, (c) neither agree nor disagree, (d) disagree, (e) strongly disagree?

What about the following statement?

"If I really try hard, I can get through to even the most difficult or unmotivated student."

To this statement do you: (a) strongly agree, (b) agree, (c) neither agree nor disagree, (d) disagree, (e) strongly disagree?

The first statement is designed to measure a teacher's belief in the efficacy of teaching. If you chose option (a) or (b), you probably believe that teaching is *not* a powerful technique to change the ways in which students perform. If you answered (d) or (e), you probably are a believer in the efficacy of teaching and the powerful role that schooling can serve.

The second statement measures whether a teacher thinks he or she can *personally* affect the way that students behave. A choice of options (a) or (b) identifies those who believe they *can* make a difference in the lives of students. A choice of options (d) or (e) indicates the opposite.

Suppose we were to study teachers who had a very high sense of efficacy, say those choosing options 1(e) and 2(a), and compared them to teachers who had a very low sense of efficacy, say those choosing options 1(a) and 2(e). How might they differ? This question was studied by Patricia Ashton and R. B. Webb of the University of Florida. They studied teachers in two similar middle schools. One was a school with interdisciplinary teaching teams, a strong advisor-advisee program, and multiage grouping wherein teachers and students stayed together for three years. The other school had a traditional departmental structure.

Ashton and her colleagues found that teachers with low efficacy scores tended to stratify their classes more by ability, and then tended to give more effort, attention, and affection to their high-ability students. These low-efficacious teachers perceived students' behavior, particularly that of their low-achieving students, in terms of its potential threat to orderliness.

On the contrary, teachers who felt highly efficacious were not as likely to be angered or feel threatened by the misbehavior of students. In addition, these teachers seemed to communicate clearly their expectations about which student behaviors were appropriate; seldom overlooked infractions when they did occur; had routine procedures for enforcing classroom rules; and were more likely to keep their students and themselves on task.

In further research, involving an additional sample of high-school teachers, Ashton and her colleagues found that teachers who believed themselves to be highly efficacious held higher academic standards, even for low-achieving students; monitored on-task behavior more frequently; built more positive and fewer punitive relations with their students; had more open communication with their students; appeared more supportive of student initiatives; and involved their students in more decisions. Thus, in this study we see how a teacher's feelings about efficacy are related to a number of other important teaching activities.

This study also allows us to examine whether the organizational characteristics of the two schools affect a teacher's sense of professional efficacy. Apparently the team-organization, multiyear grouping, and advising program in one of the middle schools did help to maintain a sense of efficacy among the teachers at that school. And, the isolation imposed by the departmental structure was apparently related to a lower sense of efficacy among teachers in the school with the junior-high-school structure.

Teachers in the two schools also held different perceptions of their roles. In the team-organized middle school they talked more about affective concerns, such as "establishing personal relationships," "listening," "helping students emotionally," and "caring." In the junior-high-school type of organization, teachers focused more on their role as instructors of subject matter. The team-organized middle-school teachers were more satisfied with teaching than were their colleagues in the other school, and were more likely to state that they would again choose teaching as a career.

Inefficacy—the feeling of powerlessness—is something every teacher has on occasion. When it is a continuing feeling, however, it is a serious problem for the teacher *and* all of his or her associates and students. It affects that teacher's family life, as well. Nevertheless, in spite of the many real and disheartening forces that are affecting teachers in these times, some teachers still manage to believe generally in the potential of the educational system, and specifically in themselves, as means to affect students in extremely important, positive ways. Their beliefs are tuned into actions that *do* foster learning in their students.

■ Practice

It may be difficult to accept the idea that teachers can increase their own efficacy in the absence of drastic changes in the educational system. The suggestion in the study described—that teachers' feelings of power or powerlessness are related to their schools' organizational patterns—may tempt us to give up, since "we can't change the system." Yet believing that is in itself a symptom of a lack of efficacy. It is also not true. Many teachers have in fact changed the system. Taking some positive steps *can* contribute to a feeling of control over one's situation. With all the pressure to promote more site-based management, teachers will increasingly be asked for their opinions about the management structures in which they work.

It is important, however, to first recognize our own limitations, not by thinking that as teachers we have no effect on students, but by setting our goals at the upper limits of what we can realistically accomplish. A realistic goal for a beginning student of Italian may be to read newspapers in that language at the end of a first year. It would be unrealistic to expect to read and comprehend Dante. To feel efficacious the goals set must be achievable.

If an eight-year-old arrives in the classroom with no knowledge of the alphabet, it is unrealistic to expect grade-level performance by the end of the year. But the setting of realistic expectations (for example, mastery of primer-level material) allows for successful accomplishment. With realistic goals a teacher can systematically work toward an accurate diagnosis of the child's strengths and weaknesses, and make separate diagnoses for different skill and knowledge areas, without regard to home background or ethnic characteristics.

Second, promoting feelings of efficacy requires a conscious determination to move toward specific goals. We have recognized this in working with the handicapped. While writing an Individualized Education Program (IEP) does mean a lot of work, it can also help in specifying realistic goals for both the child and the teacher. Writing IEPs may be a good strategy to follow, too, for nonhandicapped students who are judged, after careful diagnosis, to be unlikely to attain the general goals set for the class. The IEP should be shared with parents and the principal, so that all may understand the starting point and the expected outcome alike. It may also be discussed with students whose own efficacy may be enhanced by working toward a set of realistic goals. There is evidence in psychology that realistic goal-setting is a very powerful motivational device.

Third, teachers must learn to take credit for achieving their goals; this is part of feeling efficacious. A realistic goal for the teacher of a child who comes into kindergarten terrified and insisting on hiding under the desk may be to get that child to readily come out and remain out from under the desk by the end of two weeks. When it is accomplished, it must first be recognized as one's own success, then celebrated and shared with others. The day can be marked as special by treating ourselves in some way to recognize our efficacy as teachers and to remember: "I can make a difference." Celebrating victories is more healthy than brooding over the occasional and inevitable failure.

Fourth, we need to break down walls of isolation between and among teachers. The study suggested that collegiality contributes to feelings of efficacy. This means sharing problems, cooperating in their solution, and encouraging each other throughout. Organizational patterns may help, but basically any two or more determined teachers can establish such a relationship. As a colleague I can confess to you: "I really blew it today. Any suggestions?" And you can ask to visit my class, to get some ideas. Developing such relationships takes some risk, but they can make all the difference in the ability to handle stress.

Finally, we can reach out from our classroom to the school. We can suggest to our principal ways in which the school setting may be improved. Advice that is thoughtful, and offers alternatives, is usually welcome. It is not the principal's school, it is the teacher's as well. Efficacious individuals expect to make a difference, and therefore are willing both to share ideas for, and to assume responsibility for, improving their schools.

SECTION 2

INSTRUCTIONAL STRATEGIES

Introduction

Instructional strategies are the structures upon which teachers graft the content of instruction. Given exactly the same content, two teachers will nonetheless provide different instruction through their choice of strategies. Their choices will be guided by several considerations: the teacher's own values and philosophical orientation, the content to be presented, and both the real and the perceived individual and collective characteristics of the students.

Teachers may not always be conscious or deliberate about their philosophy and values, but by their choice of strategies they send out unintended but clear messages to the students. The choice of a strategy tells students what the teacher values. For example, a teacher's tendency to rely on lectures as the strategy of choice tends to reinforce a hierarchical relationship between teacher and student, a relationship in which the teacher "holds" the knowledge that the student is expected to "absorb." The message to students, in this case, is that they are to be passive recipients of knowledge rather than architects of their own learning. Total reliance on lectures, therefore, is likely to inhibit students' willingness to take responsibility for their own learning.

A teacher's choice of instructional strategies should be guided, in part, by the content that is to be presented. Among the vast number of possible strategies there will be some that are incompatible with the content, while others will be perfectly matched. In geography, for example, it would be highly inappropriate to choose computerized drill and practice exercises to teach about the world's cultural diversity. This is, after all, a topic that begs for *open* discussion. On the other hand, exercises based on drill and practice might be appropriate as a strategy for teaching geographic concepts, such as the names and location of land and water masses. These latter are well-structured, convergent items of information that can easily be reduced to the "yes" or "no" that are characteristic of drill and practice materials.

The third aspect to consider in choosing instructional strategies consists of the real and perceived characteristics of the learners. The student's ages, skill levels, and other pertinent individual (and collective) characteristics should all be considered when choosing a strategy for instruction. It is easy to understand why a lecture would be inappropriate as a strategy to be used in a kindergarten classroom, but is age the only consideration? On the other hand, would a lecture *always* be appropriate at the upper secondary level? Or even at the college level? We think not. A lecture would not be appropriate at *any* level if the class is quite small (three to five students, for example), or is composed of students not fluent in the language used for instruction, or is one in which students show evidence of characteristics that can impede the group's ability to concentrate and therefore benefit from such instruction.

Teachers' perceptions of their students also guide their selection of instructional strategies. When they believe their students to be slower learners, they tend to select strategies based on drill and rote learning. But when teachers believe they are working with competent learners, they tend to devote more time to open-ended discussions.

In addition to these important dimensions, a teacher's choice of instructional strategies is also limited by more practical factors, such as resources, space, and time. Regardless of a teacher's inclination, it would be difficult, if not impossible, to use cooperative learning strategies in a lecture hall. Likewise, the availability of some minimal equipment would be a prerequisite to choosing the discovery method for teaching science. Thus, the choice of instructional strategies must not be considered a casual one. Teachers should begin from a personal perspective to choose an appropriate strategy for a specific content, and in doing so be guided by what they know about students, as well as about the time, space, and resources available to them. Although, theoretically, a large number of instructional strategies are available, all the factors mentioned here nevertheless serve to constrain and limit the range of choices.

The eleven articles in this section are also but a selection from the possible choices. They are not evenly divided across different strategies—for several reasons. First, because our own range of choice was (as we explain in the Introduction) limited by the research available. Second, because we also bring to bear upon the choice *our own* philosophical orientation. We believe that classrooms are places for children to learn together, not only from the adults but also from one another. Happily, the research evidence is in our favor. It has been easy to locate interpretable studies that document the benefits which students derive from classroom environments promoting student interaction.

Five of the articles in this section report on such classrooms. They remind us that traditional family organizations which assign the older siblings teaching responsibilities for the younger have a place in our schools. In comparison to other strategies, including the currently popular computer-assisted instruction, tutoring turns out to be the most powerful strategy for increasing student achievement. Effective peer tutoring, however, requires attention to training, selection of tutors, monitoring of teachers, and close attention to student progress.

We are reminded of the importance of training to help tutors to be maximally effective. And we realize that this training is often lacking when schools begin new programs. We worry that too many new educational programs fail because the teachers who must implement them never receive the training needed to make them successful. And in this case, a double problem occurs. Teachers may not be trained in the management skills needed to supervise tutoring programs, and the students who act as tutors may not receive enough training to be as effective as they could be. Without both kinds of training, cross-age and peer tutoring programs are not likely to succeed.

In another set of articles the benefits of reading aloud are discussed, not only at the primary level but also at the secondary level of schooling. We learn from other research that it enhances comprehension for children to retell the stories they hear. And in another study, contrary to popular belief, we learn that faster reading, when it is accompanied by questions, and by leading students into drawing inferences from the text, can also enhance comprehension among at least some learners.

The three remaining articles in this section discuss instructional strategies of proven benefit. The benefits of field trips properly introduced and followed up; the benefit of play, particularly for young learners; and the benefit derived by students who arrive at school as speakers of languages other than English, when their teachers use their native language and show sensitivity to their culture.

None of the strategies covered in this chapter (with the possible exception of field trips) requires extraordinary resources. And even field trips can be inexpensive. A walk to neighborhood stores, or to a nearby park or factory, usually does not cost a cent. Yet, when properly integrated with the classroom's learning activities, such trips can be very helpful. The message here is that there are many different ways to deliver instruction, some of which are much more effective than the "traditional" strategies. Classrooms that offer a variety of ways to learn can benefit both students *and* teachers—who together can not only learn more, but also enjoy a more interesting learning environment.

Being the Teacher Helps Students Learn

■ Research

Adapted from Webb, N. M. (1989). Peer interaction and learning in small groups. *International Journal of Educational Research,* 13, 21–39.

Most of us have said that we never really understood something until we taught it. I remember saying it the first time I taught statistics, and also when I tried to teach someone about the international date line and time differences. By preparing to teach, I gained a better understanding of the subject. And, after I taught them, I felt I really understood them.

Noreen Webb of the University of California at Los Angeles (UCLA) has research that supports this common experience. Webb completed 19 studies examining how small groups operate in schools. Using student groups from second to eleventh grade, she observed youngsters helping each other to master primarily mathematical materials or problems before taking achievement tests. Some students had difficulty and requested help from their group partners. Sometimes they made obvious errors, or they may have asked high-level questions. Webb studied how students responded to these requests for help. She consistently found that students who *gave* elaborated answers had higher achievement scores than other group members. (In four studies wherein teaching experience and achievement could be examined, significant positive correlations ranged from .47 to .53.) Low-level help, such as giving an answer, didn't seem to make a difference. But teaching complicated, highly demanding cognitive materials, requiring elaborate answers, helped those who taught to achieve at higher levels.

Why is this so? Webb had some insights about this. When trying to explain something, the students who teach must review, reorganize, and clarify the material to be taught. If they discover they don't know the material as well as they thought they did, they may do additional work, or consult other sources for help.

Sometimes, even after receiving an answer, the student asking for help doesn't get the point. Then the helping student must revise his or her answer, change vocabulary, give new or different examples, or use alternative materials, such as pictures and graphs. And, because of this, like any other teacher, these students *really learn* the subject when they try teaching it.

Webb found that in groups with mixed-ability students, high- and low-ability students formed natural teacher-student pairs. Because more able students probably give the most help, it isn't surprising to learn that they also achieve the most. But in analyzing her data, Webb *controlled* for ability—which suggests that it isn't the whole story. For example, in other groups, students with *relatively* higher ability took on the teacher role. Although they weren't necessarily *high*-ability students, they were in fact more competent than most others in their group. These students also learned the most.

So, regardless of ability, most students who take a teaching role learn much more than they do when they receive instruction or work independently. These studies suggest that teachers should find ways to let students teach well so they may learn better.

■ Practice

Adapted from Aronson, E. (1978). *The jigsaw classroom.* Beverly Hills, CA: Sage; and Wells, G. (1986). *The meaning makers.* Portsmouth, NH: Heinemann.

These studies suggest that students who teach have a lot to gain. But results also warn us that the *quality* of student interaction makes a considerable difference. To benefit from working together, students must do more than just give one another answers; they must give answers that require rephrasing, explaining, and elaborating.

How can you encourage students to do this?

First, you'll have to explain that you want them to help one another. This is a new approach for many youngsters because we've traditionally discouraged helping behaviors in the classroom. So let them know when and how you expect them to help. You must also decide the limits for this exchange and then tell your students precisely what you want them to do.

Probably the best way to explain different types of responses is to model high-level ones and draw student attention to them. Make sure that students understand you're not asking them to share "answers," but to share understanding. Stress that *everyone* benefits from sharing.

To promote helping use role-play, practice, and feedback in small-group settings. During these sessions, take the opportunity to test different group arrangements, to see which work best for students.

Creating carefully structured tasks can make students give the elaborated answers that encourage helping behavior and high-quality responses. In the "Jigsaw" method promoted by Elliot Aronson and his colleagues, students study different academic materials and discuss them in "expert" groups. They then go back to their regular group and teach the material they learned to their teammates.

You can accomplish the same thing by asking students to work in pairs and giving each student specific teaching duties. This forces students to explain and develop answers, because what they learn depends on what they teach. Finally, reconsider your reward system. Individual, competitive rewards discourage students from giving responsive feedback; if they help others, they lower their chances for receiving good grades. In contrast, group rewards benefit everyone and promote helping behavior.

You can also expand student teaching roles to nongroup activities. For example, when students are working at the chalkboard, ask them to explain to the class how they solved a problem. Or assign class reports in science and social studies as well as literature. As they make presentations, ask students to explain their material clearly, so that other students genuinely understand. A healthy give-and-take atmosphere in which students defend positions spurs learning, too.

Gordon Wells, a Canadian researcher, finds that teaching roles benefit students as they develop language skills. Because the typical classroom gives students few opportunities either to start conversations or to ask questions, it creates a particularly difficult situation for students who speak other languages. But group activities and class presentations can help these youngsters to gain fluency. When pairing these beginners with more advanced learners, or even native speakers, however, be realistic—don't inhibit them with unreasonable expectations of perfect grammar and pronunciation. Vocabulary development and comprehension always precedes fine grammar and accurate pronunciation.

Remember, too, that students (particularly older ones) have skills and knowledge from their lives outside of school. Sharing what they know may result in gains in academic work and self-confidence, as well as in their enjoyment of school.

We tend to think of teaching and learning as separate activities, but these studies suggest that there's little difference. Encouraging students to teach may well be an efficient way to help them to learn.

When Are Two Heads Better than One?

■ Research

Adapted from Azmitia, M. (1988). Peer interaction and problem solving: When are two heads better than one? *Child Development*, 59, 87–96.

We've been told lately by researchers to mix instructional groups rather than keep them homogeneous, with the understanding that mixed groups help less capable students and don't hinder the able (see pages 9–13). Margarita Azmitia asked if this is true when students work in pairs. She also wanted to know if youngsters would do better working alone or in pairs at some tasks.

As a pretest in this study, five-year-olds were asked to replicate models they were shown of building-block houses. As they worked, Azmitia identified a set of low-ability children—youngsters who made many errors of location, or used blocks of the wrong size or color, when building their model house. She also identified a set of high-ability children—those who made very few errors and finished (or almost finished) a satisfactory construction in the allotted time.

Azmitia then assigned students to three experimental groups and had them work for two sessions. In the first group, low- and high-ability children worked separately at block-building tasks; in the second, students were paired homogeneously as they worked on their independent constructions; and in the third, she paired low- and high-ability children who worked together on their construction. Then she tested the children individually on a similar task and administered the block-design subtest of the Wechsler Preschool Scale of Intelligence (WPSI).

Azmitia watched the children during practice sessions and observed that high-ability ones looked at the model more frequently than the low-ability ones and spent more time on-task. In addition, during the first practice session, high-ability students in mixed pairs gave more explanations and demonstrations than when they worked with students of similar ability.

Less able children in mixed pairs seemed to learn from the more able children. They looked at the model more frequently while they tried to replicate it, and may have stayed on task a bit more as well. As a result, these students learned more than those working either in homogeneous pairs *or* alone. The overall gain in ability for low-ability children working in mixed-ability pairs totaled 78 percent from pretest to posttest!

By comparison, low-ability children working alone showed *no* gains, and pairs of low-ability children exhibited only a *small* gain. But high-ability children did well regardless of work setting. They clearly didn't suffer from being paired with low-ability children, and in fact (though the results were not statistically significant) it appears that high-ability students in mixed pairs improved more than high-ability children who worked alone or with other high-ability children. (Perhaps this is due to their teaching more; see pages 58–60.)

On the intelligence test subtest, low-ability students in mixed pairs outscored low-ability students who worked alongside or in homogeneous pairs. They scored about 17 percent higher than the other low-ability students. This is a remarkable finding for an activity in which students had only a few practice sessions with a peer expert! It seems that this kind of social interaction can improve performance on at least *some subtests* of commonly used measures of intelligence.

So, even among kids, two heads *are* better than one—especially if one of the two is more competent than the other.

▬ Practice

The need to maximize instruction within the constraints of limited time is one of the most persistent problems of teaching. Azmitia's research suggests a useful strategy for this purpose.

We all know how much children learn from each other. When we remember our own experiences, and also those of our children or younger relatives, we understand how well children can teach each other. Somehow we seem to overlook this possibility when it comes to the classroom, especially when working with younger children. We assume that they lack the sophistication and discipline to work in groups. Azmitia's research is a timely reminder of the effectiveness of a certain model of collaborative learning.

The strategy described in this research takes advantage of the benefits to be accrued while working with a more knowledgeable partner. This is in line with the theories of Lev Vygotsky, a Russian psychologist, who proposed that learning begins in social interaction and then becomes internalized by the learner. That is, we acquire new learning first in the company of others, and gradually that learning becomes a part of our own knowledge. The acquisition of speech by infants is a good example of Vygotsky's theory. Similarly, in the study described, the more capable partners appeared to model and instruct those less capable in the solution of the problem. As a result, those who were originally identified as less capable were able to extend their knowledge.

How can you take advantage of this strategy in your classroom? You can begin by identifying appropriate partners. Two things need to be remembered in this process. One, that pairs should include students who differ in their ability to perform the problem or activity at hand. Second, that children (particularly young children) differ in their abilities across the wide spectrum of possible tasks that can be used for instructional purposes. To determine which students of unequal ability should be paired off, you need first to choose the specific task in order to decide who, among your students, is more or less able to perform it.

In the study described, the task was to *copy* a model of a house, using blocks. But suppose the task would have been to use the blocks to *create* a house, without a predetermined model? Do you think the same students would have been considered more and less capable? Personally, I think not.

The point to remember here is that every student has his or her own area of expertise. If we choose to implement this strategy, we must attempt to provide opportunities for each class member to sometimes assume the more expert role in a pair. That is, we must recognize that every child has his or her own area(s) of expertise and that therefore each collaborative learning task will require a different pairing of children. We should, at different times, provide a *variety* of opportunities for students to assume different roles in the learning situation. That is why it is necessary to choose the task *before* pairing off the children.

In assigning children to pairs you must also keep in mind issues of ethnicity and gender. It will be necessary to avoid the consistent pairing of same-gender or same-ethnicity children. In fact, collaborative learning may provide you with an opportunity to bring children from different backgrounds together. In addition, you need to be alert to the possibility that children from readily identifiable groups may be monopolizing the "teacher" role in these pairs. As noted above, a variety of tasks, requiring different types of expertise, will help to avoid this problem.

And what about the tasks? The lower primary grades offer many opportunities for utilizing this instructional strategy. You want to avoid tasks that require concept development, and instead choose those that are more concrete, specific, and easily evaluated. For example, concepts of time and space would *not* be appropriate content for this type of instruction; however, learning how to tell time from a clock *would* be. Similarly, you would want to reserve for yourself instruction on the concept of codependence between animals and plants, but students could at least work together on appropriate vocabulary, such as the identification of animals and plants. In this way, paired instruction can dovetail with whole-group instruction and save precious instructional time. Also, in both of these cases it will be easy to evaluate whether your students have achieved the instructional goal you set for them.

Collaborative learning can be particularly useful in classrooms wherein linguistic differences exist. Children who are learning English as a second language can be paired with those who are native speakers of English. Conversely, speakers of other native languages can be paired up with monolingual English-speaking children. Children can then learn the value of all languages by teaching each other.

The tasks, in this case, should be chosen for their potential to generate conversation. Science and art activities are particularly suited to this purpose. For example, building an aquarium or terrarium, in addition to being an inherently interesting activity, requires cooperation and conversation. It is important, however, to also keep in mind that second-language learners also bring their own expertise to the classroom. Their lack of skills in English should not be confused with an absolute lack of skills. In fact, discovering their particular expertise, and then assigning them the lead role in a pair, may do a great deal to advance their English-language skills.

Finally: Working in pairs, for young children can provide additional benefits. They can learn to take responsibility for a peer's learning, and also to accept instruction from a peer. In addition they can begin to see learning as a joint enterprise in which expertise is shared. In doing this they may also begin to assume responsibility for their *own* learning.

For the teacher, implementing this strategy will require tolerance of the children's style of instruction—and a higher noise level in the classroom. But it appears that the rewards of more efficient use of instructional time, and more successful students, are well worth these minor discomforts.

Peer Tutoring: A New Look at a Popular Practice

■ Research

Adapted from Levin, H., Glass, G., & Meister, G. (1987). Cost-effectiveness of computer-assisted instruction. *Evaluation Review*, 11, 50–72.

Consider four practices that are supposed to increase student learning: reduced class size, increased instructional time, computer-assisted instruction, and tutoring. Which practice gets the most bang for the buck? That's the question that researchers Henry Levin, Gene Glass, and Gail Meister asked themselves in a recent cost-benefit analysis of those educational innovations.

In order to understand their findings (which may surprise you), let's create a *very* hypothetical case. Suppose there are identical twins, Inno and Trad, who are average-ability students. Whenever an innovation comes to their school, Trad remains in traditional instruction while Inno is (you guessed it) placed in the innovative program. In every analysis of math and reading, from grades two through six, Trad maintains average achievement in the traditional program by scoring at the 50th percentile. The question for us is "What happens to Inno?" Suppose he spent the same amount of time that Trad spent, but in a more innovative program—one that reduced class size, or increased instruction time, or used computer-assisted instruction, or made use of peer and cross-age tutoring: How would Inno compare with his twin brother Trad?

The researchers estimate that a class-size reduction—from 35 students to 20—would boost Inno's score to the 59th percentile in math and to the 55th percentile in reading. (Remember, these scores compare with Trad's scores at the 50th percentile in both subjects.) It was estimated that a program that increases instruction time—by 30 minutes each day in both math and reading—would have only a minimal effect, raising Inno's score to the 51st percentile in math and to the 53rd percentile in reading.

What about Inno's experience in a program of computer-assisted instruction, say one that required 10 minutes of drill and practice each day for a year? In this program, the researchers predict, Inno will score at the 55th percentile in math and at the 59th percentile in reading. And finally, let's examine what would happen if Inno went into a program that involved peer or cross-age tutoring. In comparison with Trad's performance at the 50th percentile, Inno would score at the 79th percentile in math and the 66th percentile in reading! In terms of student achievement, then, researchers found the greatest effects associated with tutoring. And when costs were estimated, the biggest effect per $100 spent was also associated with tutoring.

What can account for tutoring's powerful effects? From the theories of the previously cited Russian psychologist Lev Vygotsky, we begin to gain some insight. As we saw, Vygotsky explored the notion of learning in social settings. What ultimately becomes our own personal knowledge, he said, starts out as social knowledge. No Vygotskian would be surprised if, for example, computer-assisted learning, usually an individualized form of learning, did not achieve large effects. And his disciples would *not* expect that increased instructional time or reductions in class size would be effective innovations *if* the same workbook and independent forms of instruction were used. On the other hand, Vygotskians *would* predict that classrooms featuring cooperating learning and reciprocal teaching (see pages 13–17), as well as those that use peer or cross-age tutoring (see pages 73–77), *would* be as effective as they in fact often are.

This view calls into question the general preoccupation with individualized programs based on seatwork and workbook assignments. Too much independent work might inhibit learning, not promote it! Instead of striving for more individual activities, we should design learning environments for our children that capitalize on the natural inclination that humans have for social interaction.

Dozens of studies show positive and substantial effects of peer and cross-age tutoring. Now we also know that, in comparison with other innovations, tutoring is both theoretically more sensible, and more powerful in its effects. When we add the fact that it's also relatively inexpensive, we must wonder why we don't see peer and cross-age tutoring in the schools. It seems to provide the biggest bang for the bucks we have in education.

▰ Practice

Have you ever wanted to be everywhere in your classroom at once? A program of peer or cross-age tutoring might well give you an opportunity to multiply your effectiveness as if you *were*.

Implementation of a successful tutoring program requires close attention to five key aspects: (1) class preparation, (2) selection of tutors, (3) preparation of tutors, (4) monitoring by the teacher, and (5) continuous assessment of student progress. Prepare the class by explaining the purpose and nature of peer or cross-age tutoring in school learning. Because most students' experience with other students often is limited to social situations, it is necessary to clarify the *instructional* purpose of the process, the new roles they will be playing, and your expectations for their behavior.

Selection of tutors depends on the type of program you decide to implement. Cross-age tutoring—older students tutoring younger ones—should be determined both by students' interest and by their skills in working with younger children. Be careful not to disqualify a tutor because of poor grades. Low-achieving students often blossom when given the responsibility of a younger child's learning. Many studies show strong effects for the tutors as well as the tutees, probably because they *really* learn the material when they have to *teach* it (see pages 58–60).

If you choose an in-classroom tutoring program, avoid creating a situation whereby some students are always the tutors and others always the tutees. Effective tutors need only be slightly ahead of their tutees in the specific skill you will be emphasizing. Students should be able to assume different roles on the basis of tutoring potential and compatibility.

To prepare prospective tutors, you'll need to model appropriate instructional strategies. These may include dialogue formats or specific math problem-solving methods. Also, make clear to students the kinds of assistance you will provide. Students need to feel comfortable in their ability to handle the assignment, and confident in your support.

Implementation follows tutor training. Using what was learned when you modeled the process, tutors explain to their tutees what they will be learning, and why. They then engage tutees in the appropriate instructional strategies, and follow the lesson learned earlier from you. This lesson can be one you teach to the entire class and which tutors then expand on, or it can be one you teach just to a group of tutors—as long as you rotate tutor/tutee relationships often.

During the tutoring session, remain in the room and circulate among the groups. Monitoring should be inconspicuous but consistent. The process should include some honest information for the tutors about their performances.

Frequent assessment should be an integral part of tutoring. Both tutors and tutees should respond often to short quizzes on the lesson content. These assessments can be scored and graphed by the tutors (under teacher supervision), and the results shared individually with each tutee at a later session.

You may still be inhibited by concern about the potential for misinformation. Remember that you can decrease the likelihood of misinformation by closely monitoring each group. You can also encourage students to use reference books and to seek your help. Tutors could also exchange tips. Your biggest hurdle may be overcoming years of training and experience that have given you, for all practical intents and purposes, absolute control in the classroom. Successful tutoring programs demand the willingness to relinquish some of that control. Although this concession is not always easy to go along with, the rewards, as we have seen, can be considerable.

The Case for Peer Tutoring

■ Research

Adapted from Greenwood, C. R., Delquardi, J. C., & Hall, R.V. (1989). Longitudinal effects of classwide peer tutoring. *Journal of Educational Psychology*, 81, 371–383.

A consistent set of findings has convinced us that peer tutoring is one of the least costly, most effective teaching methods known. But we rarely see tutoring programs in the schools we visit. Perhaps the results of a four-year longitudinal study of a Classwide Peer Tutoring (CWPT) program used with poor children can convince more teachers that a powerful instructional technique is readily available to them.

The research team at the University of Kansas that developed CWPT was concerned that the instructional processes they saw in Chapter 1 classes serving poor students were not conducive to learning. They believed that school learning in the typical classroom was neither active enough nor of sufficient duration to affect the academic performance of children. They also believed that schools failed poor children, in particular, by not providing them enough engaged time with academic materials and by not giving them the opportunity to respond to that material. The system they created to increase active responding and engagement with the curriculum was CWPT.

Classwide Peer Tutoring is a highly structured tutoring program in which student pairs are assigned to work together, and each pair is assigned to one of two competing teams. Teachers have to break down material into the appropriate daily or weekly "chunks," and must also roam the classroom, helping students during the tutoring sessions. The student tutors are trained in procedures to correct the errors of their tutees, and to provide positive feedback for their correct responses. The tutor and tutee roles are reversed in every session. Tutees earn points for their teams. Daily and weekly winners are announced, and the scores of the teams are made public. Weekly social rewards are given to the winning teams that are formed anew each week.

Three groups of children from first to fourth grade were studied over a four-year stretch. One group served as the control group. They received the regular Chapter 1 program, which was the traditional instruction that teachers ordinarily provided, plus whatever benefits could be obtained through the Chapter 1 funds. The experimental group was also made up of students from low-income families attending Chapter 1 schools, but the teachers in this group had been trained in, and had agreed to use CWPT. This version of CWPT was used in only three curriculum areas—spelling, mathematics, and reading. A third group was also formed, consisting of students in schools that served a population of high socioeconomic status (SES) students. The teachers of this group, like the control teachers, taught in their usual way.

The study ultimately involved over 400 students and almost 100 teachers in nine schools within one school district. The goal of the study was to see what happened to students from a poverty background after exposure to four years of systematic CWPT, in comparison to their matched controls, and also to a control group made up of advantaged students.

The research was difficult and took years to complete. There were problems in tracking the students from school to school and from year to year. Also, new teachers at higher grade levels had to be trained every year, and some of these had not originally volunteered to participate in the study. Furthermore, classroom processes had to be monitored regularly to see if the program was, in fact, really being implemented. Nevertheless, when analyzing the performance of the 187 students who were still followed after four years, the results were amazingly clear. The experimental students who were considered to be at risk of academic failure at the beginning of this study approached or exceeded the national norms for fourth graders on the Metropolitan Achievement Test in reading, mathematics, and language arts. The students in the matched control group remained consistently below the national norms. The students in the experimental group scored between .5 and 1.4 grade equivalents, and around 10 percentiles higher, than the regular control group on the standardized tests. These differences *were* statistically significant. The students in the high SES group did score slightly higher than the students in the experimental group, but these differences were *not* statistically significant.

Not only did the experimental group's performance resemble that of their more advantaged peers, but the teaching/learning processes in the experimental classrooms were of a higher quality. The students in the experimental classes showed higher levels of oral reading, academic talk and question asking than did the students in either of the two control groups. And the experimental students did about 13 percent more writing than those in the matched control group. The students in the matched control classes spent more time in activities that were nonacademic or related to management, and their teachers were found to be more disapproving of them.

The goal of the CWPT was to increase academic engagement and responses in the classrooms of students from poor families. The program seemed to achieve that, and the children also liked the program. The changes in classroom activities that occur when this tutoring program is used appear to cause achievement gains on standardized achievement tests—gains not ordinarily seen with minority and poor inner-city children. Although such tests are not the only measure of learning in the classroom, they definitely are hurdles that these students must surmount if they are to successfully continue along the various paths that can lead to one or another kind of rewarding academic career. As teachers, we have a responsibility to help them overcome those hurdles.

▪ Practice

Peer tutoring moves the teacher away from center stage and encourages students to help each other by way of starring in the lead role as stand-ins. As with cooperative learning, the use of peer tutoring results in notable changes in classroom organization. Students appear to like these changes and, when appropriate content is presented, can achieve notable academic gains. The results of this study of peer tutoring confirm the value of this strategy for Chapter 1 students, and should encourage all teachers to implement this strategy (or one like it) for at least part of each teaching day. Of course there are hazards to be avoided in designing a program of peer tutoring—most importantly, the avoidance of patterns whereby some children consistently play the tutorial role while others are always the tutees. The Kansas research team avoided this danger through the assignment of working pairs by random procedures, through student trading of roles during each tutoring session, and by the changing of the pairs each week.

In this instructional program the tutoring relationship consisted of 10-minute sessions during which the students assigned the tutor role began by presenting the first item from a list to be learned by the tutee. Each item was written down as well as spoken by the tutee, and then the tutor would compare it with the correct response. In case of errors the tutor would immediately provide the correct answer (tutors were trained in how to correct answers), and the tutee then would practice by writing it three times.

The procedure was slightly different for reading where tutees were required to read sentences aloud, and where corrections consisted, first, of the tutor's modeling, and then of the tutee's rereading of the problem sentence. Students would trade roles for the second 10-minute session, and then, for the last five minutes, students would report aloud on their performance, and scores for teams would be recorded on a chart. The teacher then continued with the next activity.

The relatively rigid structure of the CWPT instructional model was carefully designed to avoid the pitfalls of peer tutoring mentioned earlier, and to incorporate strategies that behavioral psychologists find supportive of effective learning—for example, the immediate correction of errors. The CWPT strategy also relied on teacher preparation of instructional materials in accordance with the needs of the program. This is of course much easier to accomplish with some types of content and not others. The researchers demonstrated their understanding of this differ-

71

ence through their gradual introduction of the implementation plan. They began with spelling, which is much easier to break down into 10-minute tasks, and then added mathematics, and finally reading.

It is interesting to note that the original design of the program called for 90 minutes of CWPT activities every day. But the actual implementation fell far short of that. The use of CWPT waned, in spite of the noticeable gains that students in the program were demonstrating, and of researchers' efforts to maintain the quality and strength of the treatment during the four years of study. The researchers explain that content-preparation demands, physical effort, noise level in the classroom, and conflicting schedules were among factors that discouraged teachers' use of the CWPT model. It is important to recognize these problems for two reasons. First, because they may make the difference between the success or failure of *any* such innovation. Second, because we could argue that, given the success of partial implementation, full implementation of CWPT might have resulted in *really* spectacular results.

At least part of the problem with implementation appears to have been due to the constraints imposed on the instructional content by the tutoring format. CWPT appears to be well suited for very structured instructional activities (learning the multiplication tables, or geographic features, might be among them). It was more difficult to adapt the structure to more complex learning tasks, such as mathematical problem solving. As we have seen, some teachers also had problems with the noise level in the classroom, a factor that could be a matter of personal preference or of constraints imposed by the school environment. Finally, the problem of conflicting schedules, even in schools that had chosen to participate in the program, must be considered. It is likely that this conflict was beyond the control of the teachers, and only served as a source of further discouragement.

What is important here is to remember that *any* educational innovation is likely to require investment of teacher energy, and perhaps also adjustments in school organizational structures. The good news is that there are promising strategies out there, and they have been tested and found effective, that students do like them and learn more through their use, and that more successful students are likely to result in happier teachers. The question then is: Are you and your colleagues willing, for the sake of your students and your own well-being, to make the large investment required to institute a change in classroom practices?

How to Make Cross-Age Tutoring Work

■ Research

Adapted from Glynn, T., McNaughton, S. S., Robinson, V., & Quinn, M. (1979). *Remedial reading at home: Helping you to help your child.* Wellington, New Zealand: New Zealand Council for Educational Research; and Wheldall, K., & Mettem, P. (1985). Behavioral peer tutoring: Training 16-year-old tutors to employ the "pause, prompt, and praise" method with 12-year-old remedial readers. *Educational Psychology,* 5, 27–44.

A very basic tutor-training program was used successfully to train parents to provide remedial instruction to their own youngsters. After two and one-half months of instruction by parents (using the simple procedures discussed below), their children made six and one-half months gain in reading achievement. Moreover, and of considerable importance to those concerned about the long-term effects of such programs, the children also showed increased awareness of their own errors, correcting themselves almost twice as often as at first.

More recently the same tutorial program was brought into the schools and examined by K. Wheldall and P. Mettem of the Centre for Child Development, University of Birmingham, England. In this case the tutors were older students, equivalent to 10th- and 11th-graders in United States schools, instead of parents. These tutors all had been in their school's remedial reading program. They were taught a simple three-step tutoring technique that is very easy to learn in a short period of time. In addition, this technique is compatible with modern theories of reading acquisition, and always is easily monitored to ensure that it is used in accordance with the instructions.

In this system the tutors are taught to *pause, prompt,* and *praise. Pause* reminds the tutor to delay attention to a reader's errors for at least five seconds, or until the end of a sentence. Delaying attention to errors encourages tutees to self-correct more often, thus increasing overall accuracy and comprehension. Reading research of the past decade has confirmed that proficient readers use both syntactic and semantic clues to predict unfamiliar words, and that mispredictions or miscues are a

73

natural occurrence. Self correction, characteristics of better readers, is therefore to be expected. If the miscues of less accomplished readers are corrected immediately after occurrence, these students may lose the meaning of the prose being read, and *also* fail to learn self-correcting behavior. Thus, from the perspective of reading research, pausing after miscues makes good sense.

When a reading error is corrected, *prompts,* rather than straight-forward corrections, are desirable. Prompts require the reader to figure out the clues that must be attended to in order to predict accurately the words in the paragraph or sentence being read. If prompting fails, then tutors are urged to model for the tutees the use of clues to predict words and meanings. Prompting, and prompting with modeling, are always seen as much more desirable than the straightforward correction of errors.

The third component, *praise,* is taught because tutors generally do not give enough of it. It is particularly important that praise be given for self-correcting responses and correct responses following prompts. Praise at those times informs the tutee about appropriate behaviors. In addition, more general praise should be given for effort and progress in reading.

This simple *pause, prompt,* and *praise* tutoring method was taught to a group of older but low-reading-ability high school students in only two 30-minute sessions. They were then assigned to tutor younger students in reading. Half of their subsequent tutoring sessions were audiotaped, and then analyzed with them to ensure that they used the skills taught in this program. The tutoring program lasted only two months. Sessions were held three times a week for 15 minutes at a time. The total tutoring time for the study was only six hours.

The effect of the *pause, prompt,* and *praise* method was assessed through its effects on students that were at the British equivalent of 6th and 7th grades in the United States. These students lagged behind their peers by 3.5 years in reading achievement. They were divided into three groups. One group was tutored by the trained older students. A second group was tutored by a comparable group of older students who had re-ceived no training. A third group was allowed silent reading time equivalent to the time that the other two groups spent with their tutors. The latter two groups (those being tutored by untrained older students and those in silent reading activity) were the control groups. At the end of the two months of tutoring these three groups were compared to each other.

What was found? First of all, the 60 minutes of training changed the behavior of the tutors. the untrained tutors responded to virtually every error that tutees made, while the trained tutors delayed their responses to 58 percent of the errors made. When errors occurred, the untrained tutors supplied corrections immediately; the trained tutors used prompts 27 percent of the time. (Moreover, these prompts were successful about 50 percent of the time.) The trained tutors gave praise 8.8 times per session, the untrained tutors hardly at all. These are not bad results for such a small amount of training. But what of the tutees?

The tutees of the trained tutors self-corrected twice as often as did those of the untrained tutors. In addition, when their movement across reading levels in the graded reading program that they used was compared, the tutees working with the trained tutors had finished 36 levels, while those working with untrained tutors had finished 29. The students reading silently had finished 24 levels. Considering the latter figure as the baseline for the expected rate of completion, then, ordinary tutoring results in a 21 percent higher rate of completion.

However, when tutors are trained in the *pause, prompt,* and *praise* technique, the rate of completion is 50 percent higher! Furthermore, the tutees of the trained tutors gained over six months in reading accuracy, a gain of 700 percent over the students who simply read by themselves and whose growth over the two months was less than one month. These gains in accuracy also amounted to a 285 percent increase over gains shown by the students who worked with untrained tutors, whose growth over the two months of the study was a little over two months.

The tutees of the trained tutors not only held their advantage in gains when tested two months after the study was completed; they also registered the highest gains when comprehension was assessed. Though not statistically significant, these gains were substantial in terms of the percent increase in raw-score points on the comprehension test. In short, for a mere six hours of tutoring, over two months, many benefits accrued.

This easy-to-learn, three-step tutoring program has worked well for parents as well as for cross-age tutors who work with elementary-age students who lag substantially behind their peers in reading achievement. Furthermore, there is evidence from other sources that this kind of program might also have a positive effect on the tutors. Thus, given the elaborations and modifications necessary to meet the particular context in which you work, *you* could put this very simple tutoring program into effect. Perhaps you might want to try out some tutoring arrangements one year, and in the next introduce such a program on a more permanent basis. There is a wealth of research in this area to guide you.

■ Practice

Cross-age tutoring gives the students opportunities to work with and help each other. It also shifts the responsibility for learning beyond the teacher, to the students themselves. It is probably more comfortable for children than is peer tutoring because it more closely resembles the family situation of the older helping the younger.

Peer and cross-age tutoring are not new techniques; some of you may already have tried them. What is new here is the preparation of tutors to assume this responsibility, and the close fit of the technique recommended to our current understanding of the reading process.

To initiate a program of cross-age training in your school you will need to work with a teacher at a different grade level. One of you will provide the tutors, the other the tutees. Whoever is providing the tutors can begin training them in one school year in preparation for the next. It is not wrong to select students at the low end of the reading achievement scale. These students can benefit from what they learn about proper reading behavior, and the responsibility of helping others to learn can help them to feel more competent. In addition, students who have experienced problems in learning to read are likely to be sympathetic to the efforts of the younger classmates.

The training of the tutors can be accomplished, as in the research described, using role-playing. The teacher can act the role of the tutee and the students can take turns acting as tutors. Later the students can work in pairs and alternate their roles. It is a good idea to audiotape the training sessions so that students can hear themselves and assess their own and each other's performance. Group discussion should give students the opportunity to ask questions and clarify their understanding.

Keep in mind as you select your tutors that not all students may be suited to this role. Potential tutors should be sympathetic and nonjudgmental. They should also be self-assured enough to be comfortable in the role. In the research described above, girls were paired with girls, and boys with boys. This is probably advisable at the middle grade level and above. It is also important to avoid stereotypes by ensuring that both groups, tutors and tutees, are heterogeneous in both social class and ethnicity.

You could incorporate tutoring into your regular classroom activities, or add it to the school day. It should not substitute for your own classroom instruction, nor should it be held during the poor readers' "free time." Likewise, tutors should not lose their "free time" to tutoring, nor should they miss out on classroom instruction. Tutoring may of course be an alternative to silent reading or certain other enrichment activities. Your teaching responsibilities toward the tutees will continue in spite of the tutoring. You will need to monitor student progress through audiotapes of the tutoring session, and also through conversations with the participants.

As the students progress, you will need to provide more advanced materials for the tutors. In the study cited, the interest in tutors began to lag toward the end of the two-month period. To guard against that problem, you might want to vary activities at times. For example, you might have the tutor coach the students in preparation for a test, or perhaps sometime have the tutor play an instructional game with the tutee. Such activities, while not necessarily connected to reading improvement, are at least likely to cement the relationship between tutor and tutee.

It is also important to recognize the progress that students make as a result of their participation as tutors or tutees. Progress should be noted and successes, such as advances in reading level, celebrated. The contribution that tutor and tutee are making toward each other's progress should not go unrecognized. It is important for both participants to understand the gains to be made in teaching, as well as learning from, others.

Finally, do not forget the success noted above for parents trained in this tutoring technique. You might want to conduct training sessions for parents, in your school, and thus help them as never before to become active participants in their children's learning.

The Benefits of Reading Stories Aloud

▬ Research

Adapted from Elley, W. B. (1989). Vocabulary acquisition from listening to stories. *Reading Research Quarterly, 24,* 174–187.

We recently read about a teacher of seventh graders who claimed positive effects for reading stories aloud to her students. We also visited a mixed fifth/sixth-grade class in which the teacher's story reading was an integral part of a highly successful language arts program for poor minority children. We began to wonder if reading stories aloud in classrooms was common practice, and whether research supported the claims for this teaching activity.

Many teachers of young children read stories to their students, but not all primary teachers do. And in the intermediate grades, many teachers who might choose to read to younger children stop reading to their students because they believe the students no longer would benefit from being read a story. We found research on these issues that was conducted in New Zealand, in classrooms where all elementary-school teachers read stories aloud for about 30 minutes a day. The findings illustrate the benefits of reading aloud for elementary-school students.

In the first study, experienced teachers in seven different classrooms read an illustrated storybook to seven-year-olds. The story took only about 10 minutes to read, contained 20 unfamiliar words, and was read to the children three times over a period of seven days. Although an initial discussion of the title, cover picture, and main characters was conducted, teachers did not provide any explanations of unfamiliar words in the first study.

A test of vocabulary to accompany the book was developed. About half the items required a choice of verbal synonyms ("Which of the following words means the same as the underlined word: We summoned the teacher?") The other items were in picture form ("Which of the following pictures shows a parasol?") The gains in vocabulary from pretest to posttest, in the different classrooms, ranged from 13 to 21 percent and averaged about 15 percent. Gains on some words were as high as 40 percent ("May Day," "parasol"), although for some words the gains were much lower ("anguish," "hesitate").

The words that showed the biggest gains were those that were repeated often in the text, those accompanied by illustrations, and those that were accompanied by helpful meaning clues. Less important, but still related to gains in acquisition, were the correction of the word with the plot, its vividness, and the familiarity of the concept involved. These six variables, together, did a very good job of predicting which words in a story would be learned by the students.

This investigator also looked to see if ability was related to gains in vocabulary among the 152 children in the study. The top 75 percent of the students in ability averaged about a 15-percent gain, while the lowest-ability children averaged about a 23-percent gain. That is, low-ability children profited as much *or more* from having stories read to them as did the higher-ability children.

This investigator replicated his study using eight-year-old students, and two different books, to see how important the teacher's explanations of unfamiliar words were, and whether the same effects could occur using different storybooks. In this second study the teachers explained the unfamiliar words in half the classes, while in the other half the teachers merely read the stories. Stories were read to the children three times, over a period of a week. The gains from pretest to posttest for one of the books, when teachers explained the unfamiliar words, were about 40 percent! For the group (the group that heard only the stories) the gains were still an impressive 15 percent.

The second book used seemed to be less motivating for the students, and the gains from pretest to posttest were much less impressive. Nonetheless, the group that received the explanations still managed to gain 17 percent in vocabulary.

In this study some of the same factors predicted acquisition of vocabulary as in the first study—particularly the strength of the meaning cues, the number of occurrences in the story, and whether the word was illustrated or not. Once again the lowest-ability students gained as much as, *or more* than, the average- and high-ability students. Furthermore, three months after participating in the study, all the students received a surprise test. The results indicated that the gains they had made were being maintained.

It is clear from this study that young children can learn vocabulary from listening to carefully chosen illustrated storybooks read aloud to them. They also seem to enjoy this form of instruction. Anecdotal reports and classroom observations inform us that story reading for older students has some of the same effects, though repetitive readings and illustrations may not be as necessary for them as for younger children. Why, then, is reading so infrequent in the classroom? Why, then, is vocabulary most often taught as a workbook exercise, with work sheets to be filled out, where words are to be learned out of context? We think that with a careful choice of reading material, and with some thoughtful explanations of new vocabulary, along with elaboration of the concepts and themes of the plot by the teacher, reading aloud can be a truly powerful teaching activity.

■ Practice

Teachers are always seeking to maximize the time available for instruction and to discover instructional strategies that will be effective as well as interesting to their students. It looks like reading aloud may satisfy both of those needs. It takes only a few minutes a day, it seems to result in large gains in an important area (vocabulary learning), and it is thoroughly enjoyed by students. This then appears to be a particularly fruitful strategy for the classroom!

Now then, how to go about it? Most important will be the selection of stories appropriate to the students' age and interests. A good librarian can be a great resource in this endeavor. Librarians know which books are being read, and which new books have just arrived. They can alert you to books that may not be well-known but appear to spark children's interest. And they know authors that are especially popular with a given age group. With a stack of such books in hand, you may want to recruit some of your colleagues to help you to make a final decision about which books to use.

In choosing the books, you may want to consider using longer books than those used in the research reported here, particularly for children at the third-grade level and above. Longer books read in episodic style can provide opportunities for practice in the more sophisticated comprehension skills, such as making predictions and inferences. Episodes (as anyone old enough to remember the movie serials knows) can whet the students' appetite for the story and thereby ensure their undivided attention to the reading. In addition, longer stories are likely to provide the kind of repetition of new words that the researcher found desirable, but without the redundancy of having to listen to the same story. For example, a character may be described as melancholic several times throughout a longer story and in a variety of contexts, thereby providing repetition (and transfer) for the new word.

Finding stories that cater to the wide variety of interests represented in a classroom can be a real challenge. Be careful not to fall into patterns, such as restricting your choices to stories that focus on sports or on growing-up problems. There are many wonderful fantasies, including science-fiction and animal stories, that can be riveting if they are appropriately targeted to the students' ages. Also consider, as you evaluate your selections, the diversity of topics and characters. Make sure that females (as well as males) play leading roles; that different cultures are represented; that poor as well as middle- and upper-class situations, and different regions of the country, are included in your repertoire. As usual, successful teaching here requires an exquisite balance between responding to the students' interests and exposing them to ideas they might not otherwise encounter.

Another possibility to consider is the use of nonfictional literature. Older students may be particularly responsive to books such as *Lucy,* the true story of an anthropological quest, or to any of several books by Asimov that have to do with scientific inquiry. The latter author is particularly adept at adjusting his writing style to various age groups. Whatever the choice, one distinct advantage of nonfiction is that it can also be related to other areas of study.

It is a good idea to give a careful reading to each book before reading it to the class. In this way you will be able to identify words that might require explanation, or even illustration (if such is not available in the book itself). You may also want to think of ways in which you might extend student engagement with the text at the end of each session, such as "What do you think of the way so-and-so acted in this episode?" or "What would you have done under similar circumstances?" You might also ask students to predict what might happen next, or how they think the story should end.

Reading the story ahead of its use in the classroom can also be used to practice your delivery, especially if you record your reading and try to improve your "performance." The idea is not to present a Broadway-quality show but to make sure your delivery is clear, and that you are certain of the pronunciation of difficult words. Student comprehension can also be enhanced by your intonation and expression during the reading.

One other thing: Do not taint the enjoyment of oral reading with tests for comprehension or vocabulary. Researchers who conducted the studies of story telling have already confirmed the instructional gains that are accrued from oral reading in the classroom. You do not have to reaffirm this with more testing. The knowledge of tests to follow is likely to increase student anxiety and decrease the pure enjoyment of stories that you are seeking to encourage.

Finally, and especially appropriate as each school year ends, is the possibility for summer learning that students may gain from oral reading at home. You may want to send an inspirational letter there as the school prepares to close, in order to share these possibilities with parents and encourage them to continue what you have begun on the job. You may even want to send a list of recommended books available at the public library. And, if some of your students come from homes where another language is spoken, you may want to tell them that it is most appropriate to read to their children in their own language. There is research showing that such involved students can readily transfer gains they make in their native language to English, their second language.

Retelling Stories Can Help Kids Become Better Readers

■ Research

Adapted from Morrow, L. M. (1985). Retelling stories: A strategy for improving young children's comprehension, concept of story structure, and oral language complexity. *The Elementary School Journal*, 85, 648–661.

Reading aloud to children is a key activity in early-childhood classrooms (see pages 78–82). Research documents that when young children are read to, they gain interest in learning to read, accumulate background knowledge for interpreting what they read, and acquire more sophisticated language. But to get the most from being read to these children must clearly comprehend the stories. Children who lack a concept of *story structure*—a general mental model of what stories are like and how they can be interpreted—often have comprehension problems.

Lesley Morrow theorized that asking young children to retell stories in their own words would help them to learn story structure, and thus to better comprehend stories they listen to or read themselves. Yet a survey of preschool and kindergarten teachers showed that they rarely gave children opportunities to retell stories, because the activity was considered time-consuming, difficult, and of no educational value. Morrow hoped to show the opposite to be true. She studied a heterogeneous group of children in four public-school kindergartens. A randomly formed group of 29 became the experimental group, and 30 others served as the control. All children were read a story of about 880 words and shown the 22 illustrations that accompanied the story.

Teachers led the usual pre- and postreading activities, including a discussion of the children's favorite story parts. After the postdiscussion, the children in the *control* group were asked to draw a picture about the story. Each child in the *experimental* group was asked to retell the story "as though they were telling it to a friend who had never heard it before." No prompts were given, other than "What comes next?" or "Then what happened?"

Both groups took a comprehension test that asked questions about story setting and theme, and about problems faced by the characters. Other questions dealt with issues not derivable directly from the text— the interpretation of feelings and problem-solving strategies. The tests were scored by research assistants who were not aware of which group each child was in or what activity each had engaged in. Test results showed the experimental group's scores to be slightly above the control group's.

Morrow then wondered whether giving children practice in retelling stories would produce a greater difference in the comprehension scores of the two groups. During a second study, involving 82 kindergartners, students in the experimental group were asked to retell eight stories, and were given guidance when needed. The retellings were tape-recorded and analyzed. The same kind of comprehension test used in the first study was given after each story. By the final test, the results were stronger: From pretest to posttest, the control group improved only 9.3 percent, while the experimental group improved 27.6 percent. The experimental group outperformed the control group on such activities as discussing the setting, theme, plot episodes, resolution of conflicts, and sequence of events.

Morrow looked at the complexity of the language that the children used when discussing the stories, and found that the experimental children outperformed the control group on this measure, too. Also, children who improved the most in comprehension improved the most in retelling stories. In addition, anecdotal records revealed that, during free play, children in the experimental group indulged in storytelling more often than did control students. Experimental students also initiated in story role-playing more often and more frequently included other children in the enactments of stories. (Parents of those in the experimental group reported more often than the control group's parents that their children wanted to retell stories that were read to them at home.) Finally, the experimental group's children seemed more sophisticated at handling story questions than did the control group.

Empirical data and anecdotal reports lead us to believe that retelling stories, a very simple instructional activity, can have positive educational effects for young children. Common sense would support the idea that this activity might be of value to older children as well.

■ Practice

The past several years have seen a great improvement in the decoding skills of primary-grade children, but improvement in comprehension skills may not have kept pace. Some researchers think that children who lack comprehension skills have had little—if any—exposure to reading at home. Such children haven't had the opportunity to develop what psychologists call *story scripts* or *story structures*. The research by Morrow suggests that ordinary forms of storytelling can be enhanced to help students overcome comprehension problems and reap other important cognitive benefits.

Retelling as a comprehension-boosting technique has several strong points. First, it's easily adapted to early-childhood classrooms. Second, it requires no special materials or equipment. Third, very little training is needed to successfully implement the technique.

Begin by selecting students who have difficulty getting the point of a story or who seem to dislike listening to stories. Their dislike may be caused by comprehension problems. Next, select assistants. Because no formal teaching skills are required, aides, parent volunteers, even older students may direct the task. Give assistants an overview of the following techniques, then demonstrate their use with individual children before turning over the task to others. Tell the student the title of the story and what the story is about. Then read the story, showing the illustrations as you read. Afterwards, ask the child which part of the story he or she liked best. Then ask him or her to tell the story. A statement like "Retell the story as if you were telling it to a friend who has never heard it before" helps students to understand what is expected.

At first, students who have had little experience with story retelling may need to be prompted. But prompts should be general. The idea is to guide the youngsters through the story script by asking questions, such as: "What comes next?" "And then what happened?" "What problems did they face?" "How did it end?"

Storytelling and retelling sessions should be relaxed. Stories read to young children should be short, simple, and interesting. Look for authors who capture feelings using only a few words. Look for stories with familiar topics, characters, and situations. With a minimum of effort, you can combine interesting stories, individual attention, and language techniques to meaningfully increase your students' comprehension skills.

Should We Raise the Reading Speed Limit for First-Graders?

▬ Research

Adapted from Breznitz, Z. (1987). Increasing first graders' reading accuracy and comprehension by accelerating their reading rates. *Journal of Educational Psychology, 79*, 236–242.

Reading speed for first-graders may need to be revised as a result of studies conducted in Israel and the United States. Those studies, by Zvia Breznitz, suggest that the slow pace of reading in the first grade may be counterproductive.

Breznitz began by having Israeli first-graders read short declarative sentences, at their own self-determined pace. She recorded the speed at which each of these items was read, as well as the answers that the children gave to comprehension questions that were asked after they read each item. Then, for a second series of trials, some of the students were randomly assigned to an experimental group, wherein they were asked to read a new set of sentences that were presented on a computer screen at a much faster speed. That speed was the same as the fastest speed demonstrated by each student during the sentence-reading exercise. Each student's fastest reading speed was, generally, 20 percent faster than his or her normal pace. A *control* group of students read a new set of sentences from the computer at their *normal* reading speed.

The researcher found no change from Trial 1 to Trial 2 in either the number of oral reading errors, or the reading comprehension scores made by children in the *control* groups. However, the performance of the *experimental* group was a real surprise: The group that had been speeded up made about 50 percent fewer errors in oral reading, and

85

showed an increase of about 20 percent in comprehension! Moreover, when the experimental group was separated into those who were initially "good" and "poor" readers, it turned out that the biggest reductions in oral reading errors, and the biggest gains in comprehension, were made by the *poorest* readers. Raising the speed limit apparently helps almost all readers to read more accurately and with greater comprehension, but helps poor readers the most.

The researcher speculated that, for beginning readers, simply going at their own pace might be too slow because they could not then keep track of all the information they needed in order to answer comprehension questions. The short-term memory of children at this age is quite limited. Slowing the pace in order to attend to individual words or syllables appeared to cause a loss of meaning from the beginning to the end of the sentence. And without the adequate creation of meaning by a reader there is a higher probability of saying something inappropriate, like saying "loys" for "toys" when doing oral reading. Breznitz tested these ideas.

In a second experiment, Breznitz had students read sentences and answer questions, just as she did in the first study. Then she determined the slowest rate for each student, and used that speed when she presented a second group of sentences to a randomly selected experimental group. The slowed-down students were more accurate readers, but *comprehended* much less than did a control group.

In a third experiment, Breznitz inserted common errors into the sentences that the children read aloud. Then she accelerated the reading speed for one group, as she did in the first study. In this case, children showed the same increased comprehension as in the first study. Also, they either corrected the deliberate errors spontaneously (i.e., changing "dread" to "bread" without noticing it) or made the error that was intended, but corrected it immediately. Their rate of correcting errors was about twice that of the group that read at their own pace. And once again it was the poorest readers who seemed to be helped the most by increasing the speed at which they read. (In a fourth study done in the United States, almost identical findings to those of the third study occurred.)

It appears that, across cultures and languages, pushing students to read orally about 20 percent faster decreases their errors and increases their comprehension. Reducing their pace of reading may also reduce their error rate, but it also wreaks havoc with their comprehension. Perhaps if we stopped worrying about students' diction, accent, mispronounced words, substitutions, and other relatively insignificant reading errors, and started concentrating on increased speed, we might see better reading performance on *both* dimensions: comprehension *and* accuracy.

These studies also suggest a strategy for teaching hard-to-teach students. Perhaps by breaking up the reading task into bits and pieces, in the belief that this will help in learning to read, we are keeping the most meaningful textual materials away from the children who have the most difficulty in *making* meaning out of text. Maybe the level of the teaching materials should be raised *as well as* the speed at which we ask kids to read them.

■ Practice

A particularly good time of year to think about these results is after most students have mastered the basic skills they need for decoding text. At that point it is time both to emphasize comprehension and to try something new. Start by finding especially attractive and interesting reading materials. Magazines and newspapers may be good—and, of course, library books come in all shapes, colors, sizes, and skill levels. Use what you know about your students' interests to assemble what they'll like.

Next, show your students how to read faster, and stress the importance of understanding what the words *say,* as well as the proper reading of them. Demonstrate how to do this by having students ask questions when you finish reading. Encourage them to ask summarizing and inferring questions as well as factual ones by giving them examples of each kind of question. Encourage your students to challenge your understanding with the questions they ask. When students understand your goals of increasing their comprehension while increasing speed and accuracy, you can move to the next stage.

Pair the students, and ask them to read to each other. They should take turns being "student" and "teacher." The teacher should encourage the student to speed up, and should ask comprehension questions. The teacher also needs to note errors, and show them to the student at the conclusion. Remind them not to interrupt, and not to worry about inflection or accents (which are not reading errors).

As you start this activity, make sure the students in each team read at about the same level; you want them to help each other as equals. Also, the reading material should reflect their level and interest alike. Interesting material may motivate students to work a little harder and keep frustration at a manageable level.

To help them keep track of their progress, give the students a stop-watch to time each other, and a sheet of paper to jot down their errors. You may even want to teach them how to graph their results.

Finally, remember that an instructional strategy doesn't work with every student every time. Be ready to offer alternatives to children who do not respond well to this activity.

You may want to send letters to students' homes, describing this classroom activity. Ask parents to let their child read aloud to them at a natural pace, and to follow up with questions about the reading.

These activities capitalize on the findings of the study. They also provide a change of pace, and heightened interest in classroom processes. However, the most important benefit is to your students, who will gain more confidence as their comprehension increases.

Students who move from slow, laborious decoding to faster speeds are also likely to gain confidence in their reading skills. For the least capable readers, increased confidence at the end of the school year can prove a real boon in the year to come.

The Field Trip: Frill or Essential?

▬ Research

Adapted from Mackenzie, A., & White, R. (1982). Field work in geography and long-term memory structures. *American Educational Research Journal,* 19, 623–632; and Falk, J. H., & Balling, J. D. (1982). The field trip milieu. *Journal of Educational Research,* 76(1), 22–28.

Near the end of the school year, teachers who would like to schedule field trips often find themselves resorting to hard-sell persuasion. For the last few years, budget cuts have made arguing the merits of field trips difficult. Economy-minded school boards seem convinced that *all* out-of-school excursions create unnecessary expenditures.

Can field trips really be justified? New research data suggest they certainly can be! And the researchers also describe ways to make *sure* that such trips are worthwhile learning experiences.

Andres Mackenzie and Richard White, two researchers in Australia, studied the effects of field trips on junior-high students' retention of geography concepts. To help students learn 35 objectives about coastal land forms and plants, they first used programmed instructional materials supplemented with 60 slides of geographical features.

One-third of their students, the control group, had no follow-up activities to that course. The other two-thirds took a four-and-one-half-hour field trip to a coastal area. Half of these traveling students, designated the traditional group, went on a relatively passive trip—one that made few cognitive demands of them and that their teacher dominated. At each site their teacher called students' attention to what they were to observe. In turn they were asked to verify what they heard by checking off information in an instructional guidebook.

The second group of field-trip participants were asked to do many things: to observe, sketch, and record, and to use every one of their basic senses to generate new information. They had all their questions answered, and, in addition, participated in unusual experiences that explicitly linked what they saw and did with principles of geography. For instance, to estimate salinity, they walked through the mud of a mangrove shore and tasted the foliage. Although students in the traditional group spent the same amount of time at the site, saw all the same things, and heard important ideas more frequently, they were required to perform far fewer physical and mental activities.

Each of the three groups took an achievement test immediately following their instructional experiences. A few months later, all students took another retention test. A multiple-choice test to assess how well those who witnessed or participated in the unusual episodes (for instance, tasting bark) were able to apply that information, was also given to field-trip participants.

The results were clear: Active field-trip participants learned more! Of 35 objectives on the first test, active students scored 33.1, with the traditional group averaging 29.2 and the group who had not gone on the field trip, only 26.3.

Differences on the retention test were much more pronounced. The active group outscored the traditional group by 29.7 to 17.2. The control group retained the fewest facts (13.5). These data show that the active group—the students who engaged in the most mental activity on the field trip—retained 90 percent of the information from the class; the traditional group and the control group retained only about half the information they had acquired. In other words, the latter two groups learned less and forgot more.

Moreover, when students were tested on the material learned through their participation in "unusual episodes," the active group answered 60 percent of the questions correctly. The traditional students who witnessed but did not participate in the unusual events scored what they might be expected to score *had they never taken the trip* (about 20 percent). Students who had direct experiences linking what they saw with principles of geography not only remembered the principles illustrated in the episode, but also demonstrated greater retention of all new knowledge!

Apparently the novelty and uniqueness of the episodes made more vivid all the information relevant to that episode, resulting in greater long-term retention of information.

Two other researchers, John Falk and John Balling, both of the Chesapeake Bay Center for Environmental Studies, wanted to discover whether field trips to new settings resulted in more learning than those to familiar areas. To do this they compared students studying science in the woods adjacent to their school with those taken on an all-day field trip to a nature center. Both groups studied the same phenomena in the same way, and both retained much of what they had learned. Of particular interest was the finding that third-graders learned more in the nondisruptive, relatively familiar setting of the woods, whereas fifth-graders found the unfamiliar, more novel field trip away from the school more conducive to learning.

Thus these researchers recommend shorter, closer-to-home field trips for younger students. For older students novelty, unfamiliarity, and extensiveness are the qualities to aim for.

Both research studies clearly show that well-designed field trips can lead to new learning, reinforce what has been already learned in school, and aid greatly in the retention of information. We do not even have to mention how *enjoyable* field trips are, to defend their place in the curriculum and budget. But we will.

■ Practice

Field trips can be among the most memorable of school experiences. And research indicates that they can also help children to remember instructional material. There are two types of field trips, however; those that are simply meant to expose children to new experiences, and those with deliberate pedagogical purposes. While the categories are not totally discrete (children *do* learn from fun activities, and planned instructional trips *can* be fun) the trick is to turn the first type into the second. How can the fall trip to the pumpkin patch, and the spring visit to the museum, become deliberate learning experiences?

To get maximum benefit from *any* excursion, the teacher has first to identify those lessons that would be particularly facilitated by firsthand experience. Erosion, for example, is not only difficult to duplicate in the classroom; it is also a concept not likely to be understood by children without some direct experience. While for farm children a field trip to study erosion is probably unnecessary, it could be indispensable for city children.

Once you decide where in your curriculum a field trip would be useful, the next step is to develop a lesson plan just as you would for any other lesson. The objective must be clear: What are the students expected to learn? Without preparation and guidance, visiting a canyon can be an overwhelming and frustrating experience for ten-year-olds. There is so much to see, so much to grasp. The students need to know why they are going, and what they must attend to while there. You can help focus their attention, tease their curiosity, and provide necessary background by showing photographs of the site, teaching appropriate vocabulary, and leading preliminary classroom discussions.

Plans for the field trip itself must anchor your students ' experiences to the instructional objectives. Which unusual activities will help students to retain knowledge? On a field trip to study the desert, for instance, students might dig up one cubic foot of soil in an apparently desolate field and then find and count the number of living things within it. They could carry out a similar experiment in a tide pool at the beach, within a log in a forest, or within a given stratum in a canyon.

To call on their higher-order thinking skills, ask them to make up their own definition of a desert and justify it with their own observations. Later they can discuss and analyze their discoveries, and record the differences between the environment they visited and others they have studied.

Such active experiences will focus students' attention, engage their thinking processes, and enhance retention. But, when planning the activities, don't forget they should be teacher-*directed,* not teacher-*provided.* Although you will need to guide students' explorations, don't forget to encourage their questions and speculations.

This brings us to the return destination of any field-trip experience, the classroom. This is where experiences can be relived, speculations analyzed, unanswered questions researched, and collected materials examined. If you don't discuss the field trip in relation to the content being studied, you'll lose an important lesson—and so will they. And students who find they are not held as responsible for knowledge gained through a field trip as they are for textbook information will not be very attentive travelers the next time. Failure to require classroom follow-up devalues the field trip's instructional purpose.

A closing thought: Teachers often encounter a host of problems in planning their field trips. The bus shows up late; a helping parent cancels at the last minute; a child lacks a permission slip. All of these real problems may have an impact of one sort or another on the success of the trip. These, however, really should be considered outside your direct control. What you *can* be expected to control is adequate planning. And that is what will ensure that each and every field trip will prove a valuable instructional activity for your students—*and* you.

Play Is the Work of Childhood

▬ Research

Adapted from Connolly, J. A., Doyle, A. B., & Reznick, E. (1988). Social pretend play and social interaction in preschoolers. *Journal of Applied Developmental Psychology, 9*(3), 301–313.

With increasing pressure to start academic studies at earlier and earlier ages, it is important to remember that play—particularly "pretend" play—is one way by means of which children learn. A recent study of preschool and kindergarten-age children illustrates this clearly. It also suggests that pretend play may be a *desirable* part of education.

Researchers watched four- and five-year-olds in seven 40–minute play sessions. Although group membership constantly changed, the researchers always observed youngsters in groups of four. About half of the observed sessions were pretend play sessions; the rest, nonpretend. Researchers observed each child in both contexts. They measured how long the children played, how often they tried, and what methods they used to influence each other, how often they complied with each other's requests, their social competence, and so forth. The researchers provided toys and other props for each play group, selecting some (such as telephones, dress-up clothes, and puppets) that encouraged pretend play. They chose others (such as small blocks, puzzles, and coloring materials) to elicit nonpretend play.

The results—consistent with existing theory and previous research—probably are not what the general public would predict: In pretend play, children acted *more mature* than they did in nonpretend activities!

In this study, children played pretend activities 21 percent longer than other forms of play, suggesting that youngsters enjoyed pretend play more. Pretend play also had significantly fewer negative affective ratings (71 percent lower). That is, during pretend play the children demonstrated many fewer negative emotions, such as anger and frustration. And—although this is not statistically significant—in the pretend context these researchers also noted about 17 percent fewer refusals to play. They also found that children played together more, and were more social, in pretend settings than in nonpretend settings.

Communication patterns differed in the two settings as well. Children made about 16 percent more requests of their playmates, and their playmates agreed to these requests about 35 percent more often during pretend play. Youngsters also talked more about what they were doing, and had more success influencing others in pretend settings than in other contexts—although these findings also were not statistically significant.

Such results suggest that pretend play can bring certain desirable changes in social behavior. The authors reported that children moving from nonpretend play to social pretend play demonstrate "more positive, more successful and more developmentally mature peer social interaction." They also indicate that the social benefits were apparent for *each* child, regardless of gender, usual play preferences, or usual play partners.

It appears that providing young children with toys and activities that foster social pretend play may in fact also significantly promote social competency—an important goal of early education, indeed.

▬ Practice

Play and work are often seen as antonyms in our society. In general, work is positively valued; play is not. This study reminds us that the apparently obvious distinctions between the terms really are not so clear, particularly for children. This is especially so for young children who are developing new social skills.

If you teach in preschool classrooms, you are likely to have sufficient time and space for pretend play. Make sure that you have materials on hand that encourage pretend-play activities. Some common kindergarten toys (such as small blocks, crayons, puzzles, and gross motor games) tend to lead to nonpretend activities. But dress-up clothes, large blocks, tools, doctors' kits, dolls, and robots encourage pretend play. Don't limit children to toys, though. Rather allow them to incorporate classroom furniture—wastebaskets, chairs, tables—into their games, and therefore their fantasy world.

Although at the primary level it is generally more difficult (and less acceptable) to incorporate pretend play into classroom activities because of the need to teach "the basics," it continues to be a very effective way for primary youngsters to learn social skills. Thus you should do what you can, given your circumstances, to integrate *some* amount of pretend play with other learning activities. Playing "store," for example, can help students to master basic computation. Likewise, play-acting, whether from textbook stories or from the children's own stories, can be a powerful vehicle for developing both social skills and reading comprehension.

To maximize the benefits of pretend play, minimize adult guidance. Give students guidelines about what they are to do, provide a time frame, and allow them to work the details out among themselves. Remember that the process, as much as the end result, is the learning activity.

Of course, technology also offers advantages (some of them unique) to teachers interested in fostering pretend play. Video cameras and VCRs let children "try out" roles that can be recorded and displayed.

Television can be an accessory to reading and writing, and as a special incentive for children who are less than willing to engage in more traditional classroom activities. Writing their own commercials, for example, lets students apply basic skills as well as the analytical and synthesizing skills required to determine what will sell a particular product or service.

For older children, too, play-acting is another form of pretend play that can be extended to academic areas. Use it in the study of history, for example, by reenacting such important events as the Constitutional Convention, a presidential debate or convention, a summit conference, or other historical events.

Older primary- and middle-school children can also benefit from participation in simulation games. Many such games allow children to "walk in someone else's shoes"—that is, to understand the interaction between social context and human behavior, or to simulate civic meetings or personal-conflict situations. You may want to review available resources and request that some of these games become part of your school library.

There are many ways to learn. For most of human history, people have learned from each other during social activities. By observing rites and rituals, people can learn proper behavior before they themselves experience a certain situation.

Children, too, need opportunities to try out their social skills, and classrooms are safe places in which they can develop. Working together, understanding the effects of behavior, and developing leadership and persuasive skills all require *group* experience. As teachers, we have both an opportunity and a responsibility to provide situations that allow students to learn these skills—as well as the more traditional academic ones.

Bilingual Instruction: Which Strategies Work Best?

▰ Research

Adapted from Tikunoff, W., Fisher, C., et al. (1984, November/December). *Bilingual instruction: What strategies work best?* San Francisco, CA: Far West Laboratory for Educational Research and Development.

In the late 1960s Congress took note that large numbers of American school children spoke a language other than English. Many of the legislators recognized that these children needed to develop English-language proficiency in order to participate fully in American economic and cultural life. According to many scholars, this could be accomplished most effectively by initiating instruction in the children's home language while they acquired oral competency in English. This was the concept behind the Bilingual Education Act.

A few insightful members of Congress saw, also, a need to preserve foreign languages in order to have a citizenry capable of participating effectively in world trade and diplomacy. Such instruction would support native-language development beyond initial literacy. To be more informed, they asked for research on bilingual instruction.

One of the studies they requested was completed at the Far West Laboratory for Educational Research and Development by William Tikunoff, Charles Fisher, and dozens of colleagues at bilingual sites around the country. The focus of the study was how bilingual teachers can improve *both* the English-language proficiency and the academic skills of children who speak other languages. For the most part, the researchers studied children from families with limited educational backgrounds.

The first phase of the study examined bilingual instruction in classrooms with Mexican, Puerto Rican, Cuban, Chinese, and/or Navajo children. The 68 teachers who were studied had all been nominated as effective bilingual teachers by fellow teachers and community members.

Three major findings were evident. First, these teachers were found to behave *exactly* like teachers who provide high-quality instruction in monolingual classes. For example, they always had a strong focus on academic work. They allocated a good deal of the school day to subject matter, and never allowed too much time off-task. They communicated clearly what they intended to happen by giving accurate directions. And they expressed high expectations for their own and their students' performance. In short, good teachers are good teachers, whether in a monolingual or a bilingual setting.

A second major finding from this study was that the effective bilingual teachers used the students' native languages extensively for instruction. These teachers did not just use token amounts of the students' native languages. They did not just use the students' languages for comments of little significance, or to call attention to inappropriate behavior. They actually integrated the native language into their instruction—and this action in their part was found to correlate positively with desirable student classroom behavior. The implication of this finding is that the instruction of students who are speakers of other languages requires teachers with sophisticated linguistic skills in the students' native languages, over and above the pedagogical and content expertise normally required of competent teachers.

The third major finding was that the effective bilingual teachers made extensive use of the students' cultures, both in interpreting student behavior and in modifying instruction. Cultures differ in subtle ways that often lead to misunderstandings among teachers and students. These teachers, however, were found to be very sensitive to such issues. One of them was overheard explaining to another teacher that a Hispanic student who had looked down and would not respond to the teacher during a scolding was not being disrespectful but was, in fact, showing culturally appropriate respect to an elder who was reprimanding him!

Another teacher learned that in classes with Navajo children you should not assign boys and girls from the same tribal clan to the same reading group. Also, because repeated direct questioning calls attention to an individual child, this age-old teaching method is actually inappropriate to use with most Native American children. Effective bilingual teachers of such children instead learn to do more small-group work and use more choral responding techniques.

The findings noted above were validated in another study of 89 bilingual teachers. Filipino, Vietnamese, and Hispanic children were added to the sample. Thus, these findings were well supported.

The study did not come to general conclusions about instruction in multilingual classrooms. In some low-income urban areas many diverse language groups were served simultaneously. And of course teaching a classroom with four language groups complicated the problems of instruction enormously. Instruction was carried out differently, too, depending on the size of the linguistic community in which the child lived. Bilingual instruction for Vietnamese in Iowa was necessarily different from that of speakers of Spanish in Miami.

Nevertheless, no matter how the school districts accommodated their instruction to local circumstances (whether with special bilingual teachers for part of the day, the use of bilingual aids, multilingual teachers all the time, or whatever), the issues of effectiveness as a teacher seemed to be the same. Effective teachers apparently need to have native-language proficiency such that they can integrate certain students' mother tongues into instruction. They also need lots of cultural sensitivity. And they must demonstrate nothing short of excellence in pedagogical skills and content knowledge.

■ Practice

What do these findings about effective bilingual education mean for the classroom teacher? They remind us, first, that the language a child brings to school must not influence the teachers's expectations of the student's academic performance. Speakers of languages other than English have often been assumed to have learning deficiencies. At their worst, these assumptions have led to their disproportionate assignments to special-education classes. Often they have also led to self-fulfilling expectations for lower academic performance from these students.

More times than not it is a lack of comprehension, not inherent academic deficiency, that results in low achievement. Effective teachers know this, and so never stop maintaining high expectations.

It follows, of course, that instruction in academic skills must be delivered in a language that the student can comprehend. It is not surprising to find that integrating the student's native language into lessons increases the effectiveness of instruction. Too often, the use of the student's language has been assumed to be a hindrance to the development of competency in a new language. It is only to be expected that students who speak a language other than English will require instruction in the English language. But they will also need clarification of their many other lessons in *their own* language.

When an English-speaking child doesn't understand what the teacher has explained, an effective teacher will repeat the explanation *in other words,* and will seek to match those words to the student's level of understanding. For a child who speaks a different language, those "other words" need to be in his or her *native* language.

Effective interpretation of two languages requires a high degree of bilingual competency—a level which too few teachers are capable of, unfortunately. Teachers who are working with students who speak a language in which they sometimes are not proficient cannot provide this integration. Such teachers can, however, request such assistance from school administrators, in accordance with federal policy. Their professional responsibility for their students' achievement should make them strong advocates for this assistance.

This study also points out the need for teachers to be sensitive to their students' cultures. For example, teachers in rural and inner-city areas are likely to modify their instruction in order to make the content of instruction more relevant to their students. Teachers who work with children of a different cultural background have an additional problem. They may recognize the need to be culturally sensitive, but be unaware of just where the cultural differences lie. With the best intentions, teachers may trample on a student's (or a parent's) cultural values—for example, simply by praising a child in public.

For most of us, the understanding of cross-cultural differences must be achieved secondhand through books and by means of the advice of those who are native to the culture. A teacher needs to seek out as much information as possible—but, most of all, a teacher needs to observe students in and out of the classroom, and take time to reflect on those observations. When a child behaves inappropriately, a teacher needs to suspend judgment temporarily, because such behavior might be guided by different cultural values. A child's willingness to respond to questions or to sit on the floor, for example, might be related to home-taught values.

Teachers working with culturally different children also need to make explicit expectations that they have for behavior that might appear "obvious" to members of the majority culture. For example, in some cultures parents feel free to remove children from school when they are needed at home. The school's expectations and state laws for attendance need to be explained to these families. Teachers cannot assume that keeping a child home is indicative of the parents' lack of interest in the child's learning. The parents just might not see the link between attendance and academic progress.

Finally, the teachers in this study emphasized academic tasks and used techniques that have been found effective in monolingual classrooms. This suggests that many features of pedagogical effectiveness can be generalized. Good classroom teachers of students who are speakers of other languages apparently are good classroom teachers who possess two other important skills: They are proficient in the child's native language, and they show special sensitivity to the child's culture.

SECTION 3

LEARNING

Introduction

Although schools admittedly are artificial environments, learning is most assuredly as natural to humans as breathing. The trick we face is to learn how people go about learning, thinking, and remembering naturally, and then develop curricula and schools that are compatible with the ways in which knowledge is acquired, processed, and stored. Cognitive science, a new discipline aligned with psychology, computer science, and anthropology, is beginning to do just that. And some of the pertinent cognitive research is reported in this section.

We start with a discussion of how memory works, noting implications of these ideas of how knowledge is derived. Memory is crucial for teachers to know about because we want what we teach to be held in the students' minds long after we finish our instruction. Just how individuals *organize* their memories has become an important topic in recent times. Many scholars agree that domain-specific knowledge (that is, the organizational information about some domain of knowledge that is held in memory by a person) is one of the key factors in learning *new* information in that domain. Perhaps, some say, it is the most important factor of all: In a sense, you learn best when you already know best.

The second article points out how such domain-specific knowledge in an area—say soccer or auto mechanics—is likely to be a better predictor of new learning in that area than intelligence! This finding has a great deal to tell us about how we organize instruction and treat students.

The next two articles also explore the role of background knowledge on learning. One is about learning mathematics; the other concerns learning science. They look at the ways in which students think in these important domains of knowledge. In both cases we learn that teachers can improve their students' *learning* if they learn more about their students *thinking*. This sets the stage for an article about what happens when teachers learn to understand their students' thinking better. Students can fool teachers sometimes by getting test items right although they may not really have organized their thinking in the particular domain in the most productive ways. For this reason, teachers need to probe the thoughts that underlie their students' answers.

In the area of literacy—writing and oral-language development—we also present two articles. The first informs us that substantial gains in learning to write well can be made through explicit instruction. The second warns us that language development may be stifled in school. We may have created such an unnatural environment in school that the kind of language learning we hope will take place actually cannot, at least in schools as we now know them.

The last two articles continue the theme that environments for learning are quite important to consider. The first of these suggests a problem with the learning environment in school. It is about seatwork in elementary schools. Here it is suggested that there is less learning going on in such settings than most teachers think. The final article in this set is more positive. It is about setting an intellectual environment that produces sophisticated learning in very young children. These last two articles suggest that we look not just at how to improve learning by focusing on the individual students, but that we look also at how we set up environments that can inhibit or promote the kind of school learning we want our students to experience.

How Memory Works: Implications for Teachers

■ Research

Adapted from Lura, A. R. (1968). *The mind of a mnemonist*. New York: Basic Books; and Neisser, U. (1982). *Memory observed: Remembering in natural contexts*. Columbus, OH: W. H. Freeman.

The Russian psychologist A. R. Luria asked a man he was studying to memorize the following fictitious equation:

$$N . \sqrt{d^2 X \tfrac{85}{VX}} \cdot \sqrt[3]{\tfrac{276^3 \cdot 86 X}{n^2 V \cdot W264}} \quad n^2 b = S \sqrt{32^2/1624} \cdot r^3 s$$

The man, whom we know only as "S," stared at the equation for seven minutes and put it aside. When requested, he recited if from memory flawlessly. Fifteen years later, without any intervening activity with it, Luria asked S to recall the equation. S recited it perfectly. He said that he remembered it by thinking of his friend Nieman (N), who tapped the ground with his cane(.), next to a crooked tree that looked like a square root sign. Under the tree branches were two doors (d2) that he wanted to get rid of (X), and so on.

S was a mnemonist—a memory expert. His unique natural ability to remember (and seemingly never forget) anything sheds light on how memory works for those of us with less natural ability. His memory prowess was based on synthesis, a melding of senses. Every word or number heard or seen involved also a sense of smell or touch! He heard or had visual associations for all of the symbols he encountered. He said he even experienced the taste, weight, and texture of words. Apparently S made use of imagery and depended heavily on multiple-sense impressions to encode new material into memory.

Researchers have found that normally anyone can store visual images distinct from verbal/symbolic images. Many of them say that we actually have *separate storage systems* in our brains, for verbal information and for piecemeal information. (The recent discovery that the left hemisphere is used primarily for processing visual imagery seems also to be related to this notion.) The research implies that the more ways you can enhance imagery when teaching verbal material, the more likely it is that your students will remember what you taught. That is probably why concrete words *(water, dog, corn)* are learned quicker and remembered longer when young children are learning to speak and read than are abstract words *(legal, neatness, sensible)*. Concrete words convey images; abstract words do not.

But visualization through imagery was just one way that S remembered. He used his other senses, too. Perhaps that is why foreign-language vocabulary is learned quicker and remembered better when students learn to move to commands and speak the foreign words, as well as learn them from a book or by a teacher's speech. In one study, foreign-language teachers taught the commands for "stand up," "sit down," "pick up your pencil," and "open the book." Students remembered the meaning of the commands far better when they actually carried out the commands, and said them out loud, than when they only learned them through their written symbolic form. Apparently the melding of the senses—movement and sound—with the verbal symbolic form of the information, as with S, was what helped students in this study to learn the foreign vocabulary.

Maria Montessori reached the same conclusion a century ago. The Montessori method of instruction is *heavily* dependent on multiple-sensory approaches. Such theorists as Jerome Bruner and Jean Piaget talk of children developing sequentially from a motor stage, dependent on movement and touch; through an iconic stage, dominated by the visual senses; to a symbolic stage, dominated by symbols such as the words and numbers that are taught in schools.

What contemporary research on long-term memory reminds us of is that we never stop learning through movement, touch, and imagery, even when the verbal/symbolic learning mode becomes dominant. Thus, if we want to help children remember the things that we deem important, we should help them whenever we can to construct visual representations and give them some multi-sensory experiences during learning.

■ Practice

To make sure of our insights about memory we need to begin by determining what information our students need to remember. What must be retained now so it can be built upon later? Some concepts we teach need to be understood, not memorized—for example, the concept of mutual dependence in a community. Other facts and ideas have immediate value but need not be remembered forever. Still others, (and these are the ones we need to identify) just *have* to be remembered—for example addition facts, letters, and the days of the week.

The next step is to think of ways we can help children to learn the content we want them to remember. The easiest way to think about this is to remember that we have five basic senses. We can see, hear, feel, taste, and smell. Most of our efforts in school are directed at getting children to see and hear, and we usually miss the other three senses. Yet studies of children pretty much agree that young children in particular learn best while using *all* their senses. This then should be an important part of our lesson plan: *How many senses can we involve during instruction?*

The visual sense is concerned not only with using our eyes, but also our minds, to see. Creating vivid imagery in our students' minds can be a powerful memory aid. A visual image of an alligator with an open mouth, from one of my elementary teachers' classroom bulletin boards, has helped me to remember the proper direction for the "less than" symbol, even through advanced statistics.

The senses of touching and feeling are related to movement, which can be associated with the content we are teaching to enhance retention. One such activity, learned in my early primary years, has been a continued aid to my memory. A clever teacher taught me that if I made a fist with one hand and recited the months of the year in order while touching with a finger, in turn, each knuckle space between the knuckles until all the months were included, I could tell the length of the months. Months with 31 days would fall on the knuckles, while those with 30, or fewer days would fall in the spaces between.

How many senses can we tap? What visual images can we create? What kinds of physical activities can we incorporate into the learning process? Coming up with new ideas to enhance retention can make both learning *and* teaching more enjoyable. One beginning reading program asks children to relate visual images to phonetic sounds; first-graders enjoy spelling out words by holding up the visual images that accompany the sounds. Some teachers use letters and numbers made of different materials for the children to handle while the kids say their own names or make the sounds, thus adding the sense of touch to the visual and sound cues.

For older children, grammar can take on a new life if we use physical activities to get the information across. After all, verbs are active words, aren't they? And prepositions have a designated place in a sentence. Students can be assigned the different roles of words in the sentence and asked to make up grammatically correct sentences as their classmates arrange them in whatever ways seem appropriate.

We can borrow some of these techniques to get students' attention. Try oversize letters, or perhaps very tiny ones in a large area. Or perhaps go overboard on something children *have* to remember—for example, the date 1776. Stick it all over the room (on the floor or ceiling, in the closet) or in the wastebasket—or on yourself!

Audiovisuals can also be used effectively to relate visual images to content. *Sesame Street* has done this successfully, and in the process has taught many children letters and numbers.

Children also enjoy the unexpected and dramatic, and they remember what took place when these are used in teaching. I know a teacher who dressed up as a pirate and brought a treasure chest to class to introduce a story. Another teacher hatched baby chicks in her classroom during a science unit.

Less dramatic but also effective (and perhaps necessary) is the use of manipulatives in math instruction. Young children are not always ready for the abstraction of workbooks. Blocks, rods, abacuses, and beads can provide a concrete experience of abstract concepts before children attempt workbooks filled with abstract symbols.

The use of imagery, movement, and multisensory experiences are but three of the many ways in which retention can be enhanced during instruction. Try sharing your ideas with your colleagues and see how quickly good teaching strategies can be found to benefit your students.

Rethinking Intellectual Aptitude

■ Research

Schneider, W., Korkel, J., & Weiner, F. E. (1989). "Domain-specific knowledge and memory performance: a comparison of high- and low-aptitude children." *Journal of Educational Psychology, 81,* 306–312.

Teachers worry about students who show low aptitude for learning. Because of their apparent slowness, lack of understanding, inadequate background knowledge, and so on, these students are a challenge to instruction. Teachers also fear for these children's future in a world that is so technologically sophisticated. However, some recent research about low-aptitude children may help us to rethink our beliefs about both their skills and their potential for learning.

Today, some researchers believe that most standardized aptitude tests severely *under*estimate the abilities of children who score the lowest. The researchers believe that these children do not always lack innate ability or skill in cognitive processing; they may only lack previous knowledge, and/or may be unfamiliar with the content of the tests. Thus, the researchers see low test scores as possible deficits in knowledge previously acquired—not necessarily in aptitude to learn. This is a provocative finding, and it is supported by recent data.

Approximately 100 third-graders, 235 fifth-graders, and 235 seventh-graders from middle-class rural and urban schools were the subjects in the first study. The children were assessed on their knowledge of soccer rules, and highlights in the field of soccer history. On the basis of their scores, they were divided into two groups: soccer experts and soccer novices. Their aptitude was also assessed using a standardized verbal intelligence test. Again the group was divided into high- and low-aptitude students. Now there were four groups of students: high-aptitude soccer experts, low-aptitude soccer experts, high-aptitude soccer novices, and low-aptitude soccer novices. All students were then exposed to a story about a young soccer hero's big match. The story contained some contradictions, and some of the information was vague and required the reader to make inferences. Researchers read the story aloud, and the students referred to a written version as well.

Three tests of memory and comprehension were administered. The students' memory for textual details, their ability to detect contradictions, and their ability to draw inferences all were assessed. One might expect that older children would perform better on all three tests than younger children. And they did. One might also expect that the soccer experts would perform better on all three tests than the novices. And they did. Most might also expect that the students with the highest verbal intelligence would perform better than the students with the lowest verbal intelligence. Yet *this* was *not* the case. Low-aptitude students who were soccer experts actually outperformed the high-aptitude students who did not have much previous knowledge of soccer. That is, students with low measured verbal intelligence—an accepted indicator of low aptitude—outperformed students of higher intellectual aptitude. And they did so at every grade level and on every test!

The researchers decided to conduct another study, using the same materials and 165 students with characteristics similar to those of the students used in the previous study. But this time the researchers relied on a number of different outcome measures: understanding of metacognitive strategies, recognition of sentences from the text, measures of free and structured recall, and so on. Even with these different outcomes measured, however, they found *no* overall differences between the most and the least intellectually able students. This time also, the highly knowledgeable, low-aptitude students outperformed the less knowledgeable, high-aptitude students. The unexpected had occurred again!

In both studies the low-aptitude students with expertise in the field of soccer were practically indistinguishable from the high-aptitude students on virtually every measure, and in every grade. So the low-aptitude, highly knowledgeable students not only outperformed the high-aptitude, less knowledgeable students, but they also generally performed as well as the high-aptitude, highly knowledgeable students.

They seemed, in this domain of knowledge, to possess all the cognitive skills of the high-aptitude students.

The researchers concluded that children's prior knowledge about an area is a much more powerful predictor of their comprehension and recall in that area than is their general intellectual ability. A rich store of background in an area may be most important for learning, and intellectual aptitude may not be nearly as important as we thought.

What does this mean for education? First, we need to find students' areas of expertise, such as local history, local geography, biology as learned from the care of animals, and so on. Then we have to make efforts to teach cognitive abilities, such as inference-making, organizing, and comprehension, through the subjects in which our children *already* have interest and expertise.

▬ Practice

When children enter school we ask them about letters and numbers, and make decisions, based on their responses, about their ability to learn. Although most of our questions are solely about schoolwork, too often we assume that the children's responses are indicative of their ability to learn, even when our observations tell us otherwise.

The research described above suggests that we ought to be more cautious in making our judgments. It also suggests that asking students about what they *already* know might lead us to different conclusions regarding their ability to learn. What does this mean for the daily work of the classroom? It means that the more we can connect classroom activities to our students' prior knowledge, the more successful the students are likely to be.

To do this, teachers must first try to determine what students know. What are their interests? What is life like for them outside of school? Students in rural areas may arrive at school with a great deal of knowledge about animals, crops, and natural cycles. City students may already be very competent shoppers, or they might have already mastered a complicated transportation system. Others arrive at school as competent speakers of two or more languages.

The best way to find out what students know is to *ask them*. Many teachers do this naturally, but too many limit questions to the narrow range of knowledge covered by school. Let *them* tell *you;* listen to their conversations with their classmates, and to their choices in stories or play; and also talk with their parents.

As you learn more about them, you might want to keep a few notes on the special interests of your students. You can use this knowledge in various ways. You might, for example, think of your students' knowledge as a base upon which to build new learning. Children may be quite familiar with money and shopping activities, so why not use money as the basis for teaching math? As long as they already know about dollars and cents, why not teach them decimals?

Mail-order catalogs and newspaper ads can be much more interesting than worksheets, and can help students to learn new math skills. Too, weather patterns can form the basis for science lessons. A study of street fairs and country fairs—their origins, participants, and activities—can provide the content for an enlightening social-studies lesson.

Once we know the kinds of expertise our students have, we can organize activities to allow those who are knowledgeable about a topic to help those who are not. A student who is knowledgeable about computers can teach beginners, while a student who is a very good artist might teach a less skilled classmate. In this manner children can learn to value a multiplicity of skills, instead of only the ones that are related to success in school learning.

A more thorough understanding of what our students know can also help us direct and broaden their interests. A child's interest in dinosaurs, for example, can easily extend to geology or biology. Another's delight in rap music can be channeled into a wider range of poetry. Those who enjoy sports might find athletic statistics an interesting avenue into mathematics.

Finally, a better understanding of our students' knowledge and interests can help us to avoid the dangers of improper labeling. School knowledge is but a narrow band of all the knowledge available. This does not make it less important; it only makes it incomplete as a measure of all knowledge. Yet this is all that is tested by our official measures of competence! We need to recognize the value of our students' knowledge, and to use what they *already* know as a bridge to more thorough and useful classroom learning.

Use What Students Already Know to Teach New Things

▬ Research

Adapted from Ross, S. M. (1985). Influences of adapting the context of mathematics instruction to student background. *Journal of Instructional Psychology,* 11, 17–27; and Au, K., H., & Jordan, C. (1981). Teaching reading to Hawaiian children: Finding a culturally appropriate solution. In H. T. Trueba, T. P. Guthrie, & K. H. Au (Eds.), *Culture in the bilingual classroom: Studies in classroom ethnography.* Rowley, MA: Newbury House.

In the early nineteenth century the German philosopher–psychologist J. F. Herbart presented the idea that new things can be learned *only* as they can be related to what is already in a person's mind. Herbartians in education were strong on systematically relating new knowledge to what students already knew, because that was how they thought (a) the mind worked, and (2) student interest could be gained.

We err, sometimes, in not thinking about the breadth of Herbart's ideas. We forget, sometimes, that students know vast amounts about great numbers of things unrelated to the particular math, science, or reading and language-arts programs that we teach. All that they already know can be used to help them to learn what we must teach!

Recently this lesson was taught to us again by S. N. Ross, who conducted experiments during which instruction was adapted very precisely to what students already knew. Ross taught preservice teachers and nursing students a unit of instruction on probability theory, in one or the other of two ways. In one version of the unit, all examples were placed in familiar contexts capitalizing on things the students already knew. Educational or medical examples were used extensively. This was called the adaptive version of instruction. A version of the unit was also prepared that used abstract language to describe events. No familiar classroom or medical contexts and examples were used. All the students were then tested with three kinds of items. One kind of test item capitalized on their previous knowledge and their special instruction by using teaching or nursing contexts extensively. A second kind had contextual information but was outside the student's area of knowledge. (That is, nursing students received items written with teaching contexts in mind, and preservice teachers received items that used medical contexts.) A third kind of item was the abstract type. All of these were straight probability items, in which no particular contexts were provided.

What happened was very interesting. In comparison to the more abstract instruction, when the student's previous knowledge was taken into account during instruction and test items were written to provide contexts that were very familiar, students scored significantly higher on their achievement tests. Moreover, students who had the instruction that was adapted to either their education or nursing knowledge scored very high on the abstract items as well. Furthermore, the students in the adaptive program scored higher on the items that were written with alternative contexts in mind. That is, preservice education students taught in a way that capitalized on their educational experience did very well answering the test items that reflected medical contexts. And nursing students taught with examples that reflected their medical knowledge did very well answering test items that used educational contexts. It appeared as if the special instruction capitalizing on what the students already knew helped them to learn and transfer that knowledge quite well. This was demonstrated by their high performance on test items that either were abstract or used unfamiliar contexts for framing the problem.

Ross also used some special items in his studies to test transfer to problems that required higher-order thinking and problem-solving skills. Those students who had instruction that capitalized on what they knew generally scored higher on these items of transfer than did students who had the more traditional/abstract instruction. Students apparently must incorporate new ideas into their existing knowledge base before they can manipulate and transfer those ideas to demonstrate higher-order skills and transfer. Herbart's ideas obviously have validity even today!

Instruction and testing in mathematics using contexts that are familiar to students results in about a one-half standard deviation advantage when compared with the performance of students taught with a more abstract style. Students taught and tested in an adaptive manner are, therefore, likely to score at about the 69th percentile on an achievement test in mathematics. Students taught in a more abstract, context-free manner, are estimated to score at around the 50th percentile. It seems to pay to take into account *all* of what our students know when we teach them.

113

One last point. This study was about mathematics instruction at the college level. The same conclusion, however, was reached when reading and language-arts were the subject matter, and first-graders were the students. Educators working with low-income Hawaiian students had little success in raising reading achievement scores until they adapted instruction to the culture of the children. They used the children's preexisting knowledge about how to behave with adults and other children to redesign their reading program. It was then that reading achievement soared. The lesson is clear: Our students always have lots of knowledge about their own culture and about different domains of knowledge—be it baby care, baseball, bugs, or blintzes. Our job as teachers is to use that knowledge to teach them *new* things.

■ Practice

The results of the research reported above remind us of how important it is to relate new learning to the learning we have already acquired. It is easier to see this relationship when considering competent adults who are acknowledged to have a rich store of knowledge and many skills. Most of us have probably complained about teachers who fail to take this into account in advanced studies and "treat us like children." But children also bring to the classroom a rich store of skills and knowledge. Indeed, by the time children enter kindergarten they have already come close to mastering at least one language. Furthermore, they have learned the rules for behavior in at least one culture. (These are, after all, among the most complicated tasks that all human beings really should master.) They have also learned some mathematics, science, and social studies. Our task then is to build on what they already know, in order to help them learn what they *don't* know.

Where to begin? First, of course, you need to know what you *want* them to learn. But immediately next, you need to know what they have *already* learned. You need to spend time getting to know your students, and to provide them with opportunities whereby they can display their *existing* knowledge. Kindergarten teachers, conscious of this, usually include "show and tell" in their daily routines. (Unfortunately, this activity, which can easily enough provide opportunities for the students to discuss their own interests and concerns, often is too ritualized for the teacher to learn much about what the students know.) You also need to provide opportunities for your students to talk freely—and you must listen very carefully to what they say.

Most children have had experience as family members, have gone to the store, have played children's games, have watched television, and may have had pets. Through these activities they have learned about people, animals, and "things." This tacit knowledge can provide a context for new learning. For example, from the time we are very young we learn about shortcuts. Instead of going around a square, we try to cut diagonally across (sometimes to the detriment of lawns). Children do it all the time, but what they don't realize is that they are applying a principle of geometry: "The shortest distance between two points is a straight line." You might teach them this principle as stated here, as a flat-out geometric abstraction— but you probably would do a better job by asking them to think about shortcuts they take, and why. And even find out with them which paths are more often used in the schoolyard. It will be much easier for them to remember any old schoolyard path than that particular abstract principle (after which the principle will come to them more quickly).

You must also remember, however, that children often *don't know* that they know. If you ask Mary, a second-grader who is always talking about errands to the store, if she knows about money, she may respond that she does not. But if Mary knows that one piece of candy is 5 cents and 2 pieces are 10 cents, then Mary knows *something* about money. She also knows something about decimals if she knows that 10 pennies make one dime, and 10 dimes make one dollar. It is therefore important not only to get information from the students, but also to interpret that information and translate it into school learning. What I mean by "translating" is this: relating those everyday experiences of children to classroom learning.

It is also useful for children to become aware that they are the bearers of knowledge. Awareness that they already know something about the lesson that is coming up (say fractions) can contribute to a more receptive attitude on their part. A high expectation of one's own achievement is more easily developed when teachers take the time to make students aware that the topic really is one they already know something about. In that way we also help children to have respect for their own knowledge, and to understand that learning is not only a school activity, but one in which they are *almost always* engaged.

Beyond the common knowledge that most children share, there is the more individualistic knowledge that is determined by their environment and cultural background. If your students live in a rural area, for example, they are more likely to respond to examples related to farm life.

If they are city children, urban examples are likely to help them retain new information. The use of examples that draw on the student's individualistic knowledge is particularly important when working with the culturally different child. Instructional materials often are designed for a generalized "American" child who typically lives in a suburban environment. The Native American child who lives on a reservation may find reading difficult not because of the symbols but because the language and the settings are so alien. Stories that take place in a more familiar environment may make a significant contribution to a student's learning and retention.

Remember, also, that students who acquire new learning through a context that is familiar to them also have been shown to transfer this learning to unfamiliar situations. This is what you want from the students—not just the ability to respond to questions in class, but also the wherewithal to apply what they learn there to new situations. It will be, for example, much easier for a child who grows up in the desert to understand and transfer the concept of evaporation if it is taught in the context of what happens in a desert wash during and after a rain, than when it is taught (as it usually is) in relation to a lake. The desert wash, and not the tundra, is also a better context to use when writing test items to assess these children's learning.

This discussion is not intended to suggest that children ought to learn only within a context that relates to their own lives. It *does,* however, mean to propose that we should both take account of children's current knowledge and use it as a bridge to new knowledge. It also means that concepts that are particularly difficult can be better understood by our students when presented within a *familiar* context.

Challenging Misconceptions in Science

■ Research

Adapted from Anderson, C., & Smith, E. (1987, November/December). Teaching science. In V. Richardson-Koehler (Ed.), *Educator's handbook: A research perspective.* NY: Longman; and Posner, G. J., Strike, K. A., Henson, P. W., & Gertzog, W. A. (1982). Accommodation of a scientific conception: toward a theory of conceptual change. *Science Education,* 66, 211–227.

As young children grow in their awareness of the world, they develop theories about how the world works. Basing their findings on sensory experiences and everyday language, kids create what researchers term *naive theories.* By the time children encounter science in school, many of these personally adequate (but frequently inaccurate) accounts of the world are both in place and rigidly held. Researchers are finding that these misconceptions are highly resistant to change. And they interfere with learning.

In one study, Charles Anderson and Edward Smith of Michigan State University looked at how teaching styles affect *conceptual change*—the process of discarding a previously held belief and accepting a new concept based on scientific fact. Anderson and Smith observed 215 fifth-graders of average ability and background as they were taught a well-designed unit on photosynthesis. Before instruction, a diagnostic quiz revealed that most students believed that plants got food from soil, water, fertilizer, or sunshine. After eight weeks of traditional textbook-based instruction, combinations of quizzes and follow-up showed that 90 percent of the students failed to give up their misconceptions! Most had not learned that plants get their food only by making it themselves.

Another lesson involved the relation of light and vision. The same fifth-graders were given a drawing showing a tree, the sun above it, and a boy to the side of the tree looking toward it. The students were asked to draw arrows to show how the boy saw the tree. The correct answer was to draw one arrow from the sun to the tree and another from the tree to the boy, to indicate that what we see is reflected light. But most of the students drew arrows only from the sun to the tree, or from the boy to the tree. Five weeks later, after textbook-based instruction, three-fourths of the students still could not complete the diagram correctly.

As a result of conversations with children, Anderson and Smith observed many similar misconceptions. Kids believed their shadows were made of "stuff," that sugar disappears when dissolved in water, and that Styrofoam has no weight. Kids also thought that light travels faster at night (something I once believed, too) and that electricity gets used up in a light bulb.

The researchers concluded that such theories resist change because they make sense to kids. You can buy plant "food," and we say, "The boy sees the tree," not "The boy sees the light reflected from the tree."

When children start school, we ask them to give up the theories that have served them well—to make a conceptual change. Yet Anderson and Smith found that teachers seldom took into account the existence of their students' naive theories. Instead, most seemed to assume that their students were simply accepting the new information as presented (and teachers often could point to good test scores to prove it). But research suggests that when children's own notions conflict with scientific explanations, they may compartmentalize. That is, they may go along with the idea that what teachers tell them is true, and may even do well on tests, but they may also continue to apply their own theories to things outside of school.

G. J. Posner and his colleagues looked at how to effect conceptual change in students. They identified conditions that need to exist. First, a student must be dissatisfied with his or her existing concept. Second, any new concept must be comprehensible to the child. Third, a new concept of explanation must appear as plausible as the child's own misconception. And, fourth, a new concept has to be more useful than the previously held theory—for solving problems or for making predictions.

This perception of science instruction is different from most current models. The underlying strategy for achieving conceptual learning acknowledged the role that students' naive theories play in learning new concepts. Knowing this, we can devise instructional techniques that start with the child's concept of the world, then replace his or her inaccurate assumptions with on-target scientific knowledge.

▬ Practice

You may have assumed that your science teaching has been effective because your students are passing tests. But, as noted in this research, test scores may not assess genuine student understanding. Many grasp enough to pass a test while remaining unable to apply a concept. How then do you determine the effectiveness of your science program—and increase it?

You might begin by identifying a recently taught concept, then construct a probing open-ended question around it. For example, young students who have been taught about the movements of planets and satellites may still believe that the moon increases and decreases in size throughout the month. Present children with an open-ended question, such as: *The moon is always changing in shape. First it gets bigger and bigger, then it gets smaller and smaller. How does it do this?* Use the responses of your students to diagnose their understanding.

To contribute to conceptual change in your students, you must first help them to become dissatisfied with their misconceptions. Students' erroneous beliefs must first be revealed, then challenged. When theories fail to hold up to challenges, students will be more likely to accept scientific explanations.

Devise your presentation so it taps students' prior understandings about some phenomena and challenges any misconceptions they have. In discussing the phases of the moon, you acknowledge that the moon does *appear* to change in size during the month, but it is *what we see* of the moon that changes, not the moon itself. By contrast, a presentation that begins by describing the movements of the earth and the moon—without challenging students' odd beliefs—may leave those students still tied to their naive theories.

Your questions are crucial to the change model. Try to ask students for explanations of scientific phenomena rather than recollections of facts. Encourage them to *clarify* explanations. Ask them to construct scientific explanations *in their own words* rather than parroting textbook language.

Follow with applications to situations familiar to students. You might remind them and even demonstrate to them, that objects often appear to change size as they move toward us or away from us, just as the moon appears to change in size throughout its cycles.

Expand upon the importance to the students *themselves* of grasping the gist of basic scientific concepts as you present them. For instance, children need to view photosynthesis as a process on which all life, *including theirs,* depends—and not just as a vocabulary word. Students should be made aware of why concepts are important things to understand and remember.

Conceptual change is a challenge, not only for students but also for teachers. Rising to that challenge may require you to extend your own scientific knowledge through additional course work, reading scientific publications, and working with colleagues to find more effective science teaching methods. Teachers need to do whatever within reason is necessary first to make visible, and then challenge, students' misconceptions.

How Children Think About Mathematics

▬ Research

Adapted from Carpenter, T. P., Fenneman, E., Peterson, P. L., Chiang, C. P., & Loef, M. (1989). Using knowledge of children's mathematics thinking in classroom teaching: An experimental study. *American Educational Research Journal*, 26, 499–531.

Some teachers have been found to possess the kind of extraordinary knowledge of their students that allows them to predict quite accurately which items on a test each of their students can do and which they cannot. In one of my own research studies we found a strong positive correlation between teachers' ability to predict their students' scores and the actual achievement of those students. The ones who knew more about their students' abilities were the ones whose students achieved more. But we did not know what to do to help teachers gain increased knowledge of their students.

Fortunately, researchers at the University of Wisconsin have developed a training program to help teachers learn a lot more about at least their students' mathematics knowledge—how they think mathematically and what they know about it, and what they can do with their knowledge of it. The students of teachers who have received this training, a workshop on Cognitively Guided Instruction (CGI), have achieved at a higher level than those of teachers who have not participated. Let us look at what these teachers have learned, and what has happened with their students' scores as a result.

Forty first-grade teachers in and around Madison, Wisconsin were recruited for this study. Half of the volunteer teachers served as the control group, receiving almost no instruction before the new school year began. The other half attended the CGI workshop for 20 days during one month of the summer. These latter teachers learned to classify mathematics problems, and how children think about them. For example, the problem "X had 3 marbles. Y gave X 5 more marbles. How many marbles does X have?" is considered a *join* problem. It is considerably different from a *compare* problem, such as "X has 5 marbles. Y has 3 marbles. How many more marbles has X than Y?" While learning to classify math problem types during the workshop, teachers also learned how children *think* about mathematics problems such as these. Findings from research about children's thinking were used to inform the teachers (e.g., if children can represent the numbers with a direct model, say a counter, they can solve a problem easier; or, problems like the second one, above, throw students off because of the word "more" in the problem).

Teachers were taught to take a problem-centered approach, not a fact or skills approach, to mathematics, and also to let their students think aloud when giving answers to problems in that subject. The teachers watched videotapes of students solving mathematics problems, and analyzed their responses. They explored new curriculum materials, talked about their instruction and its compatibility with how young children learn about the world, and planned for the next year. The experimental and control groups of teachers were not contacted much during the following year by the trainers, but were observed by the research team throughout the year.

The teachers who had attended the CGI workshop later spent 66 percent more time on word problems than the control teachers did. The control teachers, however, spent 55 percent more time than the workshop-trained teachers doing basic number fact problems. The workshop-trained teachers spent 61 percent more time posing problems to students, and 53 percent more time listening to the students' thinking processes as they answered those problems, than did the teachers in the control group. Thus, the training changed the way that some teachers taught mathematics.

On tests of knowledge about students' strategies for solving problems, the CGI teachers also scored higher. Moreover, the students of the CGI teachers also scored better than the students of the control teachers on end-of-the-year tests of achievement in every one of the outcome measures used—computation skill, complex addition and subtraction,

Iowa Test of Basic Skills subtests on computation and problem solving, and so forth. Not all these differences were statistically significant, but they all favored the students of the CGI-trained teachers, who professed greater confidence and greater understanding of mathematics than did the students of the teachers who had no CGI training.

While the results are consistent, the magnitude of the results was not great. On the other hand, the training was not continued during the year, and teachers did pretty much what they wanted to do in each of their own classrooms. So a small effect would be predicted, compared to what might have occurred if there had been a more tightly focused training program running throughout the year. It is really the two major themes of training that seemed to pay off, and these can be learned by teachers individually, or (preferably) through discussion with some colleagues. The first theme is that problem-solving should be the organizational framework for teaching first-grade mathematics, with skill learning of mathematics embedded in the problem-solving approach. The second theme is that instruction should build on the students' existing knowledge. Teachers need to regularly assess students' thinking and the processes that the students use to solve different kinds of problems. Regular assessments will help teachers to understand what their students really do know, so that those teachers can adapt instruction accordingly. Implementing these two themes in your classroom should pay off in terms of more positive student responsibility and greater achievement in mathematics.

■ Practice

Mathematics, perhaps more than any other subject, seems to present the most challenge to elementary-school teachers in the United States. In international comparisons our students tend to rank below those in most other industrialized countries in mathematical skills. Public alarm generated by the consistently low performance of our students has led to many recommendations for improvement. One response to this concern has been to increase the attention given to basic skills in mathematics in elementary classrooms. This has often translated into many more hours of practice in computational skills for our students. The research presented here suggests another route to improvement in mathematics—a route that is contrary to much of what we have learned.

Traditional training in the teaching of mathematics has been based on the assumption that children must learn mathematical facts in order to learn to solve problems. However, researchers who study children's thinking have found that it is really the other way around. They have learned that before children enter school, they learn to invent informal strategies for solving problems in addition and subtraction. Thus, formal instruction should begin with the knowledge that students have already acquired on their own, build upon it, and help students to *construct* mathematical knowledge rather than merely *absorb* it. That is, in the classroom, as well as in real life, the solution of the problem, rather than the rote learning of facts, should be the goal.

Better knowledge about students' existing knowledge, and emphasis on the relationship between skills and problem solving, are at the core of the strategies described. How can you, as an individual teacher, take advantage of these ideas?

First, you will want to test your own ability to predict student performance. Before you administer the next test, try to complete a test of your students, or at least for about a third of them. Then compare your predicted answers with their own. For each incorrect answer you failed to predict, ask the students to explain to you how they understood the problem, and how they went about solving it. Try to understand their logic so that you can predict when and where they are likely to make mistakes. Then you can emphasize those problem areas in your instruction.

Listening to your students explain their problem-solving strategies can also help you to gain an understanding of what they *do* know. Students may sometimes learn on their own, or in other settings, *nontraditional* ways to solve problems. Although their ways might be different from yours, they may be equally effective, and your insistence on one particular style might confuse and discourage them. Children who have attended schools in Mexico, for example, learn a different process for division. It is as accurate as the one taught in schools in the United States, but often they are forced to unlearn it and substitute the one taught here. In those cases, form is emphasized over function, often with disastrous consequences. Having students share their own ways for accurately solving problems is a good way to help them learn that mathematics is a collection of systems for solving problems, *not* a collection of standard forms. Too many teachers unsophisticated in mathematics themselves make this mistake.

Your students can also tell you how they use mathematics in their everyday lives, and how they solve math-related problems they encounter. By the time they enter first grade, many children, particularly in urban areas, have had occasion to handle money, perhaps by running errands for their parents. They may already know the coins, and how to calculate change, though their system may be quite different from the one you teach. Researchers in Brazil, for example, found that many poor children working as street vendors, selling gum and other items, could make complex computations of inflation and the relative value of Cruzeiros against dollars. However, they were failing elementary mathematics in school. Knowledge of children's experiences outside of school can help you to design activities that respect their knowledge and needs, and avoid the lack of relevance that so often haunts instruction in mathematics.

The next thing you might want to do is assess your current style of mathematics instruction. How much time are you spending in different activities? Are you depending too much on practice of skills while neglecting problem-solving activities? Are you providing meaningful manipulative activities for your students? This assessment is best done in conjunction with some of your colleagues. You may want to construct together a list of different aspects of instruction, then conduct a self-assessment followed by observations of each other in your classrooms. In this way you can determine the accuracy of your self-assessment.

You will want to decide what and when you want to change, set individual goals, and then help each other to reach them. You cannot do it all at once, but you can try to work toward those two basic principles— that is, gaining a better understanding of students' knowledge, and putting your emphasis on problem solving. In doing this you will also be exercising your full potential as a teacher. Teaching is sometimes reduced to the lowest common denominator, to the giving and correcting of assignments. But teaching is really about thinking, both student and teacher thinking. By continually assessing your students' knowledge, and planning appropriate instruction that builds on that knowledge, you will be thinking your way through instruction rather than replicating patterns that are often devoid of meaning for both you and your students. You are also likely to enjoy your work more. Drills can be as deadening for the teacher as for the students. On the other hand, there are few things that are more fun than listening to children's explanations.

Finally, you and your colleagues may want to start discussion groups that focus on relevant research about children's thinking. This line of research is developing quickly and can be of assistance to teachers in the interpretation of student explanations, and in analysis of student errors. This research is not limited to mathematics, and indeed much of it crosses content areas. For example, researchers studying reading comprehension and science instruction have learned the importance of understanding the knowledge that students possess in the acquisition of new knowledge (see pages 112–116). Principles such as those can be applied across the curriculum.

Attention to evolving research is as important to your teaching as it is to your family doctor, and collegial study groups can make the process much more interesting—as seemed to be true for the CGI group of teachers.

Are Your Students Getting the Most from Their Writing Revisions?

■ Research

Adapted from Fitzgerald, J., & Markham, L. R. (1987). Teaching children about revision in writing. *Cognition and Instruction*, 4, 3–24.

We have found in the last few years that some children need clearly targeted instruction in order to learn. For instance, some teachers assume that students will "pick up" comprehension skills as they learn to decode text. But many never quite get the knack of it, so need direct instruction in comprehension to better understand what they read (see pages 13–17).

Researchers Jill Fitzgerald and Lynda Markham thought it appropriate to apply the ideas of direct instruction to writing. They assumed that students could write better if they were taught explicit revision skills.

A group of average sixth-grade writers were divided into two groups. The *control* group read good literature. They were instructed in such a way as to represent a popular educational belief (sometimes correct) that students who read good literature will learn good writing. This "pickup" or "osmosis" theory of learning works well in the case of some students, but not all.

The experimental group received direct instruction in revision skills for 13 days during one month. Teaching consisted primarily of four 3-

day cycles of 45-minute lessons. Each cycle focused on a different aspect of revision: additions to text, deletions, substitutions and arrangements. The researchers did not want students to see revision as boring and punishing. Instead, they led students to see it as a problem-solving process in which one cunningly detects discrepancies between what actually is written and what is intended; where sophisticated decision making is called for to choose which changes should be made; and where decisive action is needed to fix the inadequacies identified.

Each lesson cycle followed the same general sequence. On the first day, the teacher gave an overview, using charts to model the revision. Students were led through a revision problem. On the second day, after a review, students worked *in pairs* to revise a portion of text. They also wrote a brief story. On the third day, students worked *individually* to revise a portion of text, and then to revise stories they had written on the previous day.

The researchers assessed the stories that each student in the control and experimental group had written at the beginning and at the end of the study. They found that students who received direct instruction were able to suggest more places in their stories (per 100 words written) that needed revision. That is, the trained group scored 79 percent higher for seeing more discrepancies between what they intended and what they actually had written.

When the researchers rated students on how specific their revision goals were, the trained group scored 28 percent higher. They also scored 58 percent higher for the specificity of actual changes they said they would make on their papers. Changes that the untrained group indicated should be made were more vague.

Did the trained students actually make more revisions on their papers? The researchers studied five kinds of revisions: changes in the story's surface structure, changes in meaning, deletions, additions, and substitutions. For each kind of revision, trained students outperformed untrained students. They made 42 percent more revisions overall.

Did revisions improve the quality of writing? Here results were promising, although not statistically significant. The trained group, which scored 13 percent *below* the control group on a measure of story quality when the study began, finished up at the end of the study scoring about 11 percent *above* the control group. The quality of the control group's stories was rated about the same at the beginning and end. On the other hand, students who received direct instruction in the revision process increased about 20 percent in ratings of story quality.

126

Some students, no doubt, learn to make revisions and improve the quality of their writing inductively. Reading good literature and receiving teacher feedback on their writing provides them with enough information to improve. But other students, perhaps far more, might better profit from direct instruction. When students receive carefully prepared instruction targeted toward clear goals, even in an area this complex, substantial learning apparently can take place in a relatively short period of time.

■ Practice

Teachers often place more responsibility for identifying revisions on themselves than on students, by requiring rewrites based on teacher corrections and suggestions. Perhaps the most important aspect of Fitzgerald and Markham's study is that responsibility is shifted from teacher to student, and students are taught the necessary skills to exercise that responsibility.

If you use this approach, your students will spend more time reworking writing samples than producing new ones. Solving writing problems and producing a high-quality final product will become more important than neatness and following directions. This practice is similar to demands that students will face in the "real" (business) world, where rewriting is an integral part of the writing process. In fact, those who write for a living often point out that writing includes rewriting, rewriting again, and rewriting *yet* again.

This study used focused and intensive instruction. The teacher first explained, then modeled, then guided the students through the revision process, focusing on only one type of revision each time. Students tried out their skills on a sample text, and then on their own brief stories. To use this approach, you also must begin with a certain high level instructional intensity, after which students can incorporate revision processes into *all* their writing. Be sure to conduct reviews to maintain skills, and assess revision when evaluating written assignments.

Other teaching strategies can help too. Try assigning writing of a particular type, for a specific purpose. Purpose determines style and tone, and goals are of primary importance. Assess writing based not only on what the author intends, but also on how successfully the message is conveyed to the reader.

Writing assignments should address students' *real* needs, so that writings can be seen as a *useful* tool. Sixth-graders usually have complaints to write about—a TV toy that didn't live up to expectations, the lack of a neighborhood baseball field, and so on. They may want to persuade the principal to permit a school-wide rock concert, or convince parents that they need bigger allowances.

This kind of writing assignment requires students to pay very close attention to their audience: Peer tutoring forces kids to *take turns* being the audience and critiquing their classmates' writing. All of this helps the writer to understand whether the message is appropriate and effective, or whether it needs to be revised. In evaluating the final product, base your findings on how successfully students have achieved their intended purposes.

Computers make editing easier, eliminating much of the drudgery associated with rewriting, and encouraging some students to be more daring and creative. Using the computer's thesaurus can expand vocabulary, and the spelling checker helps the students to avoid errors and focus more on the communicative purpose of writing. Remember that although some students have *home* computers, others must rely solely on *school* computers for this kind of work. Thus the school's computers may need to be scheduled in such a way that your class gets sufficient time to carry out all their assignments. You may even need to wait a few months to teach writing, having first to teach keyboarding and wordprocessing.

Writing instruction can be made both to relate better to students' present concerns, and to provide a closer match to future requirements in the workplace. By switching the focus of teaching it, writing can change from a tiresome, mechanical activity to a thinking, problem-solving process. Moreover, with this kind of writing instruction, students learn to take personal responsibility for communicating accurately with their readers.

Schooling and the Reduction of Linguistic Competence in Children

■ Research

Adapted from Wells, G. (1986). *The meaning makers*. Portsmouth, NH: Heinemann.

What kind of article title is this, anyway? How could schooling *reduce* a child's linguistic competence? Where would that be allowed? Schools are for expanding the skills that kids have—they certainly don't constrict them. And children can't *lose* competence in schools: That's where we ensure that they *gain* it!

Well, no. Or at least not always. Although we might tend to disagree with the findings, data from both American and British studies suggest that we may in fact be *inadvertently restricting* children's chances for displaying their linguistic competence in schools! Gordon Wells, of England, headed a fascinating longitudinal study describing how over 100 pre-school children acquired language in their home settings. He then went on to study how 32 of these children acquired linguistic skills and used language when they entered elementary grades. We will, however, consider only a small piece of the enormous amount of data collected concerning them, from the time they first started talking, to the end of their elementary-school years.

Let us simply look at some ordinary 5-minute samples of language taken both at home and school. What do you think we might notice when we compared the language used in the two settings? At home, according to the language samples obtained, the average number of utterances by a child to an adult was 122. At school such opportunities are, of course, much more rare. Indeed, in this sample that number was only 45—a reduction in children's speech to adults of 63 percent!

The reduction in the number of "turns" taken in a conversation by the children as they moved from home to school was about 40 percent. This means that chances for *genuine* communication were pretty much lost in classrooms; short interchanges took place much more frequently than meaningful and extensive conversations. And therein lies Wells's major point: Children must create meaning out of the language community *in which they find themselves.* In comparison to that of the homes, the language community found in Wells's sampled classrooms seemed to be impoverished!

Evidence of this was seen in other comparisons of home and school, too. For example, the number of *different types of meaning* expressed by children in their conversations dropped by about 50 percent in school. Worse, the number of times that *a conversation was initiated* by a child dropped from home to school by 64 percent. And even worse yet, the number of *questions raised* by children dropped from home to school by 70 percent. That is, genuine requests by children for help, information, clarification, and so forth, dropped dramatically *when they entered their schools.*

Apparently, conversations are not started and questions are not asked in school in the same ways that they are at home. References to events other than those in the immediate environment—conversations relying on memory and imagination—also go down by 30 percent. Furthermore, in classrooms, teachers do not as frequently extend the meaning of a child's utterances as do the adults in the child's home. That is, teachers too seldom find the opportunity to engage a young student in conversations that will elaborate and enhance the communications they both are attempting. And, as if all this hadn't proved bad enough, the number of fragments of speech and of incomplete utterances by the children have been found to *increase* in school by almost 70 percent!

All of this shows the impoverished nature of the environment for language use in school as compared to the environment created at home. And what is remarkable, also, is that in this study (and others), the home-school differences in the ways that children used language seemed to be much greater than any social-class differences in such use. Which is to say that the least enriched home environments (by our traditional academic standards and middle-class values) still appeared to be richer *linguistic* environments for children to practice and learn language in than those in the typical classroom. According to Wells, then, schools *do* seem to reduce children's chances for the development of linguistic competence. And for the least affluent, this may be all the more sadly significant.

Underlying our personal reasons for valuing rich linguistic environments for children is Wells's quite reasonable belief that *talking* to learn (which, after all, came first) is just as important as *reading* to learn. Both are exercises in "meaning making." But making meaning through conversations with a child is of necessity a *joint* effort—of teacher *and* students. Meaning is not inherently in any teacher's utterances, or on the pages of any book. Ultimately, meaning is created in the mind by way of negotiation—literally, back-and-forth. An urgent task for educators, therefore, is the creation of school environments that enhance, rather than restrict, the making of meaning through oral-language development.

■ Practice

A traditional teaching approach uses a "transmission" model of instruction: The teacher knows something that the student doesn't and "transmits" it to him or her. Wells argues for a different mode, one he calls "a guided reinvention of knowledge."

Wells reminds us of the barriers to effective communication that we sometimes find in the classroom. Differences in maturity between teacher and student, and/or cultural differences, may result in misunderstandings in meaning during both conversation and instruction. Adults of the same culture converse easily because the experiences of speaker and listener overlap. There are common referents for the ideas they communicate. Participants also *negotiate the meaning* of the conversation by asking questions and elaborating points. But classrooms offer few such opportunities. Students *don't* acquire knowledge simply by being *told* something. They understand what they are taught according to their own limited experience, and they develop their own explanations. And, unless specifically challenged by a teacher, these explanations usually remain unchanged. But if students are allowed to express in their own words their understanding of what they hear, they can still construct their own meanings and the teacher can then discover and (if necessary) help them to adjust their perspectives.

1. *Teachers (and other adults) should treat with careful attention what the child communicates.* They should listen to what students say as well as do. This means providing time for students to discuss material among themselves, to give their own opinions, to ask questions, and to challenge the teachers.

2. *Try to understand what the child means.* Ask questions, ask for elaboration, and ask for examples. If there are language differences, concentrate on the meaning rather than the form of what the stu-

dent is saying. Assume that what the child is saying has meaning (if not to you, then certainly to him or her) and try to find that meaning in some form—spoken, whenever possible.

3. *Use the child's meaning to decide what to say next.* Too often, teachers dismiss one child's response and call on another who is likely to provide the "correct" answer. Doing this probably doesn't change the first child's perception, nor does it usually allow the teacher to understand that child's interpretation. The teacher must come to understand the child's view of things before trying to introduce new concepts.

4. *In selecting the words and form of instruction, recognize children's ability to understand, or to derive their own interpretations of, what is taught.* We have all attended lectures by very knowledgeable individuals we didn't understand. We've usually blamed the speaker. We need to evaluate *our own* communication when students misinterpret or otherwise failed to understand our instruction!

No "solution" is easy to pull off in a classroom. We all know that. Yet we can, in this case, at least try to increase the use of open-ended questions and small discussion groups. Encourage students to analyze what they read and hear. But, above all, urge the school children to value the exchange of ideas, and to respect individual contributions. *Your* example, as listener and conversationalist both, probably is even now the most important influence on how they will respond.

Effective communication is the heart of instruction. We cannot accomplish either if we insist on using a one-way process. Students need conversations that make them equal partners in education. After all, our goal is to develop self-sufficient, thinking learners—not robots.

What Are Students Doing When They Do All That Seatwork?

■ Research

Adapted from Anderson, L. M. (1985). What are students doing when they do all that seatwork? In C. W. Fisher & D. C. Berliner (Eds.), *Perspectives on an instructional time.* White Plains, NY: Longman; and Anderson, L. M., Brubaker, N. L., Alleman-Brooks, J., & Duffy, G. G. (1985). A qualitative study of seatwork in first grade classrooms. *Elementary School Journal,* 86, 123–140.

The title of this article was chosen by Linda Anderson for a chapter in a book on the use of time in the classroom. Anderson has provided an interesting set of answers to the question she posed.

Anderson studied the reading instruction of some high-achieving and low-achieving students in first-grade, self-contained classrooms. She observed carefully and interviewed both the teachers and the students. Her observations informed her that seatwork usually took up 30 to 60 percent of the time allocated for reading. The seatwork materials— mostly commercially produced workbook materials or dittos—often focused on discrete skills, or called for repeated use of the same answering strategy.

When Anderson inquired about the students' views of the purpose of seatwork, she found them different from those of the teachers. Students said that such materials were their "work," and "That's how we learn to read." Very few had any understanding of the *reasons* for the tasks, the *goals* of instruction, or the *ways* in which any of the skills they were learning fit together. To them it all was simply work. Perhaps for these young students any other conception might be too sophisticated. Still, we must wonder about a system that teaches children to equate school work and reading with workbook pages and copying tasks.

It was also interesting that the low-ability students, in particular, viewed their task as work *to be completed,* not work from which *to learn.* It appeared that the act of finishing the work, progressing through the book, covering the content, and handing things in were the most important goals for the students. This was particularly true when play or free time was made contingent upon the completion of seatwork.

Some excerpts from the observations of Anderson and her colleagues illustrate this. One student, Randy, was heard to exclaim with delight, "It's done!" when he finished a worksheet. Later, he told an observer that he did not like longer assignments, such as writing a story, because "It takes so long, and then I can't play." Another student, Beth, kept comparing her work with her neighbor's as they engaged in a competition to finish the copying assignment that had been given. Whenever Beth reached the end of a sentence, she raised her hands in a silent cheer. Perhaps the clearest (and saddest) example of this phenomena was given by a student named Richard, who finished the work sheet and was heard to say to himself, "I don't know what it means, but I did it!"

It is not really Randy's fault that he came to like short, artificially chopped-up assignments: They were what he dealt with most. Indeed, when these researchers examined the kinds of tasks given to students, and estimated the complexity of the thinking required to determine the right answers, they found that 51 percent of the assignments required marking of only one out of a limited number of options. A good many tasks required copying, for which neatness and accuracy were the main criteria. Other tasks called for forming single associations between letters, sounds, words, or pictures. Yet other work required comprehension of single sentences. In fact, most of the seatwork assignments required either single associations (35 percent) or the comprehension of single sentences (40 percent). Although the students were supposed to be learning to read, only 9 percent of all assignments required having to understand two or more related sentences in order to answer a question. Despite what the teachers thought, what the students were doing does not look (to the rest of us) like reading.

In settings with worksheets like these, some students who cannot read words very well just mark randomly, often using the length of the blank offered to them as a guide for picking an answer that might be correct. In this study, various students reported a strategy of using the last remaining answer in a set as a response to the last remaining question. Still others took the picture closest to a certain word on the worksheet as a clue to reading that word, no matter how nonsensical it might sound. Lucky guessing alone could produce a correct choice now and then for the low-achieving students, thus leading them to invest minimal mental effort. Even for the higher achieving students the time required to answer some items was minimal, so they too rarely thought seriously about what they were doing. They did it pretty much to be done with it. Students' strategies to respond quickly just to get the work over with succeeded often enough to mislead their teachers into not understanding how seriously deficient their charges might be in certain reading skills.

Some students in this study were seen developing social-interaction strategies so they could copy another's work. Several found ways to overhear answers that the teacher gave to other students. A few simply learned to ask quietly what somebody else was writing. Since teachers often check student seatwork very quickly, they often gave students credit for completing assignments that were never really done by those kids. And even though most of the low-achieving students had considerable problems with their seatwork assignments, their short-term strategies to get the work done often fooled the teacher into thinking they were learning a lot more than they actually were.

So, in reply to the question "What are students doing when they do all that seatwork?" we now have a qualified answer: A significant number are not doing much at all! And what many *are* doing is being done without much thought except to finish it as quickly as possible.

Admittedly this description sounds bleak. But we should remember that the first step to solving a problem is to recognize that it exists.

▦ Practice

Anderson's study helps to explain why a child who consistently completes assigned seatwork correctly continues to make the same mistakes when reading. Often there is a big difference between what we *think* children gain from their work and what children *in fact* accomplish: Students' strategies to complete work succeed often enough for the teacher not to understand how seriously deficient they might be.

Does this mean that teachers must give up seatwork? No. Not until class size is reduced to five or fewer students per teacher! Seatwork is not only a learning tool for students, but a management tool for teachers. Teachers absolutely cannot interact individually with every student all through the school day. They must devise ways to teach them through means other than direct instruction.

Anderson calls attention to the need for careful *selection, presentation, monitoring,* and *evaluation* of seatwork. Let's consider these one at a time.

First, how can we best *select* appropriate seatwork? One factor in any choice is the accessibility of materials that supplement the basal text.

Most of these materials focus on a specific skill, such as beginning sounds. The specific skill is therefore taken out of context and not necessarily related to the child's ability to make sense of what is read. When children work on one after another of these worksheets, day after day, reading becomes disassociated from comprehension. It is no wonder that children perceive the purpose of the assignment to be the completion of the worksheet.

In selecting seatwork, consider how closely it captures your larger purpose. It is also important to match the difficulty of the task to student ability. A task that appears simple on the surface may in fact be difficult for some students to complete while working alone. You might also think about having children help other children, in some cooperative way, rather than assuming that each child should work on his or her assignment alone.

Presentation is another important factor in making seatwork effective. When you introduce seatwork, emphasize the purpose of the assignment: "This seatwork is to help you practice the words we learned yesterday. Say each word to yourself as you read it, then see if you can use it in a sentence." Too often teachers emphasize procedure ("Write your name at the top of the page," "Copy neatly," "Select the correct word from the list") over purpose.

How you *monitor* will also influence seatwork effectiveness. Low achievers in particular tend to have trouble with independent seatwork. Their restless behavior may cover up difficulties in completing assignments satisfactorily. To more effectively monitor, take a few minutes at the beginning of the assignment to note the student's response to the work. As you circulate (and we do recommend circulating!), check not only for correct completion of work, but also for how students arrived at the answer. Their responses may help you to identify problem areas. It also helps if, early on, you have established several routines that direct children to alternate activities when they get stuck. This practice avoids dead time and reduces interruptions.

Finally, proper *evaluation* increases seatwork's effectiveness. It is not enough to check for correct answers. Evaluation must include time for individual conferences with students to determine their depth of understanding of the task. (see pages 5–8).

Students are likely to adopt the values we communicate to them. If our message is that seatwork is just something to complete with the right answers, then we should not be surprised if it is ineffective. If we want students to seek understanding, then we must encourage them through proper selection, presentation, monitoring, and evaluation to demonstrate that understanding daily.

Helping Kids Learn How to Learn

▪ Research

Adapted from Pramling, I. (1988). Developing young children's thinking about their own learning. *British Journal of Psychology*, 58, 266–278.

A number of studies have shown that teaching people to be more aware of their thoughts during instruction has beneficial effects on learning and retention (pages 18–22). Ingrid Pramling, of Sweden, has studied how this might be done with young students (five- to seven-year-olds) who do not ordinarily think about their thinking. A young child's conception of learning is, typically, that learning is done by *doing* something. That is, one learns to sort colors, to wash hands, to cook food, and so forth. Rarely does a young child grasp that learning involves *understanding* something. That is, one might learn what cities looked like in olden days by looking at pictures of some of them in a book, and finding out what the accompanying text says. Or that, by playing shop, one could learn how shopkeepers make money.

Pramling apparently found a way for children to learn this important difference long before they might otherwise. Three classes of young students with similar characteristics were taught a unit on shopkeeping, including a field trip to observe how stores were run. Ms. A and Ms. B organized the unit first around the customer's, then around the shopkeepers' perspective. Ms. C did not provide any structure for her students.

Ms. A and Ms. B taught about the differences in the ways the customers and the shopkeepers used money. Although the goals and the structures they used were the same, they differed remarkably in the way they taught the unit. Ms. A developed metacognitive dialogues with the children, to help them to think about their learning. She asked them consistently to tell her what they learned in one shop that they didn't learn in another; what new things they learned that morning; how they recognized that they had learned something new; what different sources of information they had used to learn about shops. At the end of the unit these students were divided into groups and asked to prepare materials to teach someone else all that they knew about shops (see pages 58–60).

Ms. B's questions had right or wrong answers. For example, "What is the name of the person you pay as you leave the store?" (Answer: the cashier). Children learned to sing rhyming songs about what can be bought for a certain sum of money. In a pleasant atmosphere she taught the facts of the unit: the sequence of events, the names of things, the way to get service, and the way the shopkeeper uses the money that customers pay. Ms. C used a project-oriented approach, as do many teachers of the young. She taught her content through plays, construction of posters, the making of clay figures, and other activities.

At the end of the unit, the children were asked what they would like to learn in school. Forty-two percent in Ms. A's class talked about learning to understand things, while only 5 and 18 percent respectively of the children in the other two classes talked about learning in this way. When asked how they might teach other children what they knew about shops, 58 percent of the children in Ms. A's class conceived of teaching as having students personally experience things, while only 5 and 12 percent respectively of the students in the other classes thought of teaching in that way. The students in the other classes described teaching as *telling*.

When questioned about the activities in which they had participated while learning about shops, most of the children in Ms. B's and Ms. C's class believed that the activities were the goal of the instruction ("We played shop because it is fun to play shop!"). But three-quarters of the children in Ms. A's class saw the activities as a means to an end—namely, some form of understanding ("We went to the shop to learn how they organize merchandise." "We found out how they advertise to get us to spend money.").

Six months later, dramatic differences among the students in the three classes were still noticeable. When asked what they had learned about writing in their school books that year, between 56 and 88 percent of the students of Ms. B and C talked of learning to *do* ("To keep my pencil within the line." "To draw nicely."). Only 6 percent of Ms. A's students talked this way. Instead, 94 percent of her students talked about their books as ways to know and understand things, as vehicles to comprehend the world around them ("By drawing the bee in my book I learned about the pollen sacks on the bee's legs."). Perhaps most remarkable was that about 30 percent of the children in Ms. A's class showed evidence of reflecting about the learning they were doing ("I realized that people take away the bee's food when I thought about what the teacher told us.") *Not one* of the other young children in the other two classes showed evidence of reflective thought during the interviews.

All year long, Ms. A focused her instruction on the children's thoughts, their ways of gathering and using information, and the alternative sources available. She created an intellectually stimulating learning-oriented environment (see pages 147–150). By asking questions that stimulated thinking *about* thinking within the contexts in which the children were working, Ms. A apparently helped children to develop a sophisticated awareness of the nature of school learning. Ms. A's students learned that learning wasn't just responding to questions or naming things, but rather that knowledge was to be connected to other knowledge and to be reflected upon. This teacher created the environment that fosters development of the kind of young learners that we say we admire. Perhaps her teaching strategies can help all of us to develop more students of this kind!

■ Practice

The comparison of the three teachers described above illustrates different concepts of teaching and learning. For Ms. C., teaching was only a matter of providing the students with the opportunity to learn through activities appropriate for young children. Ms. B was more structured in her approach, but limited her questions to factual details. For this teacher, learning consisted of recalling the right answers to the teacher's questions. Neither Ms. B nor Ms. C conceptualized their teaching as helping students to learn how to learn. Only Ms. A's instruction focused on the need for children to think about their thinking in order to learn from their own learning.

What kind of teacher are you? You may want to evaluate your instruction plans, your classroom activities, and questioning techniques to find out how your instruction compares to that of these teachers. Memories of the school experience for most of us tend to be dominated by the style of teaching represented by Ms. B. We remember the tests, and the spelling lists, and the fear of being called on for "the answer" when we were not prepared. All of these examples illustrate learning as recalling the right answer.

There certainly is a place for memory in the schools. The days of the week and the months of the year have to be learned by rote. At upper levels, facts such as the periodic table of the elements, or the geological eras, also require recall. Research informs us, however, that students at all age levels learn best when they *think about* what they're learning, when they *monitor* what and how they are learning. This is called *metacognition,* and it distinguishes efficient from non-efficient learners. You might want to analyze your own instructional activities to find out how you might increase your students' opportunities for developing metacognitive skills—skills that will help them to keep track of their own learning. Remember, the idea is not to teach a set of these skills in the abstract, but rather to teach students to apply metacognitive thinking to the content they must learn every day.

The author of this study noted how Ms. A continuously focused on the children's ideas of learning. As an example, she related what happened one day after the children noticed an unusual flower growing in a garden. Ms. A asked if anyone knew its name and, since no one knew, asked them how they might find out. The children suggested a variety of sources: asking the owner of the garden, or their own mothers; finding the answer in a book; naming it themselves; calling a radio program. The teacher discussed the name as homework. Eight children brought in the flower's name the next day. Then they had to explain to their classmates how they went about finding the answer.

Notice that Ms. A could have given them the answer, or she might have just suggested they could look it up in a reference book. Instead she relied on the students to think of alternative solutions to the problem. Finally, the task did not end with the flower's name (that is, with the right answer) but rather with an explanation of the *process* used to find out the information. These young learners are in a very rich intellectual environment!

Ms. A's strategy is, of course, similar to the way in which adults approach a problem and arrive at a solution. For example, suppose you were trying to locate a florist to order flowers for a wedding. What would you do first? Obviously there is no one right answer, so you would begin by looking for alternatives. You might look in a phone book, or ask your friends or relatives for references, or perhaps ask for ideas at your church or temple. Then you would need to make a decision—perhaps by visiting a flower shop, or by ordering a bouquet to use as a sample of their work, or maybe just on the basis of talking on the telephone with a florist. At each step you would be weighing alternatives, perhaps comparing price to quality, or the possibility for courteous service against possible rudeness. Eventually you would arrive at a decision that pretty well satisfies your demands. Throughout your planning, organizing, and decision-making you may have been thinking about the processes you used—and, if so, you were in a very practical way using your metacognitive skills.

Children who are given the opportunities provided by Ms. A learn both that problems can be solved and that alternatives usually are available, but always need to be weighed before decisions are made. They learn that single right answers are few and far between, and that, more often than not, the best answer may depend on the best analysis of the specific situation. As part of Ms. A's prodding, they learn to think about their thinking, and about how to pace, monitor, and evaluate their learning activities. This all brings them quite close to the realities that they will confront as adults.

Happily, this kind of teaching does not require either special materials or additional funds. It is only a matter of establishing habits of inquiry and problem solving that will challenge our students and stimulate learning. And that, after all, is what schools really are about.

SECTION 4

MOTIVATION

Introduction

Why is it that some children like to go to school, while others do not? "Motivation," we answer—and with that word we tend to place on the students the full responsibility for their learning. But teaching and learning are *reciprocal* activities: What we do as teachers affects the learners, and the learner's behavior, in turn, affects what teachers do.

Motivation is a complex concept that is not well understood. It seems to be very individualistically defined (that is, what motivates one person may fail to motivate another). We often talk about our specific sources of motivation, and their counterparts—the things that discourage us. For some of us an approaching deadline may be an effective motivator, yet for others it may provoke paralysis. Through the years we learn what works for us, and often for those close to us as well. It is more difficult to learn what motivates each of our students. Because of this we often resort to using techniques such as grades, and we assume that in spite of what we know about ourselves, all our pupils will respond similarly to our chosen motivational strategy. Students who do not respond, or who respond negatively, are then assumed to be "unmotivated."

Motivation is not a one-way street. Whether or not we are motivated to accomplish a task depends on several conditions:

1. Do we think the task is worth accomplishing?

2. Do we feel capable of succeeding?

3. Is there some gain associated with its accomplishment?

Although these questions must be answered by the student, teachers can, through their actions, modify each of these aspects and thereby enhance student motivation.

We need to assign students tasks that they can value. It is difficult to value three pages of the same type of math problems if we already know how to solve these problems or, conversely, if we did not know how to solve the problems. We also need to ensure that students feel competent as a function of both our expectations and our careful choice of assignments for them. And that there is something to be gained by completing the tasks. This does not necessarily mean an extrinsic reward, but rather the reward that comes from learning itself. We need to connect what we do today with what we did yesterday and what we are to do tomorrow, so that students can *see* themselves becoming more competent. Thus, through our own instruction we affect the motivation of our students.

The eight articles in this section deal, either directly or indirectly, with motivation. Two of them address the importance of a class environment that communicates positive feelings about school. In learning-oriented rooms, says one researcher, the teacher makes sure that the students not only feel competent, but also that they take responsibility for their own learning. This approach contrasts with one wherein comparative grades predominate. In these studies the researcher recommends against comparative grades and instead suggests that teachers use task-involving comments that both sustain student performance and appeal to the student's *need* to perform well.

The next article discusses a potent way to sustain the interest of students—the project method. Projects have a great ability to motivate students and avoid the pitfalls of other ways to keep their attention, a subject of the following article. In that article some ways that appear to motivate are found to interfere with learning. We have also included an article that notes the persistence of policies to retain students in grades, in spite of persuasive research evidence showing that negative effects consistently outweigh positive outcomes. We know that most retained students continue to lag behind their peers, but also that even when they catch up they become increasingly alienated from school—unmotivated, if you will. Decreased motivation and increased alienation leads, then, to school dropout much more frequently than dropout occurs among their non-retained peers.

In another article we learn that our tendency to emphasize students' inborn ability as the reason for their success is not shared by some cultures that we admire for their educational achievement. In China and Japan, for example, effort (motivated behavior) *not* ability, is credited as a major contributor to success. We must remember that students' perceptions of their own ability to achieve will be affected by our expectations. If we prejudge a student's ability on the basis of our perception of his or her genetic or social characteristics, the student will never be able to get beyond that. If, however, we communicate a message that says motivation, or effort is what is important, then the possibilities are limitless.

Finally, we present two articles that discuss how students' enthusiasm is hard to maintain, and how their negative behavior can be controlled. In the latter study we learn how to turn unmotivated, unruly students into more controllable and apparently motivated students.

Though it is hard to keep enthusiasm high, and behavior in line, teachers must work on those issues as well as the cognitive ones, for they are all interwoven and are not separable.

Is Your Classroom Learning-Oriented?

▬ Research

Adapted from Marshall, H. H. (1987). Motivational strategies of three fifth-grade teachers. *The Elementary School Journal*, 88(2), 135–150.

How can you describe subtle differences among classrooms? A recent study by Hermine Marshall explored how differences in learning and motivational strategies influence the classroom environment.

In an earlier study, Marshall and her coworkers sensed that differences among classrooms might result from the teaching methods that teachers choose to use. They studied how teachers framed and maintained lessons, and motivated students by teaching them responsibility for learning. In this study they tested their impressions by observing 3 fifth-grade teachers for 11 weeks. Each teacher represented a particular type of classroom that Marshall had identified in the previous research.

Marshall termed one type of teaching milieu "work-avoidance." In this class students tried to do as little as possible, and the teacher accepted all this—just as she accepted incomplete work, disruptions, and so forth. Another type she described as "work-oriented." Here, the teacher emphasized external rewards and motivated with threats. But a third Marshall called "learning-oriented." Here, the teacher stressed personal reward, the challenge of work, and the fun of learning. This teacher seemed to motivate students in ways that are quite laudable.

Interactions differed among the three classrooms. In the learning-oriented class, the teacher started two-thirds of the lessons with motivating statements; in the other classes, only about one-third of the openings contained such statements. More importantly, more than half of the learning-oriented teacher's statements stressed the challenge, fun, and purpose of the lesson, the personal relevance of the material, and so on.

The other two teachers used these techniques only about 10 percent of the time. Instead, they motivated their students by referring to tests and other forms of student accountability, and made threats and personal demands for performance. They used such negative techniques two-and-a-half times more frequently than the learning-oriented teacher did.

Management differed, too. During instruction, about half of the learning-oriented teacher's statements attempted to maintain student interest in the task. In the other classes, teachers spent more than 98 percent of their time trying to redirect student attention; they used twice as many refocusing statements. Moreover, the learning-oriented teacher's requests to pay attention were mostly presented positively, but the same request in the work-oriented and work-avoidance classrooms was usually couched in a negative way.

How else did the teachers differ? Interviews revealed that the learning-oriented teacher thought *all* students had ability and just needed to discover that learning was fun. In other words, the problem was motivational, not intellectual. She encouraged students to take responsibility for learning. In her class, students asked for more work, and on standardized achievement tests they exhibited a full year's growth.

By contrast, the work-oriented teacher felt *she* was responsible for learning. She saw student ability as fixed, and pushed students to do their work. Since on standardized tests her class showed about a year and a half of growth, on one important level this teacher *was* a success. But on another—the classroom environment—she wasn't.

In the work-avoidance class, neither the teacher nor the students took responsibility for learning, and the class made *no* gains at all on the standardized achievement tests.

Marshall gives us much to think about: A full measure of student achievement *in a healthy, happy environment* ought to be the goal for which we all strive. Clearly more achievement, at least as measured by standardized tests, is possible. But we believe that the costs of that sort of victory are not worth the effort.

■ Practice

One of the most puzzling problems for beginning teachers is how to relate to students. Should they be tough, hard-nosed taskmasters? Should they be friendly and easy? Something in between?

Marshall's interviews suggest that our individual views of students probably guide our relationship in the classroom—and that *this relationship influences student behavior.* We establish patterns, complete with certain standard "lines," early in teaching. (In fact, we often can remember our own teachers by quoting their favorite lines—but we don't give much thought to what was, or is, really represented by such statements.) Marshall's study reminds us that these pattern choices, though unconscious, are not completely arbitrary.

In this study, the teacher in the *work-avoidance* classroom said that students lack motivation—for which she blamed parents. Because she didn't expect much, she didn't try to motivate; instead, most of her time went to refocusing student attention. She also seemed to accept students' lack of responsibility as something she could do little about. We have seen teachers like this all over the country. They seem to abdicate their responsibility as teachers.

The *work-oriented* teacher believed that students wanted rewards and recognition. She stressed drill and practice, blaming parents when student performance didn't meet expectations. Her classroom routines, and statements about her class, conveyed this emphasis on work and performance. But instead of motivating through student interest, she often directed students to their work through such negative statements as "It's not play time."

In contrast, the *learning-oriented* teacher saw students as competent and responsible. She stressed that it was *her* responsibility to *motivate* students, and *their* responsibility to *learn.* She wanted her students to discover the joy of learning for themselves. As you might expect, this teacher routinely emphasized the enjoyment and challenge of learning; motivating was central to the lesson. Her students not only felt they *could* learn, they also felt responsible for *their own* learning.

Which of these teachers do you resemble? Do you want to remain as you are? Do you want to change?

Because no one benefited in the work-avoidance class, let's concentrate on the work-oriented classroom, where students made the largest gains on standardized tests. If you have such a classroom already, or want to display such gains, use caution: Standardized tests are only *one* achievement measure. What was the price of these gains? Are threats and rewards the best way to develop student skills? Will they result in long-term interest in learning? How do you think this teacher feels at the

149

end of the day? Is this classroom's climate one you want for your students? For yourself?

And *don't forget yourself*—because *you must share the classroom* environment. Wouldn't it be more pleasant to develop a climate of high expectations, and to attempt to prepare students for a lifetime appreciation of learning, than to have them only do well on spring tests?

How much more rewarding to be remembered as "the teacher who kept insisting I could also learn!" than as "the teacher who taught me to hate school!"

Are Grades Undermining Motivation?

■ Research

Adapted from Butler, R. (1988). Enhancing and undermining intrinsic motivation: The effects of task-involving and ego-involving evaluation of interest and performance. *British Journal of Educational Psychology, 58*, 1–14.

As teachers, we want students to do well and *also* be interested in academic tasks. But Ruth Butler's research suggests that some of our habits can undermine performance and interest in the very subjects we want students to learn and enjoy.

Butler identifies two evaluation methods teachers use to tell students how they are doing. The first, the *task-involving* evaluation, gives students feedback about how they are doing on a specific activity. For example: "You got quite a few right, but I bet you can do even better the next time we work on these." This method motivates students to do well because they take pride in their accomplishments. When students work harder, they appear to try to master the tasks, or at least to improve their performance.

Ego-involving feedback is the second type of evaluation Butler identifies. It occurs when a teacher gives grades or other relative, norm-referenced evaluations. With this method, a teacher compares one student's performance with that of other students. The children may respond to this by either working harder to demonstrate high ability or to mask low ability. Either way, it's concern about personal worth, or ego, that motivates them.

Butler conducted an extensive study of fifth- and sixth-graders in the Jerusalem (Israel) public schools. In part of her study, she randomly assigned high- and low-ability students so that they received either comments or grades to evaluate their performance. Students had to perform both a convergent anagram task, and a divergent task that required creativity to do well. At the end of the first session on the convergent work task, as we would expect, high-ability students outscored the low-ability kids.

A few days later, at the second session, students received feedback about how they did the first time they worked on the task. Then they worked on another version of this task. This was the procedure used in the third session as well.

By the end of the third session, both high- and low-ability students who received comments were performing quite well. Their scores increased from the first session to the third. In the graded group, however, students' scores went down. Apparently the type of feedback they received affected their motivation to perform well.

Data from the second and third sessions on the divergent tasks which were conducted with the same procedures as the convergent tasks, indicated that low-ability students who received comments performed either significantly better than, or about the same as, high-ability students who received grades. It appears that the form of feedback enhanced the creativity of students believed to be of low ability, and undermined the creativity of those thought to be of high ability.

Students also rated their interest in the activities. At the end of the first session, students in both groups generally rated the tasks as quite interesting. After three sessions, most of the group receiving task-involving comments *still* found the tasks very interesting. But students receiving grades had lost interest.

In this study, we see that traditional comparative grading practices involve ego needs and undermine both performance and interest. In contrast, task-involving, personal comments seem to enhance and sustain student performance and interest by appealing to students' need to perform well. Perhaps this is why portfolio evaluation systems may work out better than traditional comparative norm-referenced assessment systems.

151

■ Practice

Evaluating students may be difficult, but it's necessary. We *must* correct some of our students' mistakes and help them to raise their own standards for doing their work—even though doing this effectively, and keeping students interested and motivated, often requires an exquisite balancing act.

What Butler describes as task-involving evaluation refers to comments made to individual students and is closely connected to the purpose of the task. It relies on the student's personal motivation to show mastery over the task and improve previous performance.

Changing from simple number or letter grades to individual, task-specific comments takes time, particularly in the beginning. Making supportive, genuine, interesting, and appropriate comments takes practice, too. But increased student motivation may eventually save you more time and emotional labor throughout the year.

Using task-involving comments can also help keep students interested. Because behavior problems frequently relate to lack of motivation, it's reasonable to expect fewer such problems when you use task-related evaluative comments. Start by giving comments in just one area of the curriculum, perhaps in an area where divergent tasks predominate, such as literature, writing, and social studies. Before you begin, tell students what you are doing. If they are at least middle-grade students, you might explain why you are giving comments instead of grades. Explain that comments may be more useful to them, helping them to improve their work.

When you start writing comments, keep your criteria in mind and relate your comments to them. "Your handwriting is very neat" has nothing to do with the quality of a creative writing task. A better comment would be: "Your story kept me in suspense. Perhaps your ending could be more plausible next time."

A social-studies assignment might elicit this type of comment: "Your ideas about the civil rights movement are well stated; maybe you could organize them in chronological order." A task-involving comment for a spelling dictation might be: "You got most of the words right. You might want to watch more closely your *ei* vowel combinations."

Most of us have used grades because they are an easy, fast way to communicate with students. It's also true that many districts *require* teachers to assign grades, a factor which may have discouraged many of us from finding *any* other evaluation methods. But Butler's research indicates that comparative judgments can hamper student's motivation and interest. As a professional educator, you may want to help change a grading policy that hurts your students and may contribute to student apathy.

In the meantime, take advantage of the latitude you enjoy within your classroom. Even if you must give grades at the end of the year, or even quarterly, you can *still* change your way of evaluating daily classroom tasks, weekly tests, homework, and so on.

Motivating Students Through Project-Based Learning

▬ Research

Adapted from Blumenfeld, P. C., Soloway, E., Marx, R. W., Krajcik, J. S., Guzdial, M. & Palincsar, A. (1991). Motivating project-based learning: Sustaining the doing, supporting the learning. *Educational Psychologist*, 26(3 & 4), 369–398.

In the early part of the twentieth-century the experimental movement in education stressed project-based learning. The idea never really caught on, however, and faded away as a teaching method as the testing movement became stronger. Projects took time to complete, thus slowing down the coverage of the curriculum; they were unpredictable, in terms of the outcome for students; they required a good deal of independent, unsupervised work, which could lead to behavior problems; and they were hard to assess. But times have changed, and the project method now seems to be enjoying a rebirth in education. Its benefits may yet prove to outweigh its liabilities.

Motivational researchers use three dimensions to describe classrooms and schools. They note whether a classroom is *mastery- or ability-oriented;* whether it is *learning- vs. performance-oriented;* and whether *task-involvement or ego-involvement* are promoted. Notice that each of these orientations to motivation and learning differs primarily in terms of whether students value learning as an end in itself, or as a means of avoiding negative evaluations and gaining rewards—such as approval,

153

grades, and high test scores. Students who are mastery-oriented, learning-oriented, or task-involved learn *for the sake of it,* not for the rewards they might accrue. Because they are intrinsically motivated to do well in school assignments, and to remain involved and exert cognitive effort, they develop a deeper understanding of what they study. What kinds of activities might produce such desirable student behavior? The instructional project is one answer.

Instructional projects that have the capacity to motivate and teach have three characteristics. *First* a project requires a question or a problem. The problems can originate with either the teacher or the student: Are we experiencing acid rain in this area? How do members of this community feel about the police? What would our school be like if the students were in charge of setting the rules? How many causes, besides the issue of slavery, can you find for the Civil War? *Second,* the activities in which the students engage should have a real-world quality—that is, they should not be easy or accomplished quickly, nor should they result in predetermined solutions. *Third,* the activities associated with a project must result in some artifact (a presentation, a written report, the construction of a model, a videotape, a computer program, a musical score, a poem, a play, a recital, and so forth). It is in the students' development of the artifacts culminating the project that knowledge is constructed. The learning is in the doing.

In seeking solutions to real problems, students come to understand the key concepts and principles that are related to the problems they are studying. Learning in projects is contextualized, and that is important: Too much of school learning seems to be decontextualized, abstract, unconnected to the daily existence of our students. It is not surprising that they show little transfer of what they learn in school to what they do at home and in their neighborhoods. Projects appear to break down some of those barriers to the transfer of learning. In addition, projects have the potential to convey legitimacy to the problems that children have in the real world. They can teach students that, like any of their school problems, real-life problems can also be studied—and perhaps even resolved.

Student interest is aroused, and motivation is highest, when the problems giving rise to projects have some novel elements, are authentic, and are challenging. Projects also need to have closure, so that eventually an artifact that *should* be produced *can* be. Projects of higher quality provide students with *choices* concerning what to work on and how to approach their inherent problems. They also allow students the option to work with others when the job is of sufficient complexity and depth, and requires duration. Such projects often allow the teacher to promote cooperative learning and peer tutoring, both of which are desirable characteristics of a teaching/learning environment.

Projects will not, however, automatically ensure anxiety-free and highly motivated students. Just as ambiguity is inherent in many real-world projects, students (especially those who have never participated in this type of learning activity) tend to worry about both the quality of their work and the grade they will receive. Furthermore, not all projects will pan out. (This certainly was true of Ford motor company and its Edsel, and of the first 200 or so attempts at flying in a heavier-than-air machine—and failures that seem fully as disastrous will also occur with your students.) Learning to deal with failure can, however, be quite constructive in the hands of a sensitive teacher who stresses mastery of the area studied, prizes the task involvement of the students, and rewards learning and risk-taking, and not simply final results.

The project method calls for giving up some prized beliefs about teaching that occurs in textbooks and with worksheets; that the whole class ought to be working on the same things; that competition for rewards is healthy; and that traditional tests measure learning. Project-based methods *do* motivate students, and can help keep novelty and originality in the forefront of a teacher's life in the classroom. But this all calls for radical thought—indeed, literally rethinking the very nature of schools and classroom work. And that's just for starters. But there's no time like the present!

■ Practice

Are you ready to give up some of the traditional myths about teaching and learning? Are you willing to surrender some of your control to the students? Are you able to put up with students who want to stay after school, or come on Saturdays, to finish their projects? If so, instructional projects are for you.

Instructional projects need to be distinguished from short-term activities that may require looking up something in an encyclopedia, or building a pagoda for a social-studies unit on China. Instructional projects should be based on *real* problems that *challenge* the students, and for which there may be *alternative* answers.

As you well know, drastic changes in the classroom can be disastrous without adequate preparation. It is best to start slowly if you have never tried this method before. You may want to begin with a class project which can serve as a model for the process you want your students to follow on their own, later. The whole class can brainstorm to identify a topic of current interest to them, perhaps one that is being prominently featured in the local media. You want this first attempt to be a success, so make sure that the topic is considered important—not only by yourself and the media but also by the students. Students' interests will, of course, depend on their ages, as well as on their backgrounds. In the northwestern regions of the country, older students might be interested in the controversy between animal-rights advocates and the timber industry, for example. In an urban area the interest of students of the same age might be in issues of personal safety versus gun control legislation.

Students, individually and in teams, can select different aspects of the problem to research, once a topic is selected. They will also need to agree on the final product—to which *all* will contribute. Once they agree on these issues they will need to learn the skills required to carry out their assignments. You may want to ask your school or community librarian for help in this regard. He or she may suggest practice activities designed to develop some basic skills before students begin to work independently. Most of our students have little training in research skills, and so their first attempts are likely to be halting at best. You will have to continually model and reinforce the process, and particularly the need to find supporting (as well as disconfirming) evidence for unexamined beliefs.

You will also need to be ready to resist student pressure to reduce the ambivalence inherent in this type of instruction and make it fit traditional school activities. Rather than accept the open-endedness of project activities, students unaccustomed to working this way may want to know how many books they are required to read, or how many pages they must turn in, or when something is due. Their questions display their discomfort with change, and should not discourage either your efforts or theirs. It will help if you make them aware that ambiguity and frustration are part of learning and problem solving in the real world. The Founders did not know how many pages it would take to write the Constitution of the United States when they started—and *their* progress was not always smooth.

It is important for students to understand that in project learning the process is as important as the product. Through projects they are expected to learn not only how to resolve a problem, but how they need to proceed as they seek a resolution. They should also learn that it is all right to take a risk, and that failure occurs only when we are unwilling to learn from the experience. If you make your own goals clear at every step, and provide frequent celebrations of milestones reached, you will help students to feel they are making progress.

The level of frustration that students feel will taper off as they become more familiar with your expectations and their new skills. This should happen after just one class project is completed and shared. If it doesn't, you may want to consider undertaking another class project as both you and your students learn how to best work together in these activities. It is also important that, as this type of instruction begins to predominate in your room, you answer students' and parents' questions about the evaluation process. How will students be graded? What is an "A" project? How will grades be assigned to individuals within the teams? You need to think through these questions carefully, preferably with a group of colleagues who share your interest and are perhaps ready to attempt projects as well. You will also want to gain the principal's approval for these activities before parents raise questions with the administration.

You can proceed to individual or team-selected projects once you and your students feel comfortable with the strategy. By then they should be able to work productively on their own *or* within teams, and should require only minimal assistance from adults in conducting research. You role as a teacher will then resemble that of an opera conductor who keeps the rhythm and the melody coherent while allowing the sections or individual players to make their own music.

Remember to share projects within and without the classroom. Final products can be exhibited during open-house, and written papers can be the focus of debates. Some students may want to produce videotapes to illustrate both a problem and the process they follow as they seek to understand it. In the design and execution of projects, the sky is the limit.

Fictional Inducements to Attention

■ Research

Garner, R. (1992). Learning from school texts. *Educational Psychologist, 27*, 53–63.

The motivating of students is always on the mind of teachers. One of the ways in which they do this is by throwing into the lesson interesting tidbits of information about historical characters, such as Washington's wooden teeth or the story of his cutting down a cherry tree. Perhaps students are told of Napoleon's hemorrhoids and their effect on the battle of Waterloo, or President Franklin D. Roosevelt's alleged affairs. What effect does livening up the material to be learned with these kinds of details have on students? Do they really help students to remember better, or are they just ways to maintain attention with no demonstrable effects on learning? Are these bits of knowledge like pegs, upon which other and more important information can be hung, or are they so salient themselves that other, more important ideas are missed? These were among the questions that Ruth Garner considered as she examined some textbooks that had used this strategy.

Garner found that some textbooks (generally dull and uninteresting) used what John Dewey once called "fictional inducements to attention." That is, in order to keep interest high in a particular topic, the authors laced the text with novel, personally involving, but irrelevant bits of information that did not really address the most salient ideas to be learned. Garner suspected that it was often the seductive details, the bits of irrelevant information, that were remembered, and not the main points. So she tested her hypothesis.

In a paragraph about insects that live either alone or in large clusters, the click beetle was identified as an insect that lived a solitary life. But in half the version of the paragraph a seductive detail about the click beetle was inserted: "When a click beetle is on its back, it flips itself into the air and lands right side up while making a clicking noise." When the readers' recollections of the material were assessed, it was found that only 43 percent of the readers who had the version of the text with the seductive detail remembered the main ideas in the paragraph. On the other hand, 93 percent of the readers *without* this kind of fictional inducement to keep attention high remembered the main ideas, more than twice as many as those who were exposed to the irrelevant but interesting statement about the click beetle. Apparently, at least under some conditions, high interest can lead to low achievement.

Other studies of the phenomena exist. In some versions of a text, students read about Horatio Nelson—but other versions had irrelevant details, like "During the battle, Nelson's right arm was terribly mangled, up to the elbow," or "She fell in love with this battered, one-eyed, one armed naval hero and became his mistress." The important details of the story were such things as Nelson's incredible seamanship, his navigational ability, and his talent for getting along with his men, all of which paved the way for his meteoric rise in the British Navy. It was also important to learn that this was the greatest naval battle ever won by Great Britain, and that it won a major war for them. But when the test results in this study were analyzed, it was found that interest was a better predictor of what was remembered by students than was the importance of the material per se! In fact, the category of information that was recalled the best was information that was rated as high in interest and low in importance, the kind of seductive details many authors and teachers use to enliven their books and classroom presentations.

Altogether Garner reports on five studies that demonstrate this effect. She concludes this interest is a better predictor of what is memorable than is the importance of the material. She uses the metaphor of the light switch to describe students during learning. The switch is turned on, meaning attention is high, when interesting details are presented. But the switch is off when students are exposed to relatively dry material, even if it contains the important generalizations to be learned. So it is possible that in trying to motivate our students by keeping attention high, we sometimes inadvertently work against our main interest, which is keeping students focused on the important ideas and generalizations that we want them to learn.

▬ Practice

The findings from Garner's studies should not deter you from making your lessons interesting. The important thing is to ensure that the major points you **are** trying to convey not get slighted in favor of the interesting tidbits of information that arouse student interest. One way to do this is to provide "advance organizers" for your students—that is, prepare the soil before you sow the seed.

Lord Nelson is a good case to explore. Suppose you begin with an overview of his life and his place in British history. You would alert students to the major points to remember about the topic *before* they encountered those highly interesting bits of information that might distract them. Lord Nelson's naval expertise, and his role in promoting the supremacy of the British Navy (the major points about his life) would be discussed ahead of time. Similarly, major points to remember should also be highlighted at the end. In this way the first as well as the last information heard by the students will emphasize those items you consider most important for understanding the topic.

You can also strive to develop connections between the major points to be remembered and the isolated pieces of information you use to heighten student interest. You can draw diagrams wherein the key positions are held by the important facts, and the connections include tangential information. For example, what are the characteristics that distinguish the beetle family? Those characteristics—such as the hard, shiny shield—would anchor a diagram about beetles. The novelty of the click beetle's behavior would connect all beetles to the unique characteristics of the click beetle. The emphasis, however, would be on the anchor concepts rather than on the novelty items.

You should also consider ways in which you can make the material intrinsically, rather than artificially, interesting. Lord Nelson, for example, was a dashing figure, *with or without* his arm. His naval skills were legendary and *preceded* his famous affair with Lady Hamilton. Historical characters like Nelson can sometimes best be represented through portraits or newspaper accounts of the period; textbooks can sometimes dull colorful characters and historical periods beyond repair. The same information, presented through primary sources, can be much more interesting without the assistance of titillating bits of data. As Dewey said, "Find intrinsically interesting things to learn and the whole argument is irrelevant."

This is an important point to remember. History is genuinely interesting. So is literature. But when presented in isolation, as "important things to know" unconnected to students' lives, some topics may seem dead and irrelevant *in spite of* themselves. (This often happens in textbooks.) On the other hand, when connected to students' experiences, many topics can become genuinely important. The Constitutional Convention, for example, can gain a lot of immediacy if it is presented as a conflictive political negotiation rather than as an accomplished, dry fact. Students can identify and remember the founders of the nation if they get to know them as people who could be loud, intransigent, and obnoxious as well as eloquent and committed. When the humanity of historical characters is removed from textbooks, history becomes no more than a bad movie with unidimensional cardboard characters. Those are the movies we would all rather forget.

We have to remember that the competition for children's attention is very stiff. While it should not require teachers to become performers in living color, we must try to avoid boring our students with dead facts. In recent times, historians have come to understand how the powerful have dominated history and literature through the years. Many of those scholars have searched for, and found, the stories by and of "the common people," the ones that are typically left out of the textbooks. Women, the poor, and the disenfranchised are often the focus of this literature. Look to those stories for compelling accounts of life long ago that can command your students' attention without the injection of irrelevant distractions. Those tales are now part of history's literature, as well as of our literature. And they are *genuinely* interesting and vivid. They do *not* need the help of irrelevant details to be remembered.

Do Failing Students Benefit from Being Retained?

■ Research

Adapted from Holmes, C. T., & Mathews, K. M. (1984). The effects of nonpromotion on elementary and junior high school pupils: A meta-analysis. *Review of Educational Research, 54,* 225–236.

Between the beginning and the end of the school year you will probably be asked to consider whether any students should be retained in grade, or promoted. These days there is strong pressure to uphold academic standards. The public wants to ensure that students have mastered one grade before they start another. In our own state of Arizona, school teachers and principals are being condemned by politicians for their "overly liberal" promotion policies. Nationally, the rate of nonpromotions in the elementary schools has risen dramatically in the past few years.

These issues, however, are not new. Since the turn of the century this topic has received a great deal of attention by educational researchers. Some of their research has been experimental, not just analytical, and much of it is consistent. Decisions about whether to promote or retain a child do not appear to be informed by that research.

From 650 studies of the problem, researchers C. T. Holmes and K. M. Mathews of the University of Georgia culled 44 that contained sufficient data of high enough quality for comparing the performance of nonpromoted and promoted students. Eighteen of the 44 studies controlled for differences in both the IQ and the achievement of the promoted and nonpromoted groups. Because of such controls the researcher could be reasonably sure that the promoted group was *not* superior in ability to the nonpromoted group. Altogether, the 44 studies were conducted in grades 1–6, took place all around the United States, and, in total, compared 4,208 nonpromoted students with 6,924 regularly promoted students. The question that guided the analysis was very simple: If two children were equally likely candidates for promotion, but one was promoted and one was not, how did their performance compare when achievement and attitude toward school were assessed in the next year or two?

On achievement in reading, the nonpromoted students scored about one-half of a standard deviation below the mean of the promoted students. That is, if the reading achievement of all the students in the promoted group was determined, and the average of those scores was calculated, the nonpromoted students would rank 18 percentiles lower in performance! On tests of language arts the nonpromoted group performed about 16 percentile ranks below the promoted group. On tests of mathematics the nonpromoted group scored 13 percentile ranks below the promoted group. In social studies they scored 14 percentile ranks lower. On ratings of work-study skills the nonpromoted students were 16 percentile ranks below the promoted students, and their grade-point average was 22 percentile points lower!

In the affective areas there were also some consistent findings. Social adjustment scores were 11 percentile ranks higher for the promoted students. The promoted group scored 14 percentile ranks higher on emotional-adjustment measures. On measures of positive classroom behavior the promoted students scored higher by 12 percentile ranks. The self-concept of the promoted students was higher (8 percentile ranks), their attitude toward school was better (6 percentile ranks), and their attendance was also better (5 percentile ranks).

Every year over one million elementary and junior-high students are identified as candidates for retention in grade. We estimate that if we promoted half of them, the group of promoted students would outperform the nonpromoted students on academic achievement measures by 17 percentile ranks, and that the adjustment scores of the promoted students would be higher by about 11 percentile ranks. Those who decide to keep a child in grade at the elementary level for an additional year do so despite very persuasive research evidence showing that negative effects consistently outweigh positive outcomes. Those who now advocate a general policy of nonpromotion must be willing to demonstrate how such a policy could be successful when implementation of that policy in the past has so often failed.

■ Practice

Deciding whether or not to retain pupils who fail to keep up with their peers is one of the most difficult questions a teacher faces. Conscientious teachers are aware of the side-effects of retention, and weigh those against expected gains—benefits which, according to research cited above, may be elusive. Unfortunately, each year many teachers are put under a lot of pressure to retain slower students. In considering alternatives, it is perhaps more important to think about the questions that underlie these decisions.

Why do I think the student should be retained? Is it the student's low academic achievement, or social adjustment, or both that concerns me? If academic achievement is the major concern, you might want to consider whether changes in instructional methods might make a difference. Some children are either unable or unwilling to learn through certain methods, and yet move quickly ahead with a different approach. I remember one child in a first-grade classroom wherein programmed reading instruction was being used. Almost every student in the class was progressing rapidly from level to level. This one was not, in spite of clear indications that she was quite ready to begin reading. Fortunately her teacher, an experienced and perceptive woman, decided to try another approach. By the end of the first grade this child, who might have been retained, was reading at the third-grade level!

Sometimes teachers, especially at the early primary level, recommend retention on the basis of a child's retarded social adjustment. This is a tricky category, since "social adjustment" means different things to different people. The decision to keep children considered to be immature among younger children, who are likely to be *more* immature, is also puzzling. We would expect such a child to benefit from interaction with older, *more* mature peers.

It is particularly important to avoid labeling cultural differences as "social maladjustment." Also, a student's social adjustment to school *is* closely related to his or her relationship with the teacher. It is worthwhile to give a child the opportunity to work with a different teacher for a few weeks before deciding on retention as the solution.

The interaction between academic success and social adjustment must also be recognized. A child who is continually failing is likely to feel frustrated, and often angry. In that case, the problem is not social adjustment but academic difficulties, and must be treated as such. Conversely, a child who is having problems adjusting to the school or classroom setting is also likely to display academic difficulties. Distinguishing among competing reasons for a given problem is likely to lead to more appropriate solutions.

Another child of my acquaintance was demoted from reading group to reading group because he was distracted and not completing his work. This is analogous to promoting a child who is attentive and disciplined, though retarded. Instead of improving, the boy became more and more distracted as he was given less and less challenging work. His behavior and academic performance improved radically when he was moved to a more advanced group. Thus, the problem was not immaturity but improper diagnosis of his academic level.

Another important question to consider is: *What will the student gain from retention?* In most cases the retained student "repeats" the grade. It is difficult to understand the logic behind this action. Is it likely that a student who did not learn the material the first time will do so the second time around? I think not. But perhaps you have a special program in your school, one that seeks to develop an individualized educational program (IEP) for each student. In that case, the student will be assured of new approaches to learn what he or she failed to learn earlier, and also will get recognition for whatever knowledge is attained. In that case retention is not synonymous with "repeating."

But then, why retain at all if the child is going to be participating in a tailor-made program? This logic really gets complicated. Think of it this way: If a child is "retained" it is most likely that he or she will get only a repeat performance, and surely we would place little faith in that solution to the problem. On the other hand, in those cases where retention is properly followed by a special program responsive to the student's needs, then retention really is superfluous, since a tailor-made program can be designed at *any* grade level. The logic and the data lead to decisions to promote more than they do to retain.

Sometimes we forget that grade levels are artificial divisions that do not necessarily match a child's development. What must be considered is whether or not a student is learning, how he or she can be helped to learn better, and how the school and teacher can facilitate that process. Learning is an *interactive* process. Teachers and other school staff must share the responsibility for a student's failure, unless they have taken all measures at their disposal to help advance his or her learning. Retention suggests that the student is solely responsible, and is therefore a punishment rather than a solution to a student's difficulties.

But doing time is not what schools are about. Other institutions have that responsibility.

Are We Expecting Enough Effort from Students?

■ Research

Adapted from Stevenson, H. W., Lee, S-Y., & Stigler, J. W. (1986). Mathematics achievement of Chinese, Japanese, and American children. *Science, 231,* 693–699.

For teachers, the start of a new school year is a time for "New Year's resolutions." They often reexamine fundamental goals and practices, then commit themselves anew to increasing student achievement. The next time you do that, you might think about a recent study comparing

Asian and American students. It highlights teacher, student, and parental attitudes and practices that promote academic success.

Researchers H. Stevenson, S-Y Lee, and J. W. Stigler looked at the roots of Asian students' school achievement. Their data clearly ruled out the possibility that these levels of success are due to special tutoring, superior ability, or higher IQs. Instead, they identified three key factors that contribute to the superior performance of Japanese and Chinese students compared to American: More class time devoted to academics and to direct instruction, more support of children's academic activities from parents, and more student effort encouraged by teachers and parents.

Stevenson and his colleagues studied kindergarten children and first- and fifth-graders from Minneapolis (USA), Taipei (Taiwan), and Sendai (Japan). Comparable groups of 240 students at each grade were observed for more than 1,200 hours. Culturally fair tests were administered. Teachers and parents were interviewed.

The magnitude of difference among the groups proved impressive in certain subject areas. For example, in math, the Japanese entered kindergarten already ahead of Chinese and American students. While the Chinese quickly gained parity with the Japanese, the Americans did not. On much the same note, the American fifth-grade class with the *highest* average score did not perform as well as the Japanese fifth-grade class with the *lowest* average score. Comparisons between Chinese and Americans are similar. Their best first-grade class was achieving about as well as our least-able fifth-grade class. And, only one American was included among the top 100 math students in grade five!

How do classroom practices contribute to these levels of success? For American fifth-graders, academic activities average 65 percent of the school day, compared with 90 percent for Asian students. Furthermore, for Asian fifth-graders, instruction was divided equally between reading and mathematics. United States students spent about half as much time doing math as reading.

Teachers also interacted differently with students. United States teachers used 21 percent of class time for direct instruction, compared with 58 percent for Chinese teachers and 38 percent for Japanese. Most alarming: United States teachers spent more time giving directions (26 percent) than presenting instruction.

Attitudes about homework also appeared to influence achievement. In interviews, few American teachers and parents said they believed homework is of much value. In Taiwan, teachers and parents said homework is of great importance—and children actually *like* to do it (!) The

Japanese fall between these two extremes. The result is that Japanese students do much more homework than American students, and Chinese students do *much* more than Japanese.

What role does parental support play? Follow-up interviews revealed that Japanese parents assisted their children with homework 35 percent more often than did American parents, and Chinese parents provided assistance over 90 percent more often. But home values showed in other ways, too. Of American fifth-graders, only 63 percent had a desk at home. In Japan and Taiwan, rates were 98 percent and 95 percent, respectively, despite frequently tight living space. Asian parents were far more likely than their American counterparts to purchase math and science workbooks for their children to use at home.

Researchers also noted that parents' satisfaction with their children's schools differed among the groups. American mothers were overwhelmingly pleased with their children's schools, teachers, and performance. Furthermore, their concept of an appropriate elementary curriculum didn't include much math or science. Asian mothers expressed less satisfaction with their own children's schooling and performance. Their concept of curriculum definitely included lots of math and science.

Perhaps the most striking difference was the expectation regarding achievement. Asian teachers and parents more often viewed success at school as a direct result of *effort*. In comparison, Americans related school success more often to *ability*. How odd that in more rigid Asian societies effort is seen as paying off for the individual—while in the United States, the more open society with a long history of egalitarianism and of Horatio Alger success stories, natural ability is considered to be the key to success.

▬ Practice

This study forces us to acknowledge that the superior performance of Chinese and Japanese students in cross-national comparisons, as well as the success of Asian-American students in United States schools, is not due to happenstance, luck, or even innate ability. Several commonsense factors contribute to their success—among them more time, more effort, and more support. Such are hard evidence of the values that these Asian cultures place on academic performance.

Much has been said about United States students' lag in science and math in cross-national comparisons. Yet is this concern reflected in daily governmental and school-level decisions? Do we *really* want a different type of education than we have? If so, are we—as a society, as local schools, as educators—willing to rearrange schedules and reapportion budgets to reflect the priorities we wish to espouse? These are issues of truly enormous significance.

Necessary options for individual teachers are also embedded in these findings. For instance, we need to assess our own classroom practices. Ask yourself: *Am I spending too much time on reading and language arts and not enough on math and science? Are activities, textbooks, and instructional materials challenging enough for my students? Am I expecting the most from them? How do I foster a climate in which effort leads to achievement?*

You can also help students and parents alike to learn to more fully value homework as a component of school success. Families *must* come to see homework as a way of extending knowledge and providing practice in newly learned skills, rather than as busy work.

There are many ways in which you can use the results of this study to improve students' academic performance. However, the issues discussed here require more than mere improvements in our schools. Our responsibilities as educators extend well beyond the classroom. We must call attention to the discrepancies that exist between statements that support academic excellence, and decisions to the contrary made by governments and families. We must impress on parents—and indeed also on society at large—that developing children's academic excellence requires *at least* as much modeling, practice, and parental support as is provided Little League players developing athletic prowess.

Overreliance on intelligence and ability tests has decreased our emphasis on effort. Less is expected from children belonging to racial or cultural groups presumed to be less capable. Those who come from groups presumed more capable may believe that inherent ability will get them through, regardless of effort.

As educators, we must shift attention back to the link between effort and achievement. We can do little to change students' innate abilities. We can do much to increase their degree of effort and to improve their performance on school tasks. But, for many students, encouraging learning *for the sake of learning* is not enough. They need to see that, regardless of their color, economic situation, or national origin, academic success not only is *possible,* but also is *rewarded—not* only in school, but also in the world that awaits them after school.

Can We Help Children Stay Enthusiastic About School?

■ Research

Adapted from Hedelin, L., & Sjoberg, L. (1985, June). The attrition of interests in the Swedish compulsory school. Paper presented at the meeting of the European Conference for Research on Learning and Instruction, University of Leuven, Belgium.

An enthusiastic first-grader turns into a disdainful ninth-grader. How often does this happen in schools around the world?

Lizbeth Hedelin and Lennart Sjoberg investigated how students in Sweden change their attitudes toward school, and particular school subjects, during the course of their elementary years. When the researchers presented their data at a conference in Belgium, the audience of a dozen researchers from Europe and the United States—in spite of their experience within very different national systems of schooling—recognized a common problem: In *all* of the Western democracies, students' attitudes become increasingly negative by the time they reach ninth grade.

What we can do about this phenomenon is suggested by Hedelin's and Sjoberg's study. Large samples of students in grades one, three, five, seven, and nine were asked about their feelings of well-being while in school; about their interest in reading, writing, and arithmetic; and about their perceptions of their personal relationships with their teachers. The attitude surveys revealed that, as they advanced across grade levels, children maintained only their interest in reading and writing; steadily, and to a marked degree, they became more negative about everything else.

No differences emerged when boys and girls, or high and low achievers, were analyzed separately. Regardless of gender or ability level, students' interest in school and math lessened, and students perceived that they had much less interaction with teachers as they progressed in grade level. The largest drops in attitude and interest came between fifth and seventh grade, about the time when children in our country move from elementary school to middle or junior-high school.

The data analysis suggested a simple theory of how interest in school subjects is maintained: Student's perceptions of personal interactions with teachers play a major role in determining their attitudes toward school. As one might suspect, the more positive the students' attitudes, the higher their interest in school subjects.

Though the nature and frequency of any teacher's interactions with his or her students apparently do *not* directly influence student achievement, they *do* seem to directly influence the students' self-esteem. Teachers who create an environment in which students feel both successful and personally attached to the teacher enhance their students' sense of well-being. Among students with high self-esteem and feelings of well-being, the attitudes toward school and school subjects are also very positive.

It is a well-known psychological principle that attitude influences a person's choice of activities as well as effort and persistence at tasks. This study points out that attitude and personal relationships are intertwined even when it comes to a student's approach to such tasks as fractions, essay writing, or reading a library book. The lesson from all this is that achievement in most of the Western democracies is probably determined by attitudes *as well as* by ability.

Pressure for higher student achievement comes from many sources in our society. But the data being considered remind us that unless students feel successful, hold high self-esteem, and have feelings of well-being when in school, such achievement is not likely. As we have seen, these personal feelings about school seem to come, at least in part, from personal interaction with the teachers. Yet the trends in the United States are for more seatwork, independent work, and group instruction as students go up in the grades. Maybe we can try to spend a little more time getting to know every student personally, so that each feels attached and secure. With any luck, such efforts should help stem the tide of negative attitudes toward school.

▪ Practice

Teachers are aware of how important the first few days of school are for establishing classroom atmosphere. Sometimes, however, it's difficult to decide whether to establish a no-nonsense atmosphere that will inhibit student misbehavior, or to create a pleasant atmosphere that enhances feelings of well-being and personal relationships. Evidently, according to the research, the former approach prevails as students progress through the grades.

What can a teacher do to contribute to the development of a sense of well-being in the classroom? First, we can remember that a pleasant classroom is *not* an undisciplined one. Appropriate classroom behavior is perfectly compatible with a positive classroom atmosphere; in fact, it is a necessary component.

Second, "getting-acquainted time" is not wasted time. It is a necessary part of the opening of school. It is especially important today when increased mobility almost guarantees that one-fourth of the students sitting in the classroom are newcomers to the school.

Developing a positive, comfortable atmosphere in the classroom requires the recognition that each and every year students arrive as strangers in their new classrooms. They do not know the procedures we prefer. They do not where classroom materials are, or when and how to get access to them. They need to know all these things, and more, if they are to feel at ease in their new setting.

Students also need to get to know their teacher. Spend some time telling them about yourself—not in great detail, but enough to satisfy their curiosity. Students often are particularly responsive to their teachers' stories about their own school experiences, and especially their difficulties and embarrassments. These stories help them to see their teacher as a person much like themselves.

Activities that help the students to get to know one another are also important. Try to get them to go beyond knowing names, to knowing something about each other's own specialness. They may find that someone who appears very different on the surface shares an interest with them. It is particularly important that students recognize their commonalities in classrooms that include students from different backgrounds, since preconceptions about each other are likely to exist.

Your students are also likely to develop a more positive attitude toward the new classroom if they encounter easier tasks and smaller steps at the beginning of the year than you might be inclined to assign them. This lets them learn the new routines comfortably and helps them to feel competent and successful more easily. Simple lessons will lead to more complex ones with surprising ease as student confidence increases.

The beginning of the year is also the time to set high expectations without creating undue anxiety. Speak of a demanding curriculum in positive terms that indicate the student's ability to *cope* with your demands. Instead of saying, "Sixth-grade work will be hard because I have to get you ready for junior high," tell them, "at the end of this year you will have learned so much that you will have no problems in junior high."

The research pertaining to this article shows that academic achievement depends on more than skill development. Teachers who give *no* thought to their students' needs for self-esteem are *unlikely* to improve academic achievement. Yet those who concentrate *only* on a positive classroom climate are *denying* their students the skills they need. *Balance is required.* Experiencing a sense of well-being in the classroom helps students to have a positive feeling about school. *That's* the necessary condition for their development of the motivation to work.

Changing Minds to Change Behavior

■ Research

Adapted from Manning, B. H. (1988). Application of cognitive behavior modification: First and third graders' self-management of classroom behaviors. *American Educational Research Journal,* 25, 193–212.

In recent years some psychologists have hypothesized that even though externally imposed reinforcement and punishment could modify a person's performance, more lasting changes in people's behavior would be possible if individuals were to internalize the reasons for behaving in appropriate ways, and reinforce themselves for performing in those ways. Thus it has been suggested that Cognitive Behavior Modification (CBM), whereby people learn how to change how they think about the things they do, and reinforce or rebuke themselves, might prove more potent or longer-lasting than ordinary behavior modification—whereby an external agent provides positive or negative sanctions for performance. Brenda Manning, of the University of Georgia, recently tried CBM in public schools with regular students who had been identified by their teachers as having mild behavior problems. It worked so well that we thought other teachers would want to know about it.

Thirty first-grade and 25 third-grade children were identified by their teachers as having mild but annoying behavior problems (calling out, inability to concentrate, disturbing others while they worked, not staying in their seat, etc.). No children were getting special services, and all were within the normal IQ range of 85–115. These children were randomly separated into an experimental and a control group.

Twice a week, for 50 minutes at a time over a four-week period, the *experimental* group of children received CBM. In the training sessions the trainer used modeling of appropriate verbal and physical behavior, then got the students to practice saying and doing the same things. (For example, the model would say, "I'd better not call out. It disturbs people and the classroom gets too wild for the teacher to handle us all." Then the trainer might raise her hand and say, "I'd better raise my hand. I know I will get a turn eventually and it will be best for everyone if I do it this way.") The trainer used cueing techniques and reinforcement as well. (For instance, the model might hold up a card that said "Raise My Hand" at an appropriate point in a practice session, and when the behavior and accompanying words were appropriate, the trainer might teach the student to say, "I did that right! I showed that I can wait and I am proud of myself.")

Instruction based on modeling, provision of practice, cueing, and reinforcement has a long history of success. In a self-instructional format the children were taught to analyze the behavior problems they saw on videotapes, then decide what needed to be done. They role-played responses, practiced with cue cards, and worked on how they could control and reinforce their own behavior over the eight sessions.

The *control* group, made up of children who exhibited similar behavior, received hortatory lectures during their eight sessions. They were told, "*You* shouldn't call out because . . ." At the same time, the *experimental* group was learning, "*I* shouldn't call out because . . ." The way the two approaches differed was in terms of whether they relied on *internal* processes and *self*-management, or on *external* processes, to control behavior.

At the start of the study the two groups of students were alike in three ways. According to rating scales filled out by teachers, the students in both groups had the same types of behavior problems at the same level of severity. According to a trained classroom observer, the students displayed the same percentage of time-on-task. And, on an instrument that measured the students' locus of control (to gauge whether they felt responsible for their actions or attributed their actions to external causes), the two groups also did not differ significantly. At the end of the study the two groups looked quite different.

The teachers did not know to which group their students had been assigned. Yet when they redid their behavior rating scales at the end of the study, the experimental group of first-graders, when compared to the control group of first-graders, were rated 27 percent higher (i.e., better) in their classroom behavior. They were rated 33 percent higher one month later, and 39 percent higher three months after the training ended. The third-graders in the experimental group were rated as 20 percent better by their teachers immediately after the study, 54 percent better at the end of the month, and 81 percent better at the end of three months, in comparison to the control group of students.

In terms of time-on-task, the experimental students from both grades scored higher than the control students: an average of 42 percent higher at the end of the training, a remarkable 99 percent higher after a month, and 84 percent higher than the controls at the end of three months.

Finally, when the experimental students and the controls at both grade levels were compared in terms of their locus of control, the experimental students at both grades were found to have become more internally driven—that is, they took more personal responsibility for their actions. They showed a decrease in measured externality (and a corresponding increase in internality) of 50 percent at the end of the study; at the end of a month the decrease in measured externality was 29 percent; and at the end of three months the decrease in externality for the experimental group was measured at 46 percent.

This training in self-management of inappropriate and annoying behavior through cognitive behavioral modification was remarkably successful. By getting the children to change how they thought about their behavior, the trainer got them to change how they acted in class: They became better students after less than eight hours of careful targeted instruction! CBM deserves close attention, since it apparently works well with school children who have behavior problems that interfere with both their learning and their classroom routines. The long-term effects show that children who had CBM seemed more motivated to achieve in class, and were more personally motivated to do well by internal rather than external forces.

■ Practice

You may see a similarity between CBM and the old-fashioned "write 100 times" strategy used by many teachers. But where the old strategy punished, the new emphasizes understanding the student's responsibility toward the group and developing the individual's capacity for self-instruction.

Adopting CBM requires time from both the staff and the school day—but it lends itself to a collegial approach. So begin by identifying colleagues who will work together with you on this project. Then study the technique. (Complete lesson plans and materials may be obtained from Brenda Manning, University of Georgia, College of Education, Athens, GA 30602. A small fee may be requested.)

Review the materials, and then decide who should be the instructors, how instruction will be carried out, and where instruction will be delivered to the children. Consider all the qualified adults in and outside the school—aides, counselors, parents, and teachers—as you select the instructor. He or she must be skilled at working with small groups of children (who may not be cooperative at first) and have high expectations for their success.

Finding time is the second problem. Whose time, and how much, depends on who is involved. But keep the long-range goal in mind by comparing the required two meetings each week with the amount of time lost to interruptions and lack of attention. Remember also that you *can* find the time. If the class-day schedule looks too full, consider before or after school. Parents can be very supportive of such scheduling if they know it will improve their child's school performance.

You must also decide whether you want to begin with a small group of children in one classroom, or on a more ambitious level. Whatever the case, after training begins, support students in the program in a discreet manner, and don't embarrass them in front of their classmates.

Because young children love secrets, you may find a reinforcing code a great aid. For example, a picture of an elephant with its trunk raised might cue children to raise their hands before speaking; a picture of a child with a shell to an ear might remind them to be quiet and listen. Develop and review these codes with the children in the program, and keep them as simple and obvious as possible.

Finally, plan to evaluate the program after a period of time: Too many educational innovations perish because they aren't modified to fit specific needs. (Take time to observe the children in *and* out of the classroom.) Look first at how the program has been implemented, particularly if expectations haven't been met. Is the instruction appropriate? Has enough time been devoted to it? Is the instructor pleased? Are the teachers likewise? Most important, is behavioral change noticeable? (Include observations of, and interviews with, the children and their families as you answer the last question.)

If results are acceptable to everyone, make the modifications you desire and incorporate this strategy into your routines for managing both student behavior and motivation to succeed in school. In doing so, you will have succeeded in solving a common problem through appropriate exercise of collegial decision making.

SECTION 5

SCHOOL AND SOCIETY

Introduction

The vociferous criticism to which educators are forever being subjected might lead one to believe that schools are self-contained systems isolated from prevailing social forces. This, however, is not the case. Schools absolutely are integral components of the social system. They affect, and are affected by, the social context they inhabit. Changes in demographics, economic conditions, and family structures all are reflected in the schools. Although they do not initiate these changes, schools experience their consequences and in turn exert their own influence on events.

Many of these effects are so gradual that they tend to go unnoticed until they reach a critical point. For example, the percentage of mothers of school-aged children holding full-time jobs increased enormously between 1950 and 1980. It was a gradual change, perhaps detected first by teachers who found it increasingly difficult to find their students' mothers at home when they called.

This change went by largely unnoticed by the general public until half way through the eighties. For many years, everyone had assumed that for every child at school there was a parent at home during the school day. This was indeed the image reflected both on TV and in the movies. It was not until sometime in the mid-1980s that everyone suddenly realized that, yes, a significant change *had* occurred. Then, seemingly overnight, the need for affordable, safe day-care, like public concern for "latchkey children," became hot news in the media. In hindsight, it seems all too obvious that this social revolution should have been taken into account early on, its consequences seen as predictable from the start.

Sometimes social changes come about much more abruptly (and noticeably). Such was the case, for example, at the end of the Vietnam War when the nation's doors were opened to Southeast Asians. Their arrival contributed to drastic demographic shifts in many districts across the United States, to which the schools had to respond as quickly. At other times, abrupt changes may be the result of deliberate social or legal action. Thus, as a result of the Supreme Court's decision against racial segregation in the schools the racial composition of many schools was drastically (and, again, noticeably) changed.

What does all this mean for teachers? It means that they must be continuously aware of the changes taking place in their own social milieu, and also must remain flexible, always striving to respond appropriately to not only those changes but also the inevitable shifts occurring in the larger society. Yearning for the good old days, and complaining about "today's students," will do little to improve either teachers' morale or student learning. (Even a cursory examination of those "good old days" reveals they were not so good after all!)

Understanding the social context requires more than attention to today; it also requires attention to yesterday and tomorrow. Learning about yesterday can put today in perspective. For example, why have the literacy standards been raised? Why are we so concerned with today's dropouts if, in fact, there are fewer of them in proportion to the population? We must also look toward the future. How will current social trends affect the student population in years to come? What sort of changes must schools undertake in order to respond to social changes?

Projecting into the future may be a bit scary. We all fear problems such as AIDS and drug addiction that already affect even the preschool population. But we cannot hide our heads in the sand. Our awareness can help us to prepare ourselves to deal with new situations, to adjust. All good teachers know that preparedness is the best defense against fear of the unexpected. Heightened awareness can also motivate us to counteract negative forces in our classrooms as well as in the larger social system. We cannot forget that teachers are not just passive receivers of social change, but also have an effect on society through their own actions both within and outside of the schools. As educators we must be ready to assume responsibilities beyond the classroom, to help create a society that enables all children to reach their maximum potential.

The seven articles in this section all relate to aspects of social changes in demographics—among the most talked-about social factors in recent years. For example, one article deals with parents whose experience of schooling may be quite different from our own. We learn that we need to avoid dismissing such people as uncaring. For many of these families the struggle for mere survival saps much of their energy. Others, for various reasons, may not perceive the school as a friendly environment. (Some of them are the parents of children who arrive at school speaking a language other than English.) Children from these families and others are the focus of two of the articles that force us to ask: What do we need to know about language learning in order to be good teachers to these students? How can we have effective instruction in schools where such children are becoming an increasing presence?

Other aspects of social change raise additional questions: How can we better prepare our students to be concerned citizens in a society wherein alienation seems to be increasing? Given increased awareness about gender relations, how can we ensure equity for all our students? And finally, how can we avoid the pitfalls of the past? These are among the issues dealt with in this section. In many ways they may be the *most* difficult issues for teachers.

Responses to the questions posed above require rethinking of assumptions, rejection of accepted myths, recognition of our own deficiencies under certain circumstances, and the adoption of new, unfamiliar instructional strategies. Those are difficult changes for anyone, and they are especially difficult for teachers who always seem to be operating under society's magnifying glass. The *good* news is that our ability to cope under difficult circumstances can both enrich our overall lives and increase our efficacy as teachers. And, we trust, inevitably result also in more useful and satisfying learning for our students.

Is Parent Involvement Worth the Effort?

■ Research

Adapted from Clark, R. (1982). *Family interaction, community opportunity structure and children's cognitive development.* Claremont Graduate School, Claremont, CA; and Goldenberg, C. (1985, April). *Low-income Hispanic parents' contribution to the reading achievement of their first grade children.* Paper presented at the meetings of the American Educational Research Association Meeting, Chicago, IL (ERIC No. ED 264081).

As the school year moves into high gear and workloads increase, many teachers wonder if it is worth the extra effort to seek the involvement of parents in their children's educational programs. Recent research suggests just how helpful those efforts can be, particularly for children from families with low incomes.

Reginald Clark studied the development of literacy among Hispanic, African-American, and white fourth-graders. More than 400 family characteristics were explored in his study of 32 urban low-income families in order to find out why some low-income students achieved well and others did not.

The critical influence of the family on the school achievement of children was confirmed: Families prepare the way for a child, educationally speaking. For example, children who have etiquette training in eating, talking with others, and handling social problems apparently master some of the social skills necessary to profit from schooling. Students who, from an early age, have chores, responsibility for shopping, and involvement in hobbies apparently develop some of the mathematical and reasoning skills. Those who read to others, are read to and questioned, hold conversations, and write notes at home gain an edge in language use.

Strong support systems—family stability, close friendships, stable neighborhoods—provide parents and children the role models, advice, and comfort they need for security and growth. Families that lacked these support systems, did not provide etiquette training, did not foster responsibility, and did not provide many reading and writing activities, had children who did less well in school. The parents of low-achieving students often were described by researchers as "uncommitted" and "lacking in motivation and skills to help their children in schoolwork."

Between the homes of high-and low-achieving children, conversations differed in both quality and quantity. Whether it was during television viewing, a leisure activity, or discussions of homework, the parents of the high-achieving students were much more likely to actively instruct children and provide them with feedback. Most importantly, though, parents of both low- and high-achieving students did not differ at all in their desire to help their children, or in their expectations for them. Some parents, however, simply did not possess the skills to foster their child's school achievement. (Such skills, we note, all are learnable, but need to be taught.)

The study also found that school contacts with the parents of low-achieving students were usually made for attendance or behavior problems. Contact was rarely made to create a partnership for educating the child. To compound the problem, inner-city schools sometimes placed the higher achieving students with the most enthusiastic teachers, and the lowest achieving students with the teachers who were least likely to extend themselves to create home/school relationships.

It was found that the parents of low-achieving students actually saw the teachers more often than did the parents of high-achieving students, but this was often in an attempt to patch up problems. The parents of high-achieving, low-income students made more contacts designed to avoid problems. While parents of the low-achieving students expressed willingness to be involved, they did not know precisely how to do this. The non-English-speaking and African-American parents of low-achieving students felt truly alienated from the schools. They often did not know whom to contact, or how to get beyond the school office. They in fact believed that they did not have a right to ask anything special for their children from their schools.

These factors made teachers think that the parents were unconcerned. Furthermore, on occasions when these parents were informed about their child's school problems, they disciplined the child at home but did not respond to the teacher. Once again, in the eyes of teachers, the parents appeared unconcerned.

Claude Goldenberg's study of low-income, first-grade Hispanic youths is also relevant. Goldenberg found that when parents were informed about their children's reading problems, some intervened and caused a dramatic improvement. Of note was that many were Spanish-speakers and most had only a grade-school education. Nevertheless, when asked, some *could influence* their children's school achievement. In both of these studies *parents almost always did what the teachers asked them to do.* The problem, it seems, is to find ways to get busy teachers to do the asking. These two studies make clear that the problem is not simply unconcerned parents. It is also undercommitted schools.

■ Practice

The research cited above may make you feel that here is yet another responsibility dumped on teachers. Before you put the idea aside in frustration, consider this: You *already* spend time communicating with parents.

What this research points out is not that teachers need to take on another job, but rather the already existing responsibility of communicating with parents can be carried out even more effectively. The message is that most parents *do* care, *do* want to help, but sometimes don't know *how* to be of assistance. Even better news is that most parents *will* follow the advice that teachers give them.

Oftentimes the parents of low-achieving students were themselves low achievers for whom school was a painful experience. Meetings with teachers and administrators are likely to bring back memories of punishment and rejection. As a teacher, you are *not* there to help parents work through these problems. But you *do* have a responsibility to enhance the school experience for your students. (In doing so, you *might* also have a beneficial effect on the parents—but that is of necessity a matter well after the fact.)

Start out by identifying a handful of students who are achieving below par and who appear to come from the type of home just described. Make them your target group. As soon as possible, find an academic task that each of these students did particularly well. Send home brief, enthusiastic, *handwritten* notes praising their efforts. Make sure that the student knows that the message sent home is a complimentary one: Some might discard *anything* sent from the school, for fear of consequences.

Your next task is to think of specific activities that each of these parents might be able to do at home with their child. Remember, these parents may have minimal academic skills themselves, so do not select tasks that make too many academic demands—for instance, looking up words in the dictionary. Clark's study found that the difficulty of the work that low- and high-achieving students completed at home was not really relevant. The difference was in the amount and quality of the child-adult *interaction*.

You will want to think of tasks that encourage such interaction—for example, discussing a special TV program together, or helping a child with multiplication tables. Whatever your selection, once you have activities in mind, ask the parents for an appointment. Coming to school might be difficult for some parents because of home responsibilities, work schedules, or the dread of such a visit. Remember that you may be working against a long history. Try to be flexible. Offer to go either to the home or to a neutral spot, such as a church hall (some parents might be embarrassed to invite a stranger to what they consider a shabby home). Try to work within their time constraints—at least the first time.

That first meeting is terribly important. Let the parents know that you value their help. Share your school activities with them, and encourage them to tell about their home activities. As you learn about the family, suggest helpful activities. And make them very specific: Rather than telling the parents just to read to the child, suggest also talking about the characters. Make sure that, before you all part, they know that you feel *they can* contribute to their child's progress.

Finally, maintain close communication. Compliment parents for their part in their child's success. Remember that you are trying to help to establish new family habits. Try to keep both your expectations and your enthusiasm high.

Once you have tried some of these ideas, you may want to reappraise them in light of their effects. Which are working and which are not? How can you improve on what you're doing? Are the students benefiting? Answers to these questions will help you to fine-tune your actions and even further improve your relationship with both the students and their parents.

This is not a miracle cure; these ideas will not work with every single family. The important thing to remember is that parents *do* care, and *do* listen to teachers. If you are successful in this type of vital educational work, you can make a significant difference in the life of a child, each time you try—and perhaps even in the life of his or her family. But whatever the end result, you'll gain satisfaction every time, from having given it your best shot.

Parents Can Be Great Summer Tutors

■ Research

Adapted from Heyns, B. (1978). *Summer learning and the effects of schooling.* New York: Academic Press; and Epstein, J. (1985). Home and school connections in schools of the future: Implications of research on parent involvement. *Peabody Journal of Education, 62*(2), 18–41.

As the end of a school year approaches, we always think of remarks made at a conference by Barbara Heyns of New York University. She informed us that many statisticians, using standardized tests, found summer drop-offs in reading and mathematics achievement. Moreover, the drop-off did not appear equal across social-class groups: It was much greater for those most in need of substantial academic growth, the low-achieving, low-income students in our schools. In addition, Heyns noted that elementary summer school programs (an attempt to address the problem of the drop-off in achievement) have a poor record of *either* improving or maintaining academic achievement. They often are voluntary for the students, emphasize arts and sports, run for only part of the summer and part of each week day, and employ less-qualified personnel than those who teach during the regular school year.

While statisticians debate the magnitude and significance of the summer drop-off in achievement, teachers nearly unanimously see the drop-off as a real and important issue. But what can be done? While reading Joyce Epstein's work on parental involvement in school work, we saw at least a partial solution to the problem. More and more studies are pointing out how we might be underestimating low-income and minority parents' expectations for their children, their willingness to help or have older siblings help, and the impact that such help has on student achievement. We think that such programs certainly can make an impact throughout the year, but might be especially useful in arresting the summer drop-off.

Epstein and her colleagues surveyed 3,700 first-, third-, and fifth-grade teachers and their principals, across 600 schools in 16 school districts. Eighty-two teachers who varied in the ways they used parents to foster the school learning program were interviewed. Some teachers were assertive leaders in including parents, others used parents infrequently, and some were definite nonusers of parents as a resource. Some of the simple techniques used by the leaders included asking parents to do the following: read to their children; listen to their children read; discuss stories; play certain learning games; tutor their children in specific skills; and enter into some contracts with their children to ensure that assignments are completed. Twelve hundred of the parents and 2,100 students of these teachers were also studied. What was found was that these teachers had differential effects on parents, on student attitudes, and on student achievement.

As opposed to other parents, the parents whose children were in the classes of the assertive leaders in parent-involvement programs reported that their children's teachers worked very hard to involve the parents in instructional programs; they received most of their advice about what to do with their children from the teacher; they understood more about the school's programs and goals than in other years; they felt a greater obligation to help their children at home; they thought the teacher had interpersonal skills; and they rated the teacher higher in teaching ability. Parents who were asked to become involved did so, and for this felt all the better about performing their parental role.

Two interesting side issues came up in these studies. One was that teachers who *were* leaders in parent-involvement programs made equal demands on single and married parents, and rated them as equally help-ful and responsible. Teachers who *were not* leaders made more demands on the single parents, and rated them as less helpful and less responsible that the married parents. A second issue was that school-initiated par-ent-involvement activities *definitely* dropped off from first through fifth grades, and *perhaps* drop off even more thereafter. It is at those inter-mediate grades, however, that student attitudes toward school usually do start dropping off, (see pages 169–172) and that many minorities seem to slow down in their gains. Thus it would seem that parental-in-volvement programs might well have a particularly beneficial role to play in the upper elementary grades.

The students' attitudes also were changed by programs of parental involvement. The students in classes whose teachers were leaders in creating such programs had more positive attitudes toward school; did homework more regularly; saw more similarity between their home and school lives; and believed that there *were* close relationships between their teacher and their family.

Further, student achievement in reading (especially) was found to be related to the teachers' involvement of parents in the instructional program. The students in those classes made greater fall-to-spring read-ing gains than did other children, even after statistical controls were made to account for the quality of the teachers, their years of teaching, the students' entering ability, etc. These gains in reading were statisti-cally significant, and of sufficient magnitude to be worth the effort. The same effects in mathematics were *not* found, however. This was prob-ably due to the fact that most of the requests for parental involvement were made in the context of the reading and language-arts programs. Given all the evidence, it appears possible that at least some of the sum-mer drop-off in achievement *can* be arrested by a thoughtful program of parental involvement in students' summer learning activities.

▰ Practice

Teachers often despair over the losses suffered by children during the summer—particularly by those students who can *least* afford setbacks in their learning. Before your next summer you can ask parents to help, either with the students you now have or with those you expect to get in your next batch. (Or both.) For example, you can try to identify stu-dents likely to be in your class next fall, and send letters home to their parents, telling of your concern with summer drop-off. Ask for their support in overcoming this problem, and offer some general ideas about ways they can help their children.

A simple suggestion is to encourage parents to take their children to a library and help them to choose books that they all can enjoy and benefit from. Of course, more specific activities can also be suggested, but goals for these should be very clearly stated—and you should also explain how they will contribute to the children's learning goals for the *next* year. Parents are more likely to become involved if they see how *their* contribution will help. (This is especially true for parents who have had little formal education.) You should let parents know that their help is not just incidental but, rather, absolutely vital to their child's success.

Remember to avoid teacher jargon in your instructions. Clear and simple language will help parents feel both competent and capable of assisting their children.

Epstein found that as children moved up through the grades, parent involvement decreased—as did their feelings of competence in helping their children with school work. So teachers at the upper elementary level have a double challenge: to increase parent involvement, and to help parents to feel competent enough to do so on their own.

These parents (and/or others who need extra encouragement) may benefit from attending a workshop *before* the start of summer vacation. Such workshops can give parents an early overview of the curriculum. Parents can also examine textbooks and classroom materials, and even participate in simulations of classroom activities. The aim is to help them feel comfortable enough with school activities to enlist their support for the summer (and thereafter).

One highly productive activity that parents can enjoy is to use television programs as a learning tool, especially in the development of comprehension skills and critical thinking. Provide parents with sample questions to ask children during and after viewing. For example: *Who did what, and why? What happened first, second, last? Did the program teach anything of value? If so, what? Was the commercial accurate? How can we evaluate a politician's speech?*

Teachers who wish to suggest pencil-and-paper home-learning activities should choose them carefully. Remember that summer vacation provides children with a break from school routines. Try to structure activities that strengthen children's thinking skills in a more natural setting. For example, avoid sending homework sheets that are likely to depend on specific school-learned strategies—and that will seem like regular-school work to kids. Instead, suggest activities that require the application of concepts. For summer skills, planning a week's worth of meals requires students to recall nutrition and consumer skills, and to use math to estimate quantities, calculate costs, and practice measurement. Parents can comfortably contribute their expertise to such a task.

Collecting family or neighborhood stories, making maps of the community, planting seeds and documenting their development, observing and documenting the development of a younger relative, all are interesting activities with a high level of potential for learning *if* students are prepared for them. Best of all, they provide opportunities for parents and children to learn together.

Demands on teacher time are many, but it appears that investment in parent-involvement activities usually is well rewarded. The record shows that effective use of parental support during the summer months is likely to help students avoid losing the academic progress they made during the school year. Not so incidentally, it may also greatly enhance your reputation as a caring and effective teacher.

Does Culture Affect Reading Comprehension?

■ Research

Adapted from Steffensen, M.S., Juang-Den, C., & Anderson, R. C. (1979). A cross-cultural perspective on reading comprehension. *Reading Research Quarterly,* 15,10–29; and Lipson, M. (1983). The influence of religious affiliation on children's memory for text information. *Reading Research Quarterly,* 18, 448-457.

It can't be disputed: Cultural background influences how and what we learn. Iowans and New Yorkers, Catholics and Jews, Americans and East Indians all learn and recall different things when exposed to the same instruction.

Margaret Steffensen and her colleagues made that point clear when they invited 20 **American** and 19 East Indian adults in a university community to read and answer questions about two descriptive passages. Each passage fully described a wedding—one in India, one in the United States. Both passages were equally complex and of the same length.

The Americans took about 20 percent more time to read the passage about the Indian wedding, while the Indians took about 10 percent more time to read about the American event. It also turned out that the Americans recalled about 27 percent more about the American wedding than they did about the Indian wedding. For the Indians the opposite was true: They recalled about 28 percent more about the Indian wedding. Evidently, cultural background not only affects what is coded and what is stored in memory, but also determines the ease or difficulty with which we read certain material.

Researchers also analyzed whether ideas were elaborated on, or distorted by, readers. Readers *elaborated* most often when recalling the culturally familiar descriptions. They filled gaps, deducted outcomes, and made inferences. When recalling the unfamiliar event, they *distorted* information. For example, when Indians read that the American bride was wearing her grandmother's wedding dress, they remembered that the bride wore an old and out-of-fashion dress. Because the traditional Indian marriage is a financial arrangement and helps determine family status, it is no wonder that the Indians distorted this information. Wearing one's grandmother's dress would simply show impoverishment and poor taste. The Indians, of course, were not privy to the American tradition of wearing something old and something borrowed. Conversely, American subjects read about gifts going from the bride's family to the groom's family. But what the Americans recalled was the *reciprocal* gift-giving. Because they did not have enough familiarity with *dowry* giving, they distorted its meaning to render it more familiar.

Culture apparently provides us a way to fill in the gaps in our knowledge about ambiguous situations. Information that doesn't fit our cultural templates is reworked until it does fit—whether the fit is true or not!

Another study, by Marjorie Lipson, compared fourth-, fifth-, and sixth-graders at a Catholic school and at a Hebrew day school. These Catholic and Jewish students each read about Bar Mitzvah and First Communion. Each group took less time to read the culturally familiar passage, and was able to infer events and remember explicit material better about the familiar passage. Culture, this time in the form of religion, provided the organizational framework, or *schemata*, for enhancing comprehension and also for interfering with it. Similar studies with similar findings compared Greek Orthodox students in New York with New Orleans Catholic students; African-American and white rural eighth-graders; and Americans and Australians.

In all cases we learn that both culture and subculture membership influence how and what we learn. That brings us back to our original statement. Culture, subculture, and even geographical location determine the nature of the experiences we have. Some of us learn to wrap saris and some of us learn how to tie ties; some of us learn the Torah, some learn catechism; some of us learn the differences between toboggans and sleighs, while others learn the differences between bananas and plantains.

Our cultures, subcultures, and geography provide us settings within which we gain the experience to interpret new experiences. In a real sense, each of us carries a learning history around. Teachers have no choice but to inquire into each student's unique culture and learning history, to determine which instructional materials might best be used and when a student's cultural and life experiences are compatible—and potentially incompatible—with instruction. To do less is to toss emotional blocks to communication into an already complicated instructional situation.

■ Practice

The studies above help to explain the reading difficulties experienced by minority students in United States schools. And they alert us to the difficulties that face all children confronted with unfamiliar content. As described in these studies, *culture* is not only a matter of country of origin, or ethnicity, but also one that pertains to *all* the ways in which group members handle daily life situations. (In one study the cultural difference was based on religious traditions, and in the other, social traditions.)

Our task as teachers is complicated by the cultural diversity of this nation. We need to become reasonably knowledgeable about our students' *learning histories,* and similarly cautious when making assumptions about their ability to comprehend content.

A first step is to learn about our students' background cultures. This can be done early in the school year: Older students may write essays; younger ones may prepare notebooks with text and pictures. The students should be encouraged to share information about their home culture. (This can best be accomplished if the teacher models this behavior first.) The activity may then be repeated several times during the year. The goal is to gain some knowledge about our students' learning histories that will help us in the second step: selection of instructional materials.

As teachers we usually are quite familiar with the readability level of a text, or the difficulty level of a skill (such as mastering fractions). But we do not often examine instructional material for *cultural compatibility*. And we *need* to do so in order to predict potential difficulties that can arise from unfamiliar content; to plan ways to circumvent such difficulties; and to ensure that instructional content is not limited to just one set of traditions, but inclusive of the cultural diversity in our classrooms—and indeed in our nation. We must try to put ourselves in the students' position: What, for example, must it be like for him or her to live in New York City (or wherever)? If I were a Vietnamese child, how would I interpret a story about jack-o-lanterns?

Our purpose is not to avoid all cultural incompatibility; broadening horizons and developing new schemata are important goals of instruction. What we want to do is prepare children for the material, teach needed vocabulary, and remain on the lookout for concepts explained by means of culturally loaded examples. The water cycle, for example, may remain a mystery to Sun belt kids who have never seen snow melt, and then ice back up, if that is the *only* example used to illustrate the process.

Remember, too, that cultural incompatibility can also be found in tests and classroom activities. For example, competitive activities may cause discomfort to children from cultures that value cooperation.

Lastly, we must be watchful of the possibility that, through content and activity selection, we may be limiting students' learning. Children faced with culturally incompatible material may respond to factual questions, yet be unable to respond with higher-level skills such as predicting and inferring.

In a pluralistic country we must include a variety of perspectives, including an opportunity for all to advance their learning with the help of their *home-based* knowledge—for several reasons. First, because it is important for their academic development. Second, because doing so will help students to become conversant with the cultural diversity of this country. Finally, because it will also make for a far more interesting classroom environment.

Big Gains in Reading Overnight: Creating the Right Context for Learning

▬ Research

Adapted from Diaz, S., Moll, L. C., & Mehan, H. (1986). Sociocultural resources in instruction: A context-specific approach. In Bilingual Education Office, California State Department of Education, *Beyond language: Social and cultural factors in schooling language minority students*. Los Angeles: Evaluation, Dissemination and Assessment Center, University of California–Los Angeles.

What in the world can you do to have children grow three years in reading ability from one day to the next? How can children grow in ability right before your eyes? This actually happened in a study conducted by Diaz, Moll, and Mehan, who studied a group of children capable of working at much higher levels than their teacher expected. After these researchers changed their instruction, the children showed *immediate* gains in ability, equivalent to about three years' growth! The situation they describe as the setting is not uncommon, and so we ask you to think about instructional practices in your own school and district as we relate the situation.

The study began when the researchers took a Spanish-language teacher of children in a bilingual program to see videotapes of her students as they worked in the English classroom. Although she had sometimes communicated with the English teacher about particular children, the Spanish-speaking teacher had never actually seen her Spanish-speaking children at work in the other classroom. She watched a tape of the "stars" of her class—children in the highest reading group. The Spanish teacher watched, amazed, and blurted out "Those can't be my kids. Why are they doing such low-level work? They are much smarter than that!"

In the English-language classroom the children were doing word sounds, decoding, grammar, and recall exercises—the work of *first*-graders. In the Spanish classroom they were doing comprehensive exercises, including inferring events when data were missing, and predicting outcomes, as well as independently writing book reports. That is, they were doing the work ordinarily expected from *fourth*-graders.

It is not uncommon for children to show one behavior in one setting and another behavior in a different one. That happens because both teachers and students contribute to the creation of the context. (The context, in this case, refers not just to the physical surroundings, but also the interactions between teachers and students within the setting.) The influence of the context is illustrated by the following examples: In one case, lower-class black youths, seemingly inarticulate in the presence of a white adult tester, were capable of quite sophisticated language use in informal settings with a black adult. Another study showed that three- and four-year-old children in Headstart Programs asked more elaborate questions outside of the school settings than in their classrooms, wherein they appeared to be unsophisticated talkers and learners.

Other studies have shown that children who are very competent outside of school may not respond well to "classroom questions," the ones to which the teacher already knows the answer. These children, often from a lower socioeconomic class and/or rural environment, appear to the teacher to be dull—though they themselves wonder why they are asked "dumb" questions to which the teacher already knows the answers. In their homes, questions are asked because someone really *doesn't* know the answer, and they respond appropriately. (In both of the above cases, change in the children's behavior could be traced to changes in the context.)

It is not unusual, therefore, for a teacher to see smart, well-functioning readers operating at about the *fourth*-grade level, while another teacher, in a different environment, believes that the same students cannot pronounce words as well and assigns those children *first*-grade reading tasks. In this present study the English teacher had never seen her students in another context—for instance, performing as sophisticated readers and learners in their native language. She probably didn't know the native language of the students anyway, so couldn't interpret their behavior in another context. The English-classroom teacher did what almost everybody does when meeting someone with an accent or a rudimentary grasp of the other party's oral language: She underestimated their *comprehension* ability.

Teachers of reading often are trained to assume that decoding ability is a prerequisite to comprehension, and that correct pronunciation is the indicator of good decoding skills. If children have trouble *pronouncing*

English, as almost all non-native-born students do, many teachers assume that they have trouble decoding, and therefore cannot *comprehend* reading material. A logical strategy to remediate this problem is to offer a basic, beginning-level course of study in English—even though the students may actually be sophisticated readers in another language.

The researchers struggled to find ways to make apparent to the English-classroom teachers that she had underestimated the ability of many of the bilingual students. The research team finally combined the English and Spanish reading lessons into a hybrid: The students read aloud in English, providing the practice in oral-language production they obviously needed; but the comprehension questions, and their responses, were in Spanish when they had to be (say when a child had inadequate English oral-language production skills). During such reading lessons the children suddenly performed as if they were fourth-graders, *not* first-graders, in comprehension ability!

So, overnight growth in achievement *is* possible, *if* students have been assumed to have no competence in an area when in fact they do. Bilingual students, and students with handicaps that contribute to speech and pronunciation problems, all are likely to have their comprehension skills underestimated. If you provide the right context for learning, you too may someday see achievement grow, as if it were overnight, right before your eyes.

▬ Practice

Every teacher's dream is to have his or her students suddenly make a forward leap beyond all expectations. How can *you* achieve these results? In a nutshell: If your students are among those whose abilities tend to be underestimated due to the characteristics of their language production, you may want to attempt a drastic change in your classroom context. Start by asking yourself a few crucial questions.

First: Who might these students be? As pointed out above, students who are *non-native-born* (or from homes wherein English is a second language) would of course be prime candidates for this strategy. However, many *native-born* students also come from environments where the English spoken at home differs substantially from that at school. (This is true of many rural areas and inner-city neighborhoods.) Too, some students may suffer from handicaps that affect their language production, but not their understanding. Children who suffer from multiple sclerosis, or who are deaf, for example, may literally sound less competent than they really are.

Second: How can you find out whether or not you are underestimating your students' understanding of classroom language? To do this you will need to go beyond your own classroom. In some cases, as in the one described above, teachers who have special training or a different relationship with your students may be able to provide a very different context for them. (In that case the other teacher was a native speaker of the children's language; in your case another teacher may have to be experienced in working with, for example, deaf children.) Whatever the case, the situation would likely contribute to different expectations on the part of the teacher—and, therefore, to different forms of interactions with the students. In all such cases, observing the students in another classroom may well provide the necessary evidence.

You can also learn simply by listening to your students as they interact with their peers in informal settings. Try to get beyond the surface characteristics of language (such as pronunciation and grammatical correctness) to the deeper structures of meaning (like inferencing and predicting). You might even try audiotaping (with their knowledge, of course) informal interactions between students, to which you can listen later in order to conduct more careful analyses. You might also get helpful information from the students' parents. They probably would be able to provide *very* different perceptions of their children's understanding of language. Indeed, in their stories about their children, parents can tell us *a lot* about how well kids use and understand language. A Korean child who never says much in school, for example, may turn out to be the family's official translator!

It is important that you remain open-minded and very aware as you look for evidence of your students' language competence. Remember, you are looking for evidence suggesting that a student's understanding of classroom language may exceed that student's classroom performance, particularly in reading. This may not be readily apparent to you at first. As teachers we all tend to be somewhat judgmental about what is right and what is wrong. It is important, in this case, to *separate the correctness of the form from the content of the expression.* You may find your evidence in the students' rapping songs, or in their creative attempts to communicate their ideas while in the process of learning a new language—or, in the case of handicapped children, perhaps even in their intelligent *nonverbal* responses to situations.

Now, suppose you do find out that you have underestimated several of your students. Or perhaps even a whole class. What then? Then you need to adjust the instructional context so as to better respond to your students' level of competence. The strategy (or strategies) you use will of course depend on the specific situation, your own skills, and the resources at your disposal. If you are working in a bilingual setting you may want to coordinate your lessons with the teacher who provides native-language instruction.

Coordination can lead not only to more responsive instruction but also to more efficient use of time. Students are much more likely to understand metaphors, for example, if they are exposed to the concept at about the same time in both classrooms. In cases where a native-language teacher is not available, you will need to become a careful observer of students' behavior in order to accurately assess their understanding, remembering that *pronunciation is not an accurate predictor of understanding.*

If your major concern is with a handicapped student, you might want to confer with a district or school specialist who can give you an accurate assessment of the child's ability to understand, even when serious production difficulties exist. And, in the case where variations between the students' home language and the school standard are large enough to interfere with school performance (as in the case of "Black English Vernacular"), you may need to monitor your interactions with them in order to assess the condition under which they seem to learn best. Direct instruction, for example, may be less useful than cooperative learning environments in which interaction can be more informal.

All of the strategies outlined here suggest approaches that are what the authors call "pedagogical optimistic"—that is, rather than looking for the problem within the children, we emphasize the role played by the specific teaching and learning context within which children learn. Using these, we can take steps to create more effective learning environments wherein the major emphasis is on the abilities that children have—rather than on their weakness.

Are You Helping Boys Outperform Girls in Math?

■ Research

Adapted from Fennema, E., & Peterson, P. L. (1987). Effective teaching for girls and boys. In D. C. Berliner & B. Rosenshine (Eds.), *Talks to teachers*. New York: Random House.

In the United States, girls generally don't do as well in mathematics as boys. This is true whether we measure lower-level math skills that involve simple recall, or higher-level cognitive processes. Are these disparities due to gender differences in genetic endowment? Probably *not,* since girls do as well as boys in many other countries. Do differences in sex-role socialization contribute to this disparity? Studies have indicated that they *do.* Do classroom practices contribute to these different levels of achievement? Researchers Elizabeth Fennema and Penelope Peterson have found evidence that teachers *may* unwittingly help boys outperform girls in math.

In their study of fourth- and fifth-grade classes, Fennema and Peterson asked whether differences in math achievement were due to different levels of attention during math lessons, or if girls participated in different kinds of math activities than boys. Neither was true. Both boys and girls showed the same degree of attention, and both spent the same amount of time on lower-level and higher-level activities.

When the researchers turned their attention to teaching practices, they noticed some interesting differences. During math lessons, teachers interacted with boys more often than with girls. This wasn't because girls initiated interactions less frequently. In fact, the rates of student-initiated interactions were the same for both sexes. What differed was the number of *teacher*-initiated interactions.

Fennema and Peterson then asked why—given that most teachers try to be fair—were interactions between teachers and boys occurring more frequently? One answer to this question related to the way teachers taught lower-level math skills with timed tests and instructional games. Boys excelled in such activities, and so were more visible as "winners." For example, the winner of the game "Around the World" could be the first student to correctly answer a math question. Verbal aggressiveness makes for winners: The loudest and quickest wins the game. Because males tend to be more competitive and aggressive, in such a situation they have an advantage over females.

When boys participated in these competitive activities, they enhanced their achievement in lower-level math. Such competitions seemed to hurt the achievement of girls, because they tended to lose. Yet teachers acted as though they believed *all* children enjoyed the competitive games.

Teachers used cooperative learning strategies less frequently, but when they were used, girls achieved more than boys on higher-level activities. Whereas competitive activities gave boys an advantage, cooperative activities generally gave girls an advantage.

During lessons in which students worked independently, girls did well, but only under certain conditions: when they were encouraged to try to answer their own questions, and to decrease social interactions. Otherwise, researchers saw that girls were permitted more time than boys to socialize during independent math work, perhaps because girls were less disruptive. But this meant that boys engaged in more math while girls were more likely to drift into social activities.

The teacher's use of *praise* and *prompting* also affected boys and girls differently. Girls achieved more when teachers praised them, but boys were less motivated by praise. When boys gave wrong answers, a simple correction each was time was enough to get them to achieve better. When girls gave wrong answers, a "prompt" appeared to be more beneficial, allowing them to elaborate on ideas and use the teacher's cues to successfully solve problems.

In sum, teachers seem to influence the uneven achievement of boys and girls in math. By choosing equitable teaching methods and by being sensitive to the needs of most girls compared with most boys, we can reduce these differences.

▬ Practice

The differences between boys and girls in mathematics achievement have long been a source of concern for educators, students, parents, and the nation as a whole. So it is heartening to know that there are things that teachers can do in the classroom to minimize this disparity.

We need to begin by assessing our own practices. How well are our students achieving in mathematics? Do we find disparity in the achievement of boys and girls? If disparity does indeed exist, then we need to pay close attention to both the content and the methods of our math instruction before we assume innate differences in ability.

One of the important findings of the research cited was the difference in the percentage of time that teachers spent interacting with boys as compared with girls. To determine whether this is the case in your classroom, you may need to consciously change your patterns of interaction to ensure equitable opportunities for girls as well as boys. (This may best be accomplished with a colleague with whom you can exchange observations and critiques.)

It's important to note that it was not only the *amount* of interaction, but also its *type*, that contributed to lowering the performance of girls. While most boys enjoyed competitive activities, most girls did better with cooperative activities. This difference suggests the need for balance.

You may need to vary your teaching style and activities to provide *every* child with opportunities to do well. For example, structure math lessons to include a competitive, lower-level activity *and* an opportunity for cooperative problem solving. Another way to achieve this balance is to designate certain days each week for math activities that require students to work independently. Set aside other days for cooperative team activities. Either way, the important point is to eliminate the overreliance on any one teaching style—especially when you know that it might favor one group of students over another.

Girls also achieved better in mathematics when they received more praise and prompting from the teacher. You can help bolster female students' math confidence by providing specific praise for good work, and "prompts" that encourage them to pursue difficult problems rather than give up or seek teacher help.

One critical feature of mathematics instruction for all students is the balance between lower-and higher-level activities. Lower-level problems don't require students to understand, interpret, or apply mathematics knowledge. Higher-level activities do. Although Fennema and Peterson did not find differences in the amount of time boys and girls spent on these different tasks, they did find that pupils in general spent only 15 to 20 percent of math time on higher-level tasks. By increasing the amount of cooperative, higher-level activities you plan for all students, you'll do more to help all students acquire important advanced math skills. But make sure that problems designed for the application of math skills are not oriented to male interests, such as sports and cars.

Many interesting and profitable careers are closed to students who avoid, or fail to achieve in, math. As teachers, we have a dual responsibility:

to contribute as much as possible to decreasing the disparities in math performance between boys and girls, and to improve math achievement for *all* students.

Creating Better School Citizens

■ Research

Adapted from Solomon, D., Watson, M. S., Delucchi, K. L., Schaps, E., & Battistich, V. (1988). Enhancing children's prosocial behavior in the classroom. *American Educational Research Journal, 25,* 527-554.

Research in recent years has helped us to understand that certain teacher behaviors and classroom practices have greater academic payoff than do others. What with the main emphasis on academic achievement, we unfortunately have paid less attention to the classroom practices and teacher behaviors that contribute to the prosocial development of children. Daniel Solomon and his colleagues, however, have run a five-year longitudinal study describing some of the factors that influence children's social behavior. These researchers inform us about how we can create environments wherein children can become more responsible and concerned members of society—a goal shared by everyone in and out of our schools.

The training that the researchers provided to teachers participating in the study fostered two major objectives: development of highly supportive teacher–student relations, and opportunities for students to interact and collaborate in cooperative groups. The school staff and the parents of the children were informed, involved, and supportive of what was being promoted in the experimental classes. Teachers who were in the program received extensive training focusing on five elements: (1) use of cooperative learning where fairness, responsibility, helpfulness, and mutual respect were emphasized; (2) a discipline program based on self-control and personal commitment to the rules, where rules are developed out of classroom discussions and teacher-student negotiations; (3) promotion of social understanding through both spontaneous events (i.e., discussing the causes of an argument) and formal means (discussion of a book or performance of a play about a "different" child); (4) fostering helping activities through "buddy" programs, school and community-service programs, helping another student, etc.; and (5) highlighting prosocial values, such as recognizing the children who share, clean up, tutor another, or take responsibility for helping someone else. Developing these processes took time, and it required broad-based commitment and extensive work by the participating school staff. But was it worth it?

The researchers collected data in three experimental and three similar comparison classes, housed in six schools in a suburban district serving a middle- and upper-middle-class population. When classroom observations were conducted, the observers were kept unaware of whether they were collecting data from an experimental or a control classroom. The results are quite encouraging. The experimental teachers were found to implement the program. That is, they showed many more of the behaviors and characteristics that were designed to enhance prosocial behavior. Their classes were observed to be higher in the use of cooperative activities, and showed a greater number of reasonable/ negotiable approaches to discipline. There were also more examples of prosocial behavior, and more recognition for its display. Teachers also reported more student participation in rule-making, more students working jointly with other students, more independent problem solving by students, and more instances of students working out interpersonal problems among themselves.

When the students were interviewed, differences between the experimental and comparison classes were also observed. For example, when asked who made the class rules, 47 percent of the experimental students said that they did, while only 7 percent of the comparison students answered that way. The comparison students reported more often that they received punishment and warnings, or had their name put on the board when a classroom rule was violated. In contrast, the experimental students mentioned more frequently that there would be reparation, or a discussion with adults, for a violation of the rules. Significant differences also appeared when the students were asked why they thought their teacher had them work together. The experimental students mentioned more frequently than the comparison students that it was done so that each child would benefit from the others, and to prepare for adulthood. When asked what their teachers liked students to do, the experimental children answered over twice as frequently as the comparison children that they were to be helpful to others, and also were to work well with others. They had a clear vision of what was expected of them and what was rewarded in their classrooms.

But what about the actual classroom behavior of the students who were in the experimental classes, as judged by neutral observers? The students in the experimental classes were judged to be significantly higher both in supportive and friendly behaviors, and in spontaneous prosocial behavior, in each grade from kindergarten to grade four. In *every* year of the program the children in the experimental program were found on these indices to be nicer children, and yet they showed no loss in academic achievement. A replication of this study reveals the same pattern of results.

This program requires commitment from parents, staff, and teachers, as well as some restructuring of classrooms and schools. If we want more pleasant schools and classrooms, and more caring children, there are techniques at hand to help us toward those goals. The choice is ours: Pay for it now—or pay for it later.

▬ Practice

What would your students answer if they were asked what they think *you* want? Do you think they would mention a more pleasant, cooperative classroom environment? Probably not, don't you think? And yet, as you once again break up the argument of the day, or settle the latest name-calling incident, don't you wish for just such a classroom? How to bring the best out in children, in order to create a more pleasant atmosphere for everyone (including you), is what this particular research project was all about.

The formula given in the above essay is not a quick-fix remedy. You cannot start a program such as this in your classroom in September and expect dramatic change by the holiday break. Too, the type of change promoted must involve much more than just your classroom. It also requires consistent support throughout the school, and from the affected parents at home. The reason for this is that much of what children learn about appropriate behavior in school and society emphasizes cooperation and social responsibility. Interestingly, recent changes in business and industrial organizations have also led to the encouragement of teamwork and cooperation, rather than of individual achievement.

To benefit from the findings of Solomon and others, you must deal first with the need to create a *total* school environment. For this you will need your principal's support and, by extension, that of the school staff in general. You will also need to recruit your colleagues to join you in this effort—if not all of them, at least those whose classrooms are nearby or who teach the next lower and higher grades. You need to create this support system for two important reasons: yourself, and your students.

Making changes in one's behavior rarely is an easy task. It is easier to fall back on tried-and-true habits; it is easier to falter. That is why groups play such an important role in people's attempts to grapple with addictive behavior. Sharing the problems of transition from one style to another with your colleagues will enhance your willingness to withstand frustration and retain your commitment.

You want to provide a protective environment, wherein messages and values are consistent for your students. So you must ask for changes in the traditional teacher–student roles, one of which will be that your students must change the old thinking habits that have made you the tyrant and allowed them to shift to others responsibility for their behavior. They can accomplish this transition only in an atmosphere of trust and encouragement.

Once you have taken the steps to create a supportive environment for all involved, what do you do next? You need to create a demographic environment where, to paraphrase the words of these researchers, students exercise considerable autonomy and self-control, help make decisions about governance in their classrooms, discuss and help solve the problems that arise in classrooms, and in general develop a shared sense of membership in, and responsibility for, their school community.

How much autonomy are you willing to give your students? (Your answer will depend largely on their ages, and also on the support that others are willing to give you.) *Whatever* you grant them must be clearly understood from the start, and backed up all the way. They should not be told that they can make decisions that they really will not be allowed to make. For example, it might be reasonable for students to want to do away with standardized tests, but we know that no such decision is theirs to make—and we must firmly declare that. It is, however, possible for them to express their opinion on this matter to district administrators (and such actions should be encouraged). But they need to learn the distinction between expressing their opinion and having their opinion accepted.

In consultation with your colleagues, and with other school staff, including the principal, you should be able to agree on a list of things your students may be asked to decide on. Naturally, these may differ as the students grow in age and responsibility—it is reasonable to expect children to become more capable as they get older. It is also reasonable for students to determine appropriate action when their peers do not follow the commonly established rules. But that is the clue: They can only be expected to participate in solving a problem if they have had a hand in identifying what that problem is.

For example: Teachers often have rules about when students may go to the bathroom, and therefore they assign punishments to those who break the rules. Your students may not consider it necessary to have such rules. What do you do then? You have to either convince them of the need, or go along with them—perhaps on the condition that the situation may be reappraised after a certain time. This is also a good example of why it is necessary for the total school, or at least a good portion of it, to participate in this type of program. You can imagine how difficult it would be to attempt to give your students responsibility they are not allowed to take in the school as a whole!

In order to create the classrooms described here, you will also want to incorporate cooperative learning strategies into your academic program. We are convinced that such techniques give good results when properly implemented.

Students need to learn how to work in groups, and to value learning from each other in that manner. It is important that, in such groups, everyone be a contributor. Disabled children, or those who are less academically inclined, or those who speak another language, must be more than receivers of the generosity of others who are more competent. *Everyone* is competent at something, and for this good reason cooperative learning environments must provide opportunities for everyone to both be taught *and* teach.

Participation in school and community service programs is another one of the ways in which students learn to become responsible, caring adults. There are many such opportunities, even for the youngest children. They can plant a garden, or bring joy through song or play-acting for isolated seniors in the community, or they can forego their treats for Halloween in favor of donations for UNICEF, or share their excess toys with those less fortunate. Children themselves can come up with many ideas as they get older and learn that their contribution really is valued.

Finally, and perhaps most importantly, you need to create an environment in which the admirable behaviors described are rewarded, and wherein students clearly understand that giving of themselves is much more important than wearing the "right" sneakers, or designer jeans. This rewarding is best done often and consistently, as well as publicly. And "publicly" means not just recognition within the classroom, or even the school, but also community-wide. Let the whole world know that your school values cooperation as well as responsibility!

As you proceed with these ideas, keep the earlier caution in mind: Changes such as those suggested take time, patience, and determination. Also remember that the program described was very carefully constructed, and so would best be duplicated according to these researchers' direction. All we offer here are some ideas, based on their study, that may help you to approximate their success. You will know you have succeeded when your students, if asked what you and other teachers in the school like about them, include in their answers not just "academic achievement" but also "collaboration," "helping each other," and "kindness."

Effective Schools: Teachers Make the Difference

▪ Research

Adapted from Treddlie, C., Kirby, P. C., & Stringfield, S. (1989). Effective versus ineffective schools: Observable differences in the classroom. *American Journal of Education, 97*, 221–236.

For a number of years, researchers have been trying to identify and compare effective and ineffective schools. It was hoped that such comparisons could shed light on the processes that make one school more successful than another. It was always assumed that the teachers in effective schools instructed in different (and better) ways than did those in ineffective schools. A recent study has determined that this assumption was completely accurate. Perhaps we all can learn something about effective instruction from the findings that were reported.

The researchers used such information as the social class of students in a school, racial and ethnic composition therein, degree of urbanization of the community, and so forth, to predict the mean (or average) level of performance of the students within the school on a standardized achievement test. Then the research team looked for positive and negative "outliers"—that is, schools with similar demographic characteristics that scored well above or well below the level that would be predictable for a school with similar characteristics. The research team identified eight matched pairs of these "outlier" schools. Those that scored well above average were deemed to be "more effective," those that scored well below were termed "less effective."

Two observers, who did not know which school had been designated as the more or the less effective school, were sent to each of the 16 schools for three full school days. All the third-grade classes at the schools were examined. Observed were 65 third-grade teachers in the more effective schools, and 51 third-grade teachers in the less effective ones. Ten observable characteristics distinguished between the teachers in the more and less effective schools, and most of these were found to contribute to statistically significant differences.

As might be expected, time-on-task was different in the classes of the two kinds of schools. The observers' records in the more effective schools showed high levels of time-on-task, while the records showed weak or no evidence of time-on-task in the classes within the less effective schools. This is a variable that is well known to be associated with increased performance on standardized school achievement tests. Schools and teachers that do not attend seriously to this variable are likely not to have students that perform well on most of the commonly used standardized achievement tests (see pages 38–42).

A related variable—number of interruptions—was also found to distinguish between classes in the two kinds of schools. In the more effective schools, interruptions during the lessons were kept to a minimum, and were handled when they occurred. In the less effective schools, they were more numerous, and handled poorly. Interruptions take away from the instructional time that is available to each class. Schools and teachers not attending to this problem will lose some of the very scarce teaching/learning time that is available.

As was found in other research studies, the more effective schools had teachers who displayed behavior indicating that they held higher expectations for their students than did teachers in schools that were less effective. The teachers in the more effective schools treated students as if they were quite able, and the observers made note of this difference. As might be expected, discipline was observed to be less of a problem in the classes of the teachers in the more effective schools. Positive reinforcement was also more often in evidence in the classroom of teachers in the more effective schools. None of these findings is surprising, though it is nicely informative to have yet another study confirm that time-on-task, control of discipline, use of positive reinforcement, and communication of high expectations all are characteristics associated with both effective schools and effective teachers.

Instructional variables as well as management variables showed up as important in this research study. Teachers in the more effective schools were observed to present new material more frequently, and provide for sufficient independent practice more often, than teachers in the less effective schools. Some educators think that discipline, time-on-task, interruptions, and the like are unrelated to instructional variables (such as presenting new material). But other educators point out that often too much time is spent in schools reviewing things learned previously and repeating procedures until they are *overlearned*. For some students these are the conditions that create discipline problems, encourage disruptions, and promote taking time-off-task.

It is logical to assume that instructional and management issues are highly interrelated. By presenting more new work and providing appropriate opportunities, teachers in the effective schools may create the conditions for reduced management problems, and the maintenance of a more academic environment. The traditional belief that one must first have a well-managed classroom in order to develop a strong academic program is likely to have things backwards.

The classes in the more effective schools showed three other characteristics that distinguished them from the classes in the less effective ones. Although the observers did not know the achievement level of the schools, they found the more effective schools friendlier and the rooms more pleasant in appearance. They also noted more student work displayed.

The notes of the observers as they looked at one matched effective and ineffective pair of schools were instructive. In the ineffective school the faculty was seen to spend a great deal of time in the teachers' lounge. "They were escaping from the students," wrote one observer. Teachers seemed not to plan, students were often out of control, 15-minute recesses became 30-minute breaks, nonacademic themes were featured on the bulletin boards, a week-long fund-raiser took three weeks and prevented much academic work from being completed, and so forth.

The notes on the matched effective school were quite different. For example: "The principal, every member of the faculty, and the school building itself conveyed the message that students were in the school to learn and that no person, event, or excuse would be allowed to block that opportunity."

These findings are consistent with a large body of research. If high levels of performance on standardized academic achievement tests are a goal of the school, we now know how to make that happen. This is *not* to say that high scores are, or should be, the only goal. Other goals might require attention to other indicators. Perhaps you and your colleagues need to clarify the goals of your school. Then you may ask: are you and your colleagues really creating a school environment compatible with the goals you have for schooling?

■ Practice

This research poses a challenge to dedicated teachers by saying that teachers and schools *do* make a difference. But it also suggests that teaching doesn't create a consistently effective school by itself—a sense of community is needed, too.

Let us recommend what *you* can do to ensure the best learning environment for students.

"School-based management," a term we hear frequently now, means more than choosing textbooks and planning staff development activities. It also means that teachers, administrators, and parents share responsibility for creating school environments devoted to intellectual and social growth. How does your school handle this?

Anyone interested in school improvement should try to analyze the environment from the students' view. What messages do students get from school bulletin boards? Do they invite learning, or are they only colorful wallpaper? Are they filled with records of the accomplishments of athletes only?

How are special occasions celebrated? I remember an elementary school in which, during the few months before Martin Luther King, Jr.'s birthday, students and faculty would compete in oratorical contests. The activity culminated with an awards assembly. For the students in this school, both classroom activities and schoolwide celebrations were about learning. In other schools the same holiday might be celebrated by no more than a day off.

Fund-raising, in most schools, can be either a source of interruption or an opportunity to learn. To make it a learning activity, let students organize the campaign, write letters asking for contributions, keep track of sales, and figure the profit margin. Computers can become ever so much more interesting and meaningful through such activities. Teachers, of course, are still responsible for the funding event, but they can take the roles of overseers and guides while students take the major responsibility. The focus is on learning; raising money becomes the fringe benefit.

It's important, too, to examine the use of time, both within each classroom and in the overall school environment. Just as fire drills reduce the time it takes to empty a building, practice can reduce the time needed for children to get to classrooms first thing in the morning or between classes. And we can ensure that field trips are not just out-of-school activities, but rich learning experiences linked to the school's social and academic goals (see pages 88–92). Time also can be expanded by reducing frequent interruptions. Often the public announcement system is an important offender. Schoolwide policies can be implemented to limit its use and minimize interruptions.

What about interruptions by colleagues or parents interested in discussing a specific child? How can these be incorporated into the schedule in order to allow access while minimizing disruptions? What about the demands that many pull-out programs make on the classroom? Are their benefits diluted by the effect on the classroom program? What alternatives might be considered?

Don't forget that the schools in this study also differed in the amount of new material introduced. If adults ignore things that are repeated too often, such as TV commercials, we shouldn't be surprised if children do so as well. They get bored, and cease to learn. New material, or new ways of looking at old material, can both capture student attention and improve achievement.

Teachers communicate expectations through pacing. When the pace is brisk and the material challenging, they demonstrate confidence in students' competence. Students who are treated with respect respond in kind.

Effective school environments cannot come about with isolated teachers; it is a school-wide phenomena. Effective schools are systems in which teachers, principal, and parents work together to create a respectful climate in which learning is encouraged in every way.

SECTION 6

TESTING

Introduction

In this short section we present five articles. Although the literature on testing is enormous, most of it is technical, concerned about such measurement issues as the reliability and validity of the tests. These articles are related, instead, to the problems of teaching.

The first article is concerned with ways of getting an accurate assessment of your students' learning potential. A typical testing procedure is static; the one described in this article is dynamic, giving students the maximum, not the minimum, opportunity to succeed. The second article discusses test anxiety, a natural byproduct of a test-driven, achievement-oriented school system. We hope you will think about ways to reduce the anxiety associated with testing, including reducing the number of tests and severity of their consequences. The third article is about a controversial topic: test-wiseness. Should teachers and students spend valuable instructional time learning test-taking skills? This is a tough question with which teachers must grapple, and this article provides some ideas about these issues.

The fourth article is about the consequences of high-stakes testing—many of which are awful. So we need to think about the benefits and costs of such testing programs. Finally, we present an article about performance testing—a way of assessing students that is being promoted as an answer to some of the problems associated with standardized tests that rely too much on multiple-choice, decontextualized test items.

Getting the Best Estimate of Learning Potential

■ Research

Adapted from Delclos, V. R., Burns, M. S., & Kulewicz, S. J. (1987). Effects of dynamic assessment on teachers' expectations of handicapped children. *American Educational Research Journal, 24,* 325–336.

To be good teachers, we need to have high expectations about our student's abilities. But these must be based on the most accurate assessments that we can make, and must also not be unreasonably high. Unfortunately, although teachers are always sensitive to this criticism, they do sometimes let labels and backgrounds influence their judgment about students' ability and potential. Dynamic assessment may offer a way to help us hold our prejudices back as we determine students' learning potential.

Unlike IQ, achievement, or other aptitude and ability tests, dynamic assessment is more than presenting problems to a learner and marking the answers right or wrong. The examiner presents a novel problem, then carefully explains the rules, strategies, and principles needed to solve the problem, and finally provides feedback about the proffered solution. If the child gets the problem wrong, the examiner teaches a correct solution. Item-by-item, the cycle is teach-test-give feedback-teach, in comparison with the test-test-test pattern of traditional methods of assessment. The tutorial interaction can sometimes lead the student to unexpected success.

When parents and teachers (alike) observe the dynamic-assessment process, they often see previously hidden abilities that raise their expectations about the child's capabilities. Delclos, Burns, and Kulewicz investigated this anecdotal evidence about the changing expectations that teachers and parents experience with the dynamic-assessment process.

Through random assignment, 60 teachers taking university course work watched one of two video clips depicting the testing of physically handicapped, mentally retarded boys. In the static assessment, the examiner followed traditional testing procedures. The viewers rated "their" boy's task involvement (including his understanding of the task and his ability to learn what he needed to succeed), and the task-specific competencies he used (including working systematically or comparing his work to the model design).

After rating the student, the teachers saw a second video clip of the same child in another testing situation. Half the viewers saw a dynamic form of assessment; half saw another static assessment. Teachers who saw the dynamic assessment changed their opinions about the child's potential more than did teachers who saw a second static testing session; in fact, they rated the potential of that child *61 percent higher* in general competence (22.7 out of 30 points) than the teachers who saw the static-static sequence (13.8 points). The group whose opinions changed after viewing a dynamic assessment also rated the child higher in task involvement and task-specific behavior than the teachers who saw only two static assessments.

Dynamic assessment gives a child the maximum opportunity to succeed, and also suggests instructional alternatives. Watching children learn may create higher and more positive expectations for them than watching them take a test. Tests are often better at revealing inadequacy rather than competency. Static assessments may contribute to underestimations of potential and ability, and these may lead us to *under*challenge our students. Lack of sufficient challenge may, in turn, frustrate students and affect their feelings of competence. Since our expectations can subtly influence our interactions with students, we should create situations that help us to develop the highest, most realistic attitudes about our students that we can.

▬ Practice

If you want to find out how much and how well students learn, observing them as they learn might be the best strategy. Dynamic assessment suggests how you may do this. (Although using the ideas from Delclos, Burns, and Kulewicz's research is worth the effort, the process is not simple.) Begin by identifying students whose abilities are unclear to you. Since your expectations can have a strong effect on both instruction and student achievement, adopting the dynamic-assessment strategy can help you develop more accurate perceptions of their potential.

A realistic appraisal of a student's competence requires selecting tasks that range from very easy to very difficult. You won't be able to tell where the student needs additional help if you only select tasks that the student can already do—but you don't want to frustrate the student with tasks that are much too difficult. The tasks should be active rather than passive, and of reasonably short duration. (Your specific choice depends on the age and other characteristics of the student; for example, paper-and-pencil tasks are more appropriate for older, more mature children.) You also need to find a time and a place to conduct the assessments. If you and a colleague work together, one of you can work with your classes while the other meets with individual students. If that isn't possible, perhaps a paraprofessional or parent volunteer can supervise the classroom while you are testing students. (Use a temporary divider to create a testing area out of a corner of the classroom if other space is unavailable.)

As you present each task to the student, make sure that he or she clearly understands your expectations as well as the rules, principles, and strategies needed to solve the task. Then ask the child to complete the task independently. Give the child feedback about his or her performance, and then ask that he or she try the task again. You can then determine that student's specific problems.

Keep two questions in mind during the assessment: What does the child need to learn? How does he or she respond to various aspects of training?

As your students work on their tasks, ask them questions about what they are doing, and what would help them to do better. Remember, you are identifying learning strengths and weaknesses, not finding out what they already know about a specific task. You can also use dynamic assessment as you observe your students in a learning situation with either adults or peers. Or, ask a colleague to use it by observing you as you work with a particular student.

Dynamic assessment can distinguish appropriate levels of instruction as well as a specific point in a student's learning process. In this way, dynamic assessment is perfectly compatible with the theories of Lev Vygotsky. Vygotsky emphasized the importance of the "zone of proximal development," the region anchored on one end of what students can do by themselves and, on the other by what they can accomplish with someone else's help. He believed that teachers should concentrate their efforts in that region. The use of dynamic assessment can help you to avoid the hazards of labels, and free you to concentrate instead on each child's potential for learning.

Student Anxiety and Student Achievement on Tests

▪ Research

Adapted from Helmke, A. (1987). The role of classroom context factors for the achievement-impairing effect of test anxiety. Munich, Federal Republic of Germany: Max Planck Institute for Psychological Research.

There is a good deal of talk throughout the nation about the need for increased standards, efficient use of classroom time, development of tougher curriculum, more evaluation of students, and so forth. Some of the current criticism of schools has merit and must be taken seriously—after all, teachers are paid by society to achieve its educational goals. So if tough standards, efficient time management, and the like are what the public wants, teachers need to attend to those concerns. But the general public does not always see the negative side-effects of what appears to be sensible policy. Fragile children often are affected by such public policies. Sometimes a *too* highly academic and efficient school can cause children to perform *less* well academically than they might otherwise. And in such schools, both personality development and attitude toward school may also be negatively affected.

A study that brings this effect out quite clearly has been reported. Andreas Helmke, working in Germany, looked at 39 fifth-grade classrooms. He measured anxiety and mathematics performance. When he correlated both he found that in all but two of the classes the correlation was negative, running as high as -.81. That means that the higher the average level of test anxiety in the class, the lower the mathematics achievement in that classroom. Anxiety about test performance was seen as having, in most classes, "a profoundly detrimental effect on academic performance." But then the important question is: In what ways do classes that show these large debilitating effects of anxiety on achievement differ from those that *do not* show such effects? In this research we get intriguing answers.

When teachers show a very efficient use of time for academic purposes, without taking breaks to deal with nonacademic matters such as private teacher-to-student conversations, or administrative matters, their classrooms show much greater debilitating effects on achievement from test anxiety. When time management is less strict (when students have some breathing room, when there is not a constant pressure to attend), the debilitating effects of anxiety on achievement *are not* seen. Here we have an example of what makes teaching so difficult. Whenever the instructional density goes up, when the amount of material covered per unit of time in classrooms is higher, achievement for the classroom usually goes up as well. But at the very same time, anxiety about test performance also increases, and for some students in that class the anxiety will have a detrimental effect on their achievement. How a teacher ever learns to balance such opposing forces in the classroom is not easily understood.

Another characteristic of teachers who manage classrooms where the effects of test anxiety on achievement are minimal was found. They provide many more previewing and reviewing opportunities. They spend extra time informing students of what will happen next, where they should be whenever, what they should be studying, and so forth. Apparently this kind of structuring activity relieves some anxiety—and it is not difficult to see why. If you are a student who wants to do well, but you feel unsure of where you are and where you are going, it's *easy* to tense up! These teachers also spend extra time reviewing what has been presented. Students in their classes do not get just one shot at learning something, and that seems to reduce the otherwise strong negative relationship between anxiety and achievement.

One other factor stood out in comparing the classes where anxiety was or was not having a major detrimental effect on achievement. This was the importance placed on academic success by others. When pressure to do well was present from teachers, classmates, and peers (that is, when success and failure were very salient characteristics of the classroom environment), then the debilitating effects of test anxiety on achievement were at a maximum.

The establishment of norms to do well in tests, and succeed at various projects, is what we strive for in our schools and classrooms. Yet those norms can be too strong, too pervasive, so that anxiety about succeeding becomes so high as to be detrimental. Once again teachers are seen as having to balance forces in their classrooms. The press for excellence and the distaste for failure should certainly be fostered in our students—but, at the same time, we must see to it that the pressure to succeed and thus to avoid failure does not overwhelm our youngsters and cause debilitating anxiety. Balancing these forces can be like balancing yourself on a tight rope.

In sum: Classes differ in the magnitude of the debilitating effects of test anxiety on achievement. In some classes these effects are minimal, or even nonexistent. In others the effect is quite strong. Teacher use of time, and the density of the instruction given, are factors related to these differences. The greater the density of the instruction, the more likely that anxiety will cause a problem.

The amount of structuring and review of material that occur in the class also are important factors. The greater the amount of structuring and review, the less likely that anxiety will cause a problem.

Finally, the salience of success or failure on tests is also a factor. When teachers, peers, and classmates overemphasize test performance, anxiety will be high and debilitating. The finest teachers seem to know how to manipulate these forces as they walk that highwire.

▰ Practice

This seems to be another example of how teachers are at the mercy of contradictory forces. Just when we learn to maximize instructional time in the classroom (see pages 38–42), along comes a researcher to warn us that our efficiency may have detrimental effects.

Upon further examination, however, this is only another example of the importance of common sense in education. We know that efficiency is important because of the limited amount of time that children spend in schools. But just as larger and larger doses of a medicine will not certainly cure us faster, a larger "dose" of efficiency is not necessarily better. The critical factor in all this is *balance,* guided by common sense and perceptiveness. What's a teacher to do?

First, try to establish a classroom climate where learning, not test results or grades, is the goal. Tests are only one convenient measure to find out what students have learned. Remember that testing and learning are not the same thing! If you focus on tests you are likely to increase your students' worry about testing. When students are too anxious about tests they may not perform as well in them, and you may then have apparent cause to underestimate their learning.

If you focus on learning, rather than testing, then you enhance your students' opportunities to learn. Students in this study had minimal test anxiety when teachers used reviews, previews, and interaction strategies.

Take time to prepare students for learning. Let them know what coming lessons will be about, what your goals are for the lesson, and what you expect from them. Use teasers to whet students' appetites for what is coming. Although it is easier to interest students in some topics more than others, try to keep the excitement of learning alive.

Encourage students to discuss what they have learned, rather than their test scores or grades. Perhaps you could initiate an end-of-the-day activity during which students share what they have learned that day. Or have them set up a bulletin board, or keep lists of what they have learned, not only in school but also at home with their friends. These activities may change the climate of the classroom, and could also be referred to when talking with parents. Remember that instruction is not just the delivery of content by the teacher. Learning really requires active participation by the learner.

Covering new material may be counterproductive if students don't have the opportunity to digest and restructure, in their own thoughts and words, what they have learned. Student feedback will also help you to correct misinformation, and perhaps to redirect your efforts. The children should have the opportunity to talk about what they have just learned, and to analyze, ask questions about, and apply new learning before moving on.

Help your students to understand that evaluation is a routine part of school. They need to assess their own progress in order to focus their energies better, and you need to assess their learning so you can plan and modify your instruction.

Take the fear out of testing by routinely using a variety of evaluation strategies in your classroom: end-of-unit reports, short quizzes, experiments that require application of learned facts. Portfolios of achievement are as good an indicator of accomplishment as is a score on a test; they probably evoke less anxiety and serve the same purpose. Sometimes you should mimic standardized tests, such as timed responses and multiple-choice questions, when you give classroom tests. This utilization can increase students' test-wiseness (see pages 221–226), potentially increasing their scores and reducing their anxiety.

Consider identifying *your own* test anxiety. Recent demands for better test results have increased teachers' anxiety *as well as* students' (see pages 169–172). Are you communicating your anxiety to your students? Do you constantly remind them of tests to come? Do you introduce instruction with "I want you to listen; this is very difficult, and many students miss it on the test," or similar comments?

Focus your attention on *student* learning. If you emphasize that, you can reduce anxiety without hampering achievement. Make sure that the content you plan to cover is appropriate, that you teach it in the most effective and exciting way, and that the tests used are compatible with what you are expected to teach.

A little anxiety increases student performance. Too much interferes with it. It is your task to balance the two well enough so that a misstep need not mean a fall.

Should Students Be Made Test-Wise?

■ Research

Adapted from Samson, G. E. (1985). Effects of training in test-taking skills on achievement test performance: A quantitative synthesis. *Journal of Educational Research,* 78, 261–266; and Bangert-Drowns, R. L., Kulik, J. A., & Kulik, C. L. C. (1983). Effects of coaching programs on achievement test performance. *Review of Educational Research,* 53, 571–585.

It is commonplace throughout America for federal program managers, state departments of education, and school district evaluation personnel to require some sort of achievement testing near the end of every academic year. Administered by the millions are such standardized tests as the Metropolitan Achievement Test, the Iowa Test of Basic Skills, and the California Achievement Test. Another million or so different varieties of spring achievement tests are developed by individual teachers to measure accomplishments of their students in the hundreds of courses and curriculum areas taught from kindergarten through high school. A large body of research about the effects of preparing students for the spring onslaught on standardized and teacher-made tests now exits. The research leads us to believe that students, like farm land, need some off-season preparation if we want to see maximum growth on tests of achievement. That is, winter is a good time to get things ready for spring.

Two independent reviews have been published on the effects of coaching or training in test-taking skills on achievement test performance. Such skills are often called *test-wiseness*. Test-wiseness is usually described as the student's ability to use characteristics of the test and the test-taking situation to his or her advantage. Students can be thought of as having either very little or considerable amounts of test-wiseness. Moreover, test-wiseness exists independent of the actual knowledge a person has about a subject matter. Because these are relatively independent dimensions, when a person scores very low on achievement tests it could mean that he or she possesses a very low level of subject-matter knowledge, or, alternatively, has a very low level of test-wiseness. We need to be able to disentangle these two characteristics in order to evaluate students and our instruction.

In the dozens of studies that have now addressed this issue, investigators were interested in the effects of practice with feedback on items like those on the tests that are used to judge learning, the effects of teaching students how to use time appropriately when being tested, how to accurately read and follow test directions, how to use answer sheets properly, how to check answers, when to guess, how to guess, how to use deductive-reasoning strategies, how to infer the intent of the questions asked, how to recognize cues used by the test developers, and so forth.

The reviews of this literature excluded studies that required only practice on items like those that appear on the tests that are of interest. In such situations, students only have their own experience to learn from and receive no real instruction on how to be test-wise. Also excluded in these reviews were tutoring programs in general ability. The studies that were looked at were those that simply asked if training in a potpourri of test-making skills, including instruction on items very much like those that would be on the test, would result in increased performance on those tests. The studies reviewed included training for kindergarten students and graduate students alike. The majority of the samples used in this set of research studies were students in the K–7 range.

What was found in these reviews was clear: In the vast majority of studies, the students who received test-wiseness training acted wiser on their tests. That is, they scored a lot higher on those tests than did students of equal ability who did not take the test-wiseness training courses. Both research reviews concluded that if we think of an average student as performing at about the 50th percentile on a standardized test or on some teacher-made test, that same student would probably score at above the 60th percentile on those same tests if he or she had been exposed to a typical kind of test-wiseness training program. In grade equivalence, the average test-wiseness training program adds about 2.5 months to the grade equivalent score of the average child.

When characteristics of the training programs were examined closely, no best pattern was revealed. All we know now is that students have greater success after some general coaching in areas of test-taking skills related to the specific test that is of interest. Although an optimum training curriculum cannot now be identified, one clear pattern did exist: Those programs that had extensive duration, lasting from five to seven weeks, had greater effects than did shorter programs, those lasting one to five days.

Related to that finding was the unambiguous finding that the more actual contact hours (between teachers and students) that were devoted to learning the test-taking skills (say 20 hours rather than 3 hours), the higher the test scores. The research yields some estimates of this relationship. For two hours of instruction, a student at the 50th percentile would end up at about the 55th percentile. For a program of 3.2 hours' duration, the expected gain would be about 8 percentile ranks. Five hours of training should yield about 10 percentile ranks. Ten, 20, and 30 hours' training, respectively, should show gains of 14, 17, and 19 percentile ranks (respectively) over the average student's performance.

These data reveal bigger effects for more extensive training programs, but *also* show diminishing returns as training time is increased. It probably doesn't pay to study how to take tests for too much longer than 20 or 30 hours. Eventually, one should remember to instruct students in the content they need to know. But up to 20 or 30 hours of test-wiseness instruction seems to pay off.

There is not yet much data about the gains to be expected for low-income, low-social-class, foreign-born, and ethnic minority students. But the hit of bigger gains when training those students does exist. In nine studies wherein low-ability students were trained in test-taking skills, they showed an average gain in test performance that was higher than the gains made by middle- and high-ability students who had also taken the training. So there may actually be some extra payoff in ensuring that low-achieving students (which often means lower social-class, ethnic minority, and foreign-born students) get such training.

It also looks like this kind of test-wiseness training might need some annual repetition, because the effects appear higher right after training and considerably lower two months later. It also appears, from related research, that this kind of coaching actually results in slightly greater effects when aptitude tests, rather than achievement tests, are used. That is, the gains may be slightly higher for students when they get test-wiseness training for taking intelligence tests, critical-thinking tests, problem-solving tests, and tests for employment in a particular field.

If it is winter when you read this, then spring testing is not far behind. Winter appears to be a good time to plan for 10 to 30 hours of instruction in test-taking skills, over about 5 to 10 weeks. This might just let your students have an opportunity to display their knowledge of subject matter without being penalized for their lack of test-wiseness!

▪ Practice

The idea of training students in test-taking skills may appear abhorrent to some. Preparation of that type may seem like cheating. It is important, therefore to clearly separate content knowledge from test-taking skills: Students are taught content, and tests are used to assess whether they have learned that content. Many different types of tests may be used— essay questions, multiple-choice, and fill-in (the blanks). Some students do very well with certain types of tests, but not with others, *even when they know the content for all of them.* (Have you ever felt that a certain type of test was better for you? If so, you understand that your performance on a given test *is* related to the test format. Similarly, students respond differently to different tests.)

Student comfort and familiarity with the test format, the test-taking situation, and the conventions of the test all contribute to good performance. This is especially true for those students who have had little or no experience with testing, such as recent immigrants and ethnic minorities. We sometimes forget that tests and testing are artifacts of a certain style of schooling, and particularly of schooling in the United States of America. There are people who go through their entire academic career without ever taking an objective test. It is therefore not a skill one is born with, but rather one that must be learned.

Coaching for test-taking is not a substitute for effective instruction. We do not want our students only to be able to respond to the questions on the test. We also do not want them penalized for lack of practice in test-taking. We want them both to know the content and to be able to demonstrate that they do. Test scores are useful not only for record keeping: Successful test-taking can also help the student to feel competent *as* a student.

From the research articles described above it is suggested that a training program in test-taking skills of 10 to 30 hours be spread over a 5- to 10-week period. You may wonder where that time is going to come from, since your days are already packed with instruction. It is important to understand that this type of training need not be (perhaps should not be) a separate instructional activity. Test-taking skills can be adequately developed *within the context of other lessons* as long as you take the time to emphasize the skills of interest: using the time appropriately, reading carefully and following directions, using answer sheets properly, checking answers, knowing when and how to guess, using deduction and inferencing skills, and others. Remember that the findings discussed do not apply to situations in which students only practice taking tests but receive no specific instruction on how to be test-wise.

A coaching program in test-wiseness may begin with study of the tests to be used. You and your colleagues will need to analyze different sections of the test to determine its salient characteristics. For example, some multiple-choice tests include a response "DK" (Don't Know), while others do not. Some include responses such as "All" or "None of the Above." These responses may be unfamiliar to many students. Yours need to understand when it may be appropriate to choose them.

Answer sheets also vary—spaces for responding may run up and down or left to right, for example. Students should be familiar with the format they will be using. We have seen a student fail to answer $3 + \square = 5$, though answering quite easily the same item when it was presented as

$$
\begin{array}{r}
3 \\
+\ \square \\
\hline
5
\end{array}
$$

Once you have an idea of the important features of the test, you can devise ways in which these features may be incorporated into your own teacher-made tests. You may want to add directions to your tests, for example. These should be written in the style used in standardized tests rather than in the more informal classroom language. You may also want to practice working on timed tests—not just quick spelling and computation tests, but longer tests that simulate the timing of the formal testing situation.

Students also need to learn how to infer the intent of questions, and how to use deductive reasoning strategies (for example, crossing out all the responses that are totally inappropriate, and thereby reducing the choices). These and other test-taking skills can help them to feel in control of the situation, and frees them to concentrate on their content knowledge during test-taking.

These activities can be blended into routine discussions and/or evaluation activities. To get maximum benefit from this kind of coaching, however, it should be conducted much like sports coaching. The test should be reviewed, student responses discussed, the reason for errors analyzed, strategies practiced, and alternatives suggested. If you follow such a program, you are likely to be rewarded with less overall anxiety—and better performance from your students.

How Standardized Tests Affect Teachers

▪ Research

Smith, M. L., Edelsky, C., Draper, K., Rottenberg, C., & Cherland, M. (1989). *The Role of Testing in Elementary Schools*. Los Angeles, CA: Center for Research on Educational Standards and Student Tests. Graduate School of Education, University of California at Los Angeles.

For fifteen months Mary Lee Smith and her colleagues attempted to learn about both the ways in which tests affect teachers and the ways they go about teaching. After observing in classes; interviewing teachers, students, and administrators; attending faculty meetings; and going through the documents at two schools, these researchers painted a consistently negative picture of the effects that standardized tests can have on an educational system. They found that the tests were "high stakes"—that is, that the test results affect decisions about pay or promotion for teachers, as well as the promotion or graduation of students. Thus the newspaper accounts of the school-by-school and grade-by-grade comparisons results in feelings of shame, embarrassment, guilt, anxiety, and anger for those teachers whose students had not scored well. One source of their frustration was that teachers *knew* that the poor test scores of some students were due to socioeconomic factors, and other conditions over which they had no control. No matter *how* well they taught and nurtured children from poverty, when those students were compared with healthy, wealthy, advantaged children they (and the teachers who served them) always seemed to be deficient.

Many teachers felt that the state-mandated standardized test was cruel and unusual punishment for their children. Elementary teachers had heart-wrenching stories of how the tests induced emotional responses among some students (fighting, vomiting, crying, giving up, random marking of answers, and so forth). Teachers in the upper grades reported that students felt either frustrated by or uninterested in the tests, resulting in their simply "kissing them off." Although not all teachers held these beliefs, and many administrators dismissed these feelings as overreactions by teachers and students alike, many teachers had serious concerns about the emotional consequences to themselves *as well as* their students involved in high-stakes testing situations.

The interviews also revealed other consequences of testing, both in schools that did well on such tests and those that did not. When a principal believed that test scores were of major importance, the teachers often felt that they were kept from being creative. There was pressure not to try out new and exciting programs, and against deviating from the curriculum most related to the tests. Teachers reported that in order to keep their favorite literature or mathematics programs they sometimes drilled the children in test-taking skills for a few weeks, so that the kids could score well enough to keep the principal off their teachers' backs. But they knew that this was not useful instructional time, so they felt anxious when they did this.

The testing programs also reduced the time for genuine instruction. Teachers estimated that preparation for the tests, and the testing itself, took between three and four weeks of the school year. And because the tests were broad in scope, teachers reported that pressure to cover many different areas forced them to move through the curriculum too quickly for the good of many of their students.

Teachers also complained that sometimes their ordinarily most successful programs had to be abandoned as the tests approached and pressure mounted to practice them. The researchers noted in one school that as the year went on there was a move from laboratory, hands-on instruction in science several days a week, to more textbook-based instruction, to *no science at all* in the last few weeks before the state tests.

In the same school the students wrote about 40 minutes each day in the fall, but from January on they did worksheets in grammar, capitalization, and punctuation. In this school, in the weeks just before the tests were given, both social studies and health instruction *disappeared altogether*. Apparently every vestige of critical thinking was abandoned by this staff as children were prepared to take the high-stakes tests.

As the curriculum was narrowed, as more and more instruction was carried out through worksheets that resembled the multiple-choice format used on the tests, schooling appeared to become ever more boring for both students *and* teachers. Some of the teachers, however, became subversive. They closed their doors and returned to the programs they liked to teach and thought were good for their students. Some did this with the blessing of their principals; others hid what they were doing, or openly challenged the authorities. All of those who taught a curriculum not matched to the tests had to pay a price in terms of test scores, but some seemed willing to do this because they did not value the tests, but did value their own professional opinions. As might be expected, while some teachers dared to take such risks, others became even *more* technician-like, teaching precisely what was required for their students to do well on their tests—and losing their own professional skills in the bargain.

The effects, on teachers, of the growth in importance of standardized tests during the last part of this century was to deprofessionalize many of them, changing them into simple tellers of prescribed curriculum. This is a scary thought that gets scarier as calls for still more tests (and *national* tests!) echo throughout the halls of academe.

▬ Practice

How can a teacher deal with the pressures of standardized testing programs? Should teachers compromise their own belief systems and accept these tests, and their consequences, without question? Or should teachers ignore the tests and challenge their superiors? These are important questions that address not only the instructional authority of teachers but also their moral authority.

Let us assume that you, as so many other teachers, have serious concerns about standardized tests. Let us also assume that your concerns are not about whether or not you should be held accountable for your instruction, but about the ways in which such accountability is measured. According to Smith, et al.'s research, you have two choices: One is to put aside your professional expertise and go along with activities designed to prepare students for the tests. In that case, although it is likely that your students will do somewhat better in the tests, you will probably feel that you have cheated them out of some important learning—and also that you have been diminished in your role as teacher. You may, however, decide to follow your professional guidance and continue to teach as you know best, without regard to the tests. It is possible that your students, unaccustomed to the tests' format, and perhaps unfamiliar with much of the content, may perform less well. In that case both you, and your students, will pay the consequences of your insistence on professional standards.

Neither one of these approaches is satisfactory. As a teacher you do of course have a responsibility to ensure that your students are as successful as possible. To knowingly allow them to do anything but their best in order to help you to preserve your professional standards may not be a defensible posture. On the other hand, preserving a tradition that is pedagogically useless is also difficult to defend. And, although you may be only one educator among many, you have as much right as the most powerful to play an influential role in the definition of educational policy.

Let us now consider some alternatives to both of the above approaches. If you are very much opposed to the tests, but unwilling to take the consequences likely to follow from active opposition, you will need to ensure your students' success in the tests. You can do this by incorporating into your instruction the content and process of the tests through means compatible with your values (see pages 165–169). I believe it is possible to do so without forfeiting your standards.

The easier task will be to provide, in your instruction, activities that include test formats and testing practices similar to those used in standardized tests. Throughout the year you should be able to take advantage of many opportunities to insert the multiple-choice format into your lessons. You might have the students create their own multiple-choice tests, which could then be analyzed in class—or, if you have a peer-tutoring program you will have student tutors design multiple-choice tests for their tutees. (Their work should be reviewed and analyzed by them, with your guidance.) Old multiple-choices tests are usable either as a way to earn extra credit, or as homework. You would then review students' responses in class, analyzing why a particular answer is preferable to another.

The idea is to help students to become familiar with this style of testing in an informal way. You want to avoid giving much weight to these activities, but also ensure that your students can respond to such items competently. Notice that each of these suggestions is accompanied by analysis. In this way the students are not just mindlessly practicing techniques to answer such tests; they are learning how the tests work—and, by inference, how they can succeed with them.

You can similarly help your students to become comfortable with timed testing. Many students become very anxious about standardized tests because in the typical classroom they are not usually given a limited amount of time to complete the task. You may believe strongly that timed tests are not the best way to find out how much students have learned, yet nonetheless, students who do not have the opportunity to practice within time limitations *will* suffer during yearly examinations. The trick is to provide plenty of practice in timed exercises during activities that are, by nature, more dependent on rote learning. And, although the practice should not be associated with your own (more comprehensive) evaluation, you can encourage students to compete *with themselves* in order to increase their speed of response.

It is somewhat more demanding to ensure that students taking standardized tests are not confronted with content that is completely alien to them. You will need to become familiar with objectives of the test, and plan how you can use *your own* materials and instructional strategies to achieve *the same* objectives. While spending time teaching students how to answer the items on a test is indefensible, it is perfectly appropriate to keep the testing *objectives* in mind as you plan what to teach throughout the year. For example, an objective for elementary-school students might be being able to recognize and name the earth's land and water masses. You can achieve this objective through rote memorization, or you might prefer to undertake class projects that would allow students to learn this content as they work through their projects.

If your teaching style tends to emphasize indirect instruction (by, for example, using literature to study grammar, and dialogue journal to learn how to write), you may want to use games and homework to cover test content more directly. Flash cards may be used to review spelling and punctuation, and traditional worksheets might be utilized as homework in order to get practice in specific areas of difficulty, once students have been exposed to these activities through other strategies.

It is a good idea to be honest about what you are doing with your students. Explain to them why you prefer to teach in certain ways, and how your style may not be fully compatible with the requirements of the standardized tests. They need to know that you want to ensure their success in the test, and that therefore you will provide opportunities for them to learn what they need in ways that you believe will benefit them most.

The suggestions offered here are only partial and temporary solutions to a moral problem faced by teachers. That problem is the excessive attention that our society bestows on tests that educators at all levels consider inconsequential. This is compounded by the fact that the public gives great importance to test scores and probably will continue to do so. It is not easy to attempt to satisfy two competing ideologies. And it is very difficult for one person to effect change in areas, such as standardized testing, that have become so deeply ingrained in the social fabric. But it *is* possible for groups of teachers to become informed about these issues, and to demand that their voices be heard by policymakers. *Your* voice, when joined to the voices of many others, can swell the chorus calling for changes in policies that are detrimental to teachers and students alike. Perhaps then those who make the decisions will finally listen.

Performance Testing in Education: An Increase in Authenticity

▪ Research

Shavelson, R. J. (1991, April). Authentic assessment: The rhetoric and the reality. A symposium given at the meetings of the American Educational Research Association, Chicago, IL; and Wiggins, G. (1989). A true test: Toward more authentic and equitable assessment. *Phi Delta Kappan, 70,* 703–713.

There are many areas where we accept performance tests as natural. We engage in athletics, the arts, club work, and other activities that culminate in games we play, recitals we give, and plays and debates in which we engage. The demonstration of the degree of skills and other abilities that are called for in those activities *eventually* are made public. More-over, the standards for judging performance in a science fair, hockey game, choral recital, or debate are known *in advance*. Those preparing for such performance tests are allowed to be coached to the maximum possible. Unlike the assessment systems that we have in schools, these kinds of performance tests are transparent—that is, test takers know what is coming and how to prepare for it. There are few surprises. It is these qualities of performance tests that Grant Wiggins and others find so appealing.

Wiggins notes that if our children are judged inadequate in writing business letters, speaking in public, listening to a lecture, creating work of artistic merit, finding and citing scientific evidence, or problem solv-ing, then we should test them in such a way that they write, speak, lis-ten, create, do original research, and solve problems. If the goal is to write, then an essay *is* a reasonable culminating task. Achievement on a set of multiple-choice items about punctuation *is not*. If the goal is to have students think scientifically, then asking students to design and run a study in an area they have never before encountered is a reason-able way to assess if they have learned the skills. (For example, you could give students several different paper towels and a pan of water, and ask them to figure out which product has the most absorbency. In this kind of performance test you may be able to infer more about a student's knowledge of scientific thinking than from the same child's multiple-choice test performance.)

Performance tests have a certain kind of face validity about them that is irrefutable. They get close to the skills we really want to assess when we test our students. Performance tests of this kind can also be embedded in the curriculum, rather than kept separate from ongoing instruction. This too is an advantage over conventional testing, which is usually added on after instruction has taken place, and rarely is itself instructive for the test-taker.

An interesting characteristic of performance testing that should appeal to both teachers and parents is slowly becoming evident. That is, the student who may perform well on the multiple-choice test may not be the same child who scores well on the alternative assessment instru-ment, the one more like real-world performances. Richard Shavelson and his colleagues have studied the correlations between scores obtained by students on traditional multiple-choice tests and those obtained on different kinds of level performance assessments. In their research study, the same children took a battery of tests that had different formats for some of the same problems. A problem such as determining the absorbency of different paper towels was presented in multiple-choice format, through computer simulation, and as an actual performance test of the type described above.

The intercorrelations for student performance on the three forms of tests were low, indicating that a student scoring high on one format of the test may not score high when another format of the test is used. Apparently, different kinds of students will be identified as talented and knowledgeable, depending on which form of testing is used. Some children may suddenly appear among the ranks of the most able in a class, and some we might have thought to be very talented might turn out to be talented only in areas of the school curriculum that are less authentic—that are more abstract and contextualized from real situations. It is therefore possible (but not yet certain) that performance tests may be less biased against poor and minority students than traditional tests. What is becoming certain, however, is that performance tests identify some students who have strengths that are not demonstrated when traditional tests are used.

Videotapes and written records of performances can be stored in portfolios. These files are kept for the teachers and students to go over as they review progress, and also to share with parents. As the criteria for judging the products that students produce are developed and clearly stated, they can be shared with parents and students. This should result in student performances and portfolios alike getting better and better as everyone gains more experience with the system.

Of course, judging such performances take enormous amounts of time, and this clearly is a problem to be overcome. Moreover, the evaluation of a student's ability may not appear to be as reliable as those derived from standardized achievement tests. But the time and effort required seem to be worth it, because traditional forms of testing can be misleading, and often fail to provide useful information.

Performance tests have been around for centuries. They are suddenly being promoted because Americans *finally* are seeing the limits of multiple-choice standardized testing and how such testing negatively influences instruction. The effort to develop these tests might very well be worth whatever that takes.

■ Practice

Have you even complained about the lack of relationship between what students are supposed to learn and the tests used to demonstrate what they have learned? You probably have. If so, you are likely to welcome authentic testing. The name is well given, since such tests are distinguished by the authentic connection between what is taught and what (and how) learning is demonstrated. But being open to authentic testing is not enough. You will need to discard some deeply held myths before embarking on *this* change. And you will also have to spend time with your colleagues, defining the standards for authentic tests and learning how to get them judged.

Let us begin with the myths. The main one is the belief that *what is learned in school can be measured only through paper-and-pencil tests.* Does it make sense for a professional basketball coach to give a written multiple-choice test to find out whether the athletes can execute certain maneuvers? It sounds bizarre, doesn't it? And yet that is not far from what we do when we ask students to—for example—identify different grammatical structures in a set of sentences after attending an English lesson focused on the writing process.

Another myth that must be discarded is the assumption that *traditional standardized testing is "objectively scored," while authentic performances are "subjectively scored."* The scoring systems for ice skating, gymnastics, and diving are objective (and often highly consistent), yielding scores representing complex and aesthetic authentic performances. There are even international contests for concert pianists, where their piano virtuosity is judged. The judges in such contests are well trained and can distinguish among levels of proficiency that novices cannot usually detect fully.

There are classroom examples of this same kind of performance test. For example, Wiggins reports on an oral-history project at Hope High School in Providence, RI, where students do projects on topics like running your own business, and labor unions. The participants are judged on the presentations, which must include having their hypotheses stated and checked, proof of background research, a set of incisive questions written to ask of informants, interviews with at least four knowledgeable informants, analysis of fact and opinion in the interviewees' comments, and so forth.

An economics project in Brighton High School, in Rochester, NY, asks students to respond to a problem in business. The students are told that their firm is losing market share even though total aggregate demand for their product is growing. They are given a month to come up with a plan for the board of directors. They must define the problem; prepare data displays that show demand, supply, costs, revenues, and so forth, for the present and for one year in the future; recommend action plans; and in other ways illustrate the application of business knowledge gained in their course. A multiple-choice test could never assess their knowledge in the same way, and would not be nearly so interesting for the teacher and the students. Remember, performance tests are much more lively for the teacher involved, and this is a decided asset. The teacher can also act as a coach, helping students to get ready for their presentations—their performances—much as if for an Olympic contest. For a few weeks the work of the classroom can be focused on these projects. Community business people could be asked to judge the presentations, increasing their involvement in the life of their local schools.

To build performance tests is not easy. It would seem, however, that before you attempt to build one, you need to think about four things. First: Students must have some opportunity to demonstrate in an authentic way what they have learned. The business presentation, or a science project, or using an abacus in base 2 to demonstrate how a computer operates, all are ways to demonstrate what has been learned. Second: The demonstration must be public. It should look like an Olympic competition. This also means that students should be well prepared to perform in a public setting. Third: You must be able to specify in advance what is expected of the students and their helpers (parents, siblings, tutors, and the teacher acting as coach—not as evaluator). This makes the test transparent. Everyone will know what to expect. Fourth: The performance must be judged by well-trained people of integrity.

We think you can have a great deal more fun if you try to develop performance tests, and learn to work with portfolios. Of equal importance is the fact that your students might find school more fun as well, demonstrate higher levels of motivation, judge evaluation to be fairer, and actually learn more! No one is sure that all these benefits will occur when you develop such a system, but it certainly seems worth trying.

Epilogue

We hope that the articles in this book have informed you, given you confidence about your ability to interpret educational research and make decisions about its application, and also whetted your appetite for educational research. It is important to remember that what is included in this book is only a sampling of recently published articles in educational research. There is much more from which you can learn out there, and we encourage you to seek it out, bring it into your schools, share it with your colleagues, and examine it against your own experience.

As you read this book you probably became aware of several themes that run through many of its articles. Although the articles (and therefore the themes) are of our own choosing, the findings presented are supported by consistently solid research evidence. As you close this book we urge you to pay ongoing attention to its themes, reflecting now and again on their relevance to your own professional work, and occasionally rereading the articles by way of reminder.

Here's a list that you can look back upon when you want to review the themes that underlie the articles in this book.

- Recognizing that our educational goals include much more than test scores

- Recognizing the potential for learning that exists in all children

- Involving parents and guardians in meaningful ways in the education of their children

- Recognizing the relationship between a student's cultural background and his or her learning

- Cooperative and peer learning strategies

- Collegial relationships among educational practitioners

We regard the last theme as particularly important. Throughout this book you have repeatedly found us referring to the power of collegial work. We strongly believe that school-based study groups are the best setting for the discussion of educational research. We hope you will adopt such a process of professional development in your own schools. Within professional study groups, practitioners can bring their own experiences to bear on their readings. It is undoubtedly through that process, rather than through blind acceptance, that educational research will become truly useful to practitioners. And it is more than likely through that process that meaningful, continuous improvement also will take place in our nation's schools.

Index

There are
one-story intellects,
two-story intellects, and
three-story intellects with skylights.

All fact collectors, who have no aim beyond their facts, are
one-story minds.

Two-story minds
compare, reason, generalize,
using the labors of the fact collectors
as well as their own.

Three-story minds
idealize, imagine, predict—their best illumination
comes from above,
through the skylight.

—Oliver Wendell Holmes